THE
BROOKLYN
NOBODY KNOWS

=== AN URBAN WALKING GUIDE ===

WILLIAM B. HELMREICH

PRINCETON UNIVERSITY PRESS
PRINCETON AND OXFORD

Copyright © 2016 by Princeton University Press

Published by Princeton University Press,
41 William Street, Princeton, New Jersey 08540
In the United Kingdom: Princeton University Press,
6 Oxford Street, Woodstock, Oxfordshire OX20 1TR
press.princeton.edu

Cover and interior photographs by Antony Bennett
Cover and interior design by Amanda Weiss

Library of Congress Cataloging-in-Publication Data

Names: Helmreich, William B., author.
Title: The Brooklyn nobody knows : an urban walking guide / William B. Helmreich.
Description: Princeton : Princeton University Press, 2016. | Includes bibliographical
    references and index.
Identifiers: LCCN 2016013485 | ISBN 9780691166827 (pbk. : alk. paper)
Subjects: LCSH: Communities—New York (State)—New York. | Brooklyn
    (New York, N.Y.)—Description and travel. | Brooklyn (New York, N.Y.)—
    Social life and customs. | Brooklyn (New York, N.Y.)—Social conditions.
Classification: LCC HN80.B856 H45 2016 | DDC 306.09747/23—dc23
LC record available at https://lccn.loc.gov/2016013485

British Library Cataloging-in-Publication Data is available

This book has been composed in Adobe Caslon Pro, Futura Std
and Hayfork JNL

Printed on acid-free paper. ∞

Printed in the United States of America

10 9 8 7 6 5 4 3 2

For Helaine

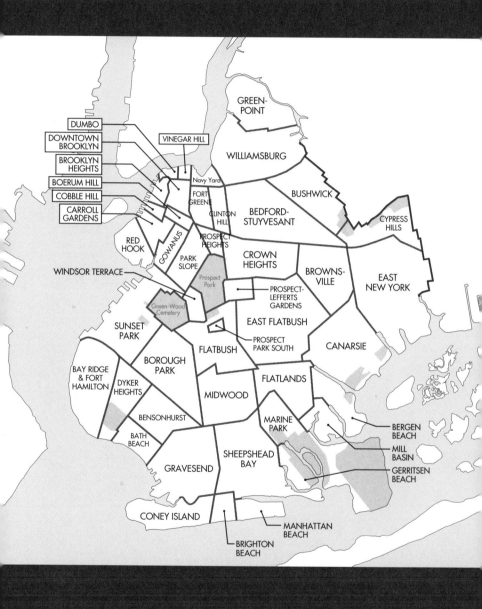

CONTENTS

INTRODUCTION

BROOKLYN. The land of *diversity, change, engagement, self-image*. These are the four core areas that, more or less, depending on the neighborhood, unite the borough. It has been called the "hottest borough," but is it really that? Can a minicity that contains within it at least forty-four distinct neighborhoods be lumped into one general category for anything other than geographical purposes? Can we really consider those who live lives of grinding poverty in East New York and Brownsville to be in the same world as those residing in a luxurious apartment in North Williamsburg or in a Park Slope brownstone? Clearly not.

Can the rhythms of life that govern Hasidic Jews who wait for the siren in Borough Park proclaiming the beginning of the Sabbath, or the calls to daily prayer for Muslims of the muezzin in Bay Ridge, be compared to the secular lifestyles of those who go clubbing along Third Avenue in the same Bay Ridge, or those attending a rock concert in Prospect Park? Clearly not.

And what about those who work in downtown Brooklyn for an investment firm or for the Department of Education? Surely their lives revolve around different matters and concerns than those that animate retirees basking in the summer sun on the benches lining Brighton Beach's boardwalk. Can recent Chinese immigrants to Sheepshead Bay, Sunset Park, or Bensonhurst be living the same lifestyle as the mostly white residents of Gerritsen Beach whose parents or grandparents were Irish or German immigrants?

Every day, tens of thousands of Brooklynites ride the trains through the tunnels and across the bridges to Manhattan and other points throughout the metropolitan area. But what do these riders share with the retired public employee who lives in Canarsie and who lets me know emphatically that he hasn't been to Manhattan in ten years and is no longer sure how to get there? What do the members of Brooklyn's only Cambodian temple in Flatbush have in common with the gay community in Brooklyn Heights? Do those who fear leaving their homes at night because of crime see Brooklyn through the same lens as those who can't wait to leave their homes in the evening for a night of partying?

The residents of Brooklyn share the same 71 square miles of land, but that doesn't make them the same. And yet, that's precisely what they have in common—their amazing *diversity*. Even within their enclaves, differences abound. Whatever remains of the Puerto Rican community of Williamsburg is acutely aware, as its members walk the changing streets, of the cultural and socioeconomic gulf separating them from the young and well-heeled newcomers who have migrated to their neighborhood. They know it when they see their dress, way of speaking, mannerisms, and general lifestyle. Specifically, they know it when they are hard-pressed to find a cup of coffee for less than three dollars, and they know it when they pass stores selling used clothing as vintage attire at exorbitant prices. And they experience the pain of seeing longtime friends and relatives depart for not-so-green pastures in the aging suburbs of eastern Long Island or the south-central Bronx. Similarly, in Gravesend and Bath Beach, older Italians look on with wonderment as ethnic succession in the form of Chinese and Russians alters the character of the communities they inhabited for generations together with Jews, Irish, and other white ethnic groups.

So it goes as well with disparate communities whose members rub elbows and shoulders because their communities border each other. Chinese and ultra-Orthodox Jews meet between Eighth and Ninth Avenues where Sunset Park and Borough Park share a border. Yet they do more than meet—they collide, competing fiercely for the homes that become available there. Similarly, the gentrifiers, Hasidic Jews, and blacks vie for the same living spaces in sprawling Bedford-Stuyvesant. These battles reveal the depths to which *change* has become a defining characteristic of the borough.

This change, which is becoming more and more pronounced, is a second unifying characteristic of Brooklyn. In fact, it has been so throughout the borough's rich and storied history, a past that has long been a beacon of hope for generations of newcomers. It was so for the Italians, Irish, and Jews, who came here from the teeming slums of the Lower East Side to escape their wretched existence in stultifying conditions so well described by Jacob Riis in his classic work, *How the Other Half Lives*. And when they came to Brooklyn, they met with prejudice, just as later black and Hispanic arrivals experienced the same treatment at the hands of those who preceded them.

In the larger sense, the story of class, race, and religion in Brooklyn is best seen through the prism of five distinct groups: blacks, Hispanics, Orthodox Jews, Asians—mostly Chinese—and gentrifiers. To clarify, these groups aren't monolithic by any means. An estimated 25 to 40 percent of the black population is Muslim, and they come from a variety of nations, especially those in the Caribbean. Hispanics also come from many different lands, and they include both Catholics and Protestants. Orthodox Jews range from modern types to Hasidim and many who are in between, and Asians are made up primarily of Buddhists, Muslims, Hindus, and Christians from every part of the continent. With the diminished presence of Italians, Irish, and more secular Jews, these new populations represent the dominant trend in Brooklyn's shifting population. They are sweeping into communities where they had never lived before. Sometimes there are clashes over territory, but overall there's an attitude of live and let live. Most newcomers are too busy carving out lives for themselves to worry about other nationalities living nearby. The gentrifiers are also a varied group. They come from a variety of ethnic and racial backgrounds and from all over the country. They are likely to be middle or upper class, and their reasons for moving into neighborhoods range from convenience to work, to a desire to be in the city's more exciting areas, and, in some cases, to a belief that they're preserving the city's heritage and authenticity by settling in its inner core.

In addition to change, a third uniting feature is an openness to *engagement* with others. Call it a melting pot, call it a salad bowl, call it a mosaic, a kaleidoscope even, but the reality is the same. To be one of this borough's estimated 2.6 million residents is to be a person who constantly encounters and is accepting of people different from oneself. To begin with, they share public space—streets, parks, housing, beaches, murals, museums, supermarkets, bars, and such. A group of Asians will play Ping-Pong in a park, while Colombians and Ecuadorians engage in a game of soccer. Walk by that same park later on in the day and you'll see these two groups playing basketball together and with African Americans as well. I saw this scene, or a variation of it, perhaps in a swimming pool or picnic area, over and over again.

In the supermarkets, people shop and interact with one another, from asking where something is or discussing the best food for their pet, to working together as employees in that same store, or restaurant, or clothing outlet. Students on a school outing from a Hasidic institution in Borough Park meet Muslim students on a school trip to Bay Ridge's Owl's Head Park. When I see them, they're playing in the same playground, side by side. But perhaps in five or ten years, they'll take that step across the line and friendships will result, just as the owners of a Turkish restaurant next to a kosher eatery interact. One of the great opportunities that Brooklyn, and the city in general, creates is the chance for groups not at all friendly with each other in the old country to get to know one another on neutral ground—Dominicans and Haitians, Pakistanis and Indians, blacks and Asians from Guyana, etc., etc.

Another arena for engagement is a concept that I call "daygration." What appears to be a map of separate communities is actually far more porous. While many people may live in more separate and homogeneous communities, they often work elsewhere. So when Russian seniors are bused to a nice center that happens to be in mostly black Canarsie, they spend time with their West Indian caregivers for many hours during the day. White physicians with practices in Bushwick serve the needs of Hispanics. Chinese employees in a take-out place have black or white clienteles in so many parts of Brooklyn. An Italian restaurateur of a famous restaurant in Dyker Heights, Tomasso's, reports that much of his clientele is Russian. The same is true for the owner of a Peruvian eatery in Gravesend. A Polish landlord in Greenpoint tells me about what it's like to deal with his gentrifying tenants. It's far different from the Holocaust survivor who explains to me how she relates to her Polish cleaning lady who is, after all, from the country that she fled because the local population was generally not sympathetic in the least to her plight. An Italian funeral director describes to me, in vivid terms, how he adjusted to a black clientele, after the neighborhood in which he grew up and worked underwent a demographic transformation. In his words: "I could have run away, but I only did so in terms of where I moved to. I kept my business here and it worked out pretty well."

Much has been written about gentrification, affordable housing, and residential segregation, and these are abiding concerns that often generate sharp differences of opinion. That debate sometimes obscures the far more important reality: Brooklyn, as well as the rest of the city, must address these challenges now if it is to retain its reputation as a borough for all, one worthy of being called a leader in innovation and tolerance. And nowhere is this more apparent than in Brooklyn because Brooklyn is indeed "hot" when it comes to being on the cutting edge of change, both socially and culturally and in terms of physical growth. The sounds of jackhammers, cement mixers, cranes lifting and balancing beams of steel, and God-knows-what-else resound through many of the communities here. This is probably the biggest challenge facing Mayor Bill de Blasio and his administration, and it will be so for future administrations as well.

What does this portend for the future? Greater engagement than ever before. The pace and direction of change is inexorable, and more and more people of widely divergent socioeconomic and cultural backgrounds will be living in closer proximity to each other. Mixed buildings, where, in varying proportions, residents of apartments are low income and live together with middle and even upper classes, will inevitably generate greater contact and awareness of each other. This will result in a more nuanced view of others whose lifestyles and attitudes diverge.

A fourth area of commonality is more subtle, and that is the importance of Brooklyn's *self-image* to its residents. I heard this again and again everywhere I walked in my journey through every neighborhood in the borough. And it is dominated by a belief that Brooklyn has become a world destination, a place that's really on the move. Every positive story about Brooklyn that appears in the media feeds that perception and causes things to snowball. Of course, it's one that's more prevalent in the areas where real estate is booming—Brooklyn Heights, Williamsburg, DUMBO. But even in areas like Marine Park, Sheepshead Bay, and Brownsville, the idea has taken hold.

People feel that this general trend will continue and will ultimately affect them. Hotels are going up, mainly to serve tourists, in areas like Gowanus and Bushwick that never had them. When locals see that visitors from all over the world are willing to stay a week in their home borough, it changes how they think about it. The same holds true when Brooklynites see all the people who travel from other parts of the United States to throng the Coney Island amusement center, with its new rides and restaurants. It's still relatively undeveloped, but definitely on the upswing.

As the prime neighborhoods for change have become more crowded, hungry investors have also broadened their views of what's a good bet for the future. Bedford-Stuyvesant is a perfect example. The area has become more diverse in terms of its population and, as a result, new businesses are constantly opening up. Hotels like the Akwaaba Mansion on MacDonough Street, an African-themed guest house, are thriving. Brownsville, long considered a no-go area because of its relatively high crime rate, is suddenly a possibility. I spoke with a black man who lives on Long Island and is rehabbing an old brownstone there. "I travel forty miles every day to get here because I know this is going to happen once Bed-Stuy becomes too expensive for a lot of people. And I want to be in here before it's too late, before the prices really go up."

In short, there's a feeling of pride that their hometown has become a focus of worldwide attention and interest. People are increasingly beginning to say they hail from Brooklyn rather than the individual communities in which they reside, especially when talking to nonresidents. Prospect Park, Grand Army Plaza, the Promenade in Williamsburg, the beaches, marinas, museums—they were all here before, but in those days these were quiet pleasures, enjoyed by locals and perhaps others in the know. But now everyone else knows about them. Before, movies like *Saturday Night Fever*, *Goodfellas*, and *The Lords of Flatbush* celebrated Brooklyn as the home of "dese" and "dem," and as stomping grounds for the Mafia.

Today, the image has changed completely. Brooklyn's streets hum with activity, its bistros and nightclubs are packed, and visitors from everywhere talk about its vibe. Brooklyn has become a place limited only by where the imagination can soar. Then again, imagination is based on reality, and the reality is that Brooklyn has come a long way in the last twenty years.

At the same time, as this book makes clear in the descriptions of its neighborhoods, Brooklyn's vitality also lies in the fact that it is home to many quiet residential communities where the pace of life is slower, its people more traditional, and where the emphasis is on family, schools, religious institutions, and a sense of community that often resembles a small village rather than a bustling center of constant activity. In this way, Brooklyn isn't one whole. Communities like Flatlands, Carroll Gardens, Mill Basin, Brooklyn Heights, East New York, and Dyker Heights still look, feel, and function in very different ways—physically, economically, socially, and culturally.

But even in these places, there's an awareness of context. Places like Prospect Park South, Bergen Beach, and Dyker Heights may be oases of tranquility. But, unlike folks who live in small towns throughout America, these residents can, in a flash, be a thirty- to forty-minute ride away, they can be in the epicenter of Brooklyn's nightlife or in Manhattan itself, something that residents of Iowa or Kentucky can't do. And Brooklynites know it. It's what gives them a dual identity of cosmopolitanism and localism, a big city and small town mentality, each influencing the other and resulting in a hybrid strain that's unique. While Brooklyn's farther reaches are somewhat protected from dramatic change by distance, this could all change if faster and more efficient modes of transportation narrow the distances to the city's core.

In general, Brooklyn, and the city as a whole, must find a way to balance the interests and needs of all socioeconomic groups, be they developers and gentrifiers, the middle classes, or the poor and working classes. Building more affordable housing, for example, has become a mantra, but it isn't just a matter of committing to the idea, but the *extent* of that commitment. Similarly, keeping crime rates low is a key factor, but it must be done in a way that guarantees the rights of all. And even when these priorities are addressed, other factors like the national economy and federal and state policies that are largely beyond municipal control could upend the city's best efforts. For the moment, however, Brooklyn remains an incredibly complex and differentiated place, one where multitudes of people coexist, largely peacefully, living their lives and dreaming their dreams.

* * *

My love for walking the city can be traced back to a game my father played with me as a child, called "Last Stop." On every available weekend, when I was between the ages of nine and fourteen, my dad and I took the subway from the Upper West Side, where we lived, to the last stop on a given line and walked around for a couple of hours. When we ran out of new last stops on the various lines, we did the second and third to last, and so on, always traveling to a new place. In this way, I learned to love and appreciate the city, which I like to call "the world's greatest outdoor museum." I also developed a very close bond with my father, who gave me the greatest present a kid can receive—the gift of time.

In walking, actually rewalking, Brooklyn, my approach was the same as when I did the research for *The New York Nobody Knows: Walking 6,000 Miles in the City*: a comprehensive analysis of all five boroughs. I walked and observed what was going on around me, all the while informally interviewing hundreds of people. New Yorkers are a remarkably open group if approached in a friendly and respectful manner—no one refused to talk to me. Sometimes I told them I was writing a book, but much of the time I didn't need to, and simply engaged them in free, casual conversation. I often taped what they were saying, using my iPhone function in front of them. Hardly anyone asked why, and if their attention lingered on the phone, I quickly explained why I was recording. No one minded. Perhaps that's a statement about what we've become—a society accustomed to cameras and recorders, and one that assumes that few things are really private anymore. Clearly, this is a great boon for researchers. Greater tolerance in general and an abiding belief that the city is safe are also contributors to this state of affairs. Indeed, it is pretty safe, certainly in the daytime.

I walked in the daytime, at night, during the week, on weekends, and in all seasons, in rain, snow, or shine, from mid-October of 2014 to mid-August of 2015. I averaged about 80 miles a month. I attended parades, block parties, and other events and also hung out on the streets, in bars and restaurants, and in parks. Most of the time I walked alone, but sometimes, my wife, Helaine, and, on occasion, our dog, Heidi, accompanied me. I began in Greenpoint and finished in Cypress Hills, walking through every community for a total of 816 miles, as measured by my pedometer. I had, of course, walked almost every block in the borough for the first book, and probably sixteen times before that, albeit more selectively. I wore Rockports, in my view the world's most comfortable and durable shoe. In fact, I was able to do most of the walk in just two pairs.

Although I'd already walked nearly every block in Brooklyn, the findings here are mostly new because the city is constantly changing. New stores, murals, and buildings go up, parks change, and there are different events every year, like concerts, comedy shows, protests, parades, feasts, and town hall meetings. Everyone with whom I spoke was new, and the conversations often led in different directions. Walking is, for my money, the best way to explore a city. It slowed me down so that I could see and absorb things and literally experience the environment as I talked to those who know it best, the residents. And the more I walked, the greater the chance I had to get really good material. I just didn't know whether it would happen in the first or the fifth hour of my trip on any given day. Bicycling is the next best option.

This book is intended to be a guidebook for those wishing to explore Brooklyn. Because the intended audience is largely tourists, curious residents of these neighborhoods, nostalgia seekers who grew up in or lived in these areas, and New Yorkers looking for interesting local trips, the book discusses every single neighborhood in Brooklyn. In order to make it a book that could be easily carried around it was necessary to limit the discussion to the most interesting points, but there's much more to see than what is mentioned here.

The focus is on the unusual and unknown aspects of these neighborhoods. The combination of quotes from interviews with residents, musings on life in general—from air conditioning, to cell phones, to careers—plus many anecdotes about all manner of things, and its focus on sociological explanations of why things are the way they are, all combine to make it what I believe is a rather unique guidebook.[1]

There's a street map for each community, and the reader can walk that community in any order, searching out whatever is of interest. To cover every area, it was necessary to be selective in what was chosen for discussion. But what was chosen is also meant to whet the appetite, to entice the reader into wandering these streets to make new discoveries. Large cities are always changing, and some of the places described here may no longer be there when you take your walks. But I'm sure there will be new things to see of equal or even greater interest. Most of the borough is quite safe, though caution may be necessary in some areas. These are identified in the appendix in the back of the book, along with some tips on how to safely explore them.

The areas are divided into seven groups and are arranged according to geography and similarities. They can, nonetheless, be walked in any order. There's some historical information in the sections, but not much. This is, after all, a book about the present. Brooklyn has an enormous number of famous residents, past and present, and a few are noted here. If a reader is interested in searching out the residences of well-known personalities, I suggest first looking them up on Wikipedia and other Internet sources. And if specific topics like parks, Italians, or bars are of interest, the comprehensive index should definitely be consulted.

The vignettes, interviews, and descriptions have one overall goal—to capture the heart, pulse, and soul of this endlessly fascinating borough.

GREENPOINT

WILLIAMSBURG

DUMBO

VINEGAR HILL

BROOKLYN
HEIGHTS

COBBLE HILL

DOWNTOWN
BROOKLYN

GREENPOINT

GREENPOINT EXTENDS FROM COMMERCIAL AND ASH STREETS and Paidge Avenue on the north, to the Queens border on the east, on Maspeth Avenue and Frost Street to the south, and roughly N. 11th, West, and Commercial Streets along the western border. It is one of the last remaining working-class enclaves in the city. In the nineteenth century, Greenpoint was an industrial area, and shipbuilding was its main activity. It was also the location of the Eberhard Faber Pencil Company, glassworks, a sugar refinery, brick foundry, chemical producing factories, a rope manufacturing company, and other industries.

The area was already home during this early period for Polish immigrants. The Polish-owned establishments are dwindling, slowly receding into the history of the neighborhood as it gentrifies. Yet one still sees Polish men, likely immigrants, trudging home in their work boots, wearing faded shirts and trousers, at the end of the day, and carrying their knapsacks, usually filled with the tools of their trade. Their weather-beaten faces are creased with the lines of hard work and perhaps the assorted worries and even disappointments that have marked their transition from the old

3

world, an ocean away. Why has Greenpoint remained so strongly Polish for 130 years? That's a really long time for a group to remain in one area, especially when it's the one in which they first settled. First, the lack of easy transportation to Manhattan creates insularity. And the G train has spotty service, so much so that it is also referred to as the "Ghost Train." Most important, successive waves of immigration from Poland, especially after World War II and in recent years, have replenished the population.

Finally, Greenpoint is a full-service community, with ethnic stores of every kind, churches, and cultural organizations that, given the inherent conservatism of the strongly identified Poles, makes them content to stay put. In fact, 13 percent of Greenpoint residents can walk to work—more than twice the New York City average of 6 percent.[1]

And yet gentrification is really on the move in Greenpoint, where it seems as though every inch of available space is being used. Glass and steel buildings, anywhere from six to nine stories high, are going up, not just on quiet, tree-lined blocks, but on busy, noisy, and not especially picturesque McGuinness Boulevard. Moreover, Greenpoint is yet another example of the segmented way in which neighborhood change occurs. Most of the stores on Manhattan Avenue and Nassau Street are Polish owned and operated. But on nearby Franklin Street it's a different story. Franklin has almost no Polish presence, dominated instead by bars, cafés, an English-language bookstore called WORD, and newly constructed apartment buildings. Manhattan and Franklin are parallel to each other and one block away, and yet it's almost as if they are two separate neighborhoods.

As I begin my walk, I'm standing in front of the Greenpoint Manufacturing and Design Center at 1155 Manhattan Avenue. Peering through a metal-grated window, I see a man working on a design for a building column. Not surprising, as this nonprofit company specializes in rehabilitating former manufacturing buildings, which it then rents out to small companies. This rehabbing is one way in which a community stays close to its historical roots. It's also an attraction for many gentrifiers who want to live in areas that have a certain gritty feel. It's almost as if they're traveling into the past, yet enjoying modern-day comfort.

This is where Manhattan Avenue dead-ends at Newtown Creek, and I see a launching pad for both kayaks and canoes. This is no small matter because the presence of boaters here sends a message—we are reclaiming this area for those who live in the world of the outdoors. No, you're not going down the Delaware River enjoying a view of the woods, but your mode of travel isn't a car or a subway either. You won't catch many, or any, ocean liners going through Newtown Creek, I think, as I watch a barge, the *Cape Laura*, laden with layers of crushed automobiles, slowly pass by a kayaker heading toward the East River.[2]

One unique place that doesn't fit into the hotel chain category is the Box House Hotel, located two blocks away at 77 Box Street. It looks pretty ordinary on the outside, but inside is a different story. It's a boutique hotel, one of a kind, and was originally a window and door factory. The unusual rooms are spacious and beautiful, with sixteen-foot-high ceilings, modern kitchens, and flat-screen TVs. Like the standard-looking hotels, the Box House Hotel caters to a foreign clientele, the room price can be as low as $219 a night, and you can be in Manhattan by subway in fifteen minutes. These moderately priced hotels in the outer boroughs of New York are becoming quite popular as more and more visitors gravitate to them.

The Newtown Creek Nature Walk is at nearby Paidge Avenue, an eastward continuation of Box Street. The nature walk was designed by sculptor George Trakas, who wanted to teach visitors how nature and industry are integrated. As I walk along Newtown Creek, metal plaques describe how the plants and small trees growing along the side are related to industry. For example: the bushy bluestem, whose stems are cut and bound together to make brooms and brushes; the horsetail, which was used as a scouring brush to polish arrow shafts, and whose roots were cooked with whaling oil and salmon eggs and eaten as a delicacy. The wood from the Kentucky coffee tree serves as material for constructing boat ribs, furniture pieces, fence posts, and railroad ties. It was also a source of coffee during the Civil War. There's the American cranberry bush, used to treat high blood pressure. Not to be omitted is the Joe-Pye weed, a remedy for bladder and kidney stones. It was named after a Native American traveling medicine man in Maine. Of course, the use of natural products in industry is nothing new, but to see the plants next to end users in this industrial section of Greenpoint makes it all the more real, especially when on an outing with the kids.

Retracing my steps, I exit the park and head back to Manhattan Avenue. This portion of Manhattan Avenue, from Box Street until Greenpoint Avenue, does not have much of a Polish presence. It's fairly nondescript, with walk-up apartment buildings, take-out joints, Hispanic-owned grocery stores, and Laundromats lining the avenue.

I spot an unusual name for what turns out to be a Yemeni-owned place, the God Bless Deli. A worker there tells me: "I hate this whole business with 9/11. We, in the grocery business, didn't do it and Islam doesn't agree with killing innocent people." It's a view I've heard many times in the city, and he admits to having told this to many non-Muslim customers. Such interactions on the job between people of different nationalities is an example of *daygration*, the daytime contacts that people of different cultures have with each other as they meet on neutral ground. However superficial they may seem, they provide people of varied backgrounds, in this case Hispanics, Poles, Yemenis, and gentrifiers, with a chance to meet and engage each other in commerce and chitchat.

As I cross Greenpoint Avenue, I notice, halfway up the avenue, an unusual name for a fairly nondescript restaurant—the Chinese Musician. I am unable to associate Chinese food with anything musical, except the name of the waltz, "Chopsticks." I wonder how and why it got that name, but the cashier inside is not too helpful. "I just work here," she says. "The restaurant is owned by a man who is now living in China." She tells me that many have asked her about the name but she hasn't a clue.

An Internet search is similarly unenlightening, though one site called "Lost City," titled its review of the place: "A Good Sign: Chinese Musician Restaurant." Concluding (as did many other reviewers) that the food was, at best, average, it observed that the joint "has one of the better, and more curious, names in the city. You sorta want to eat there simply because it's called Chinese Musician. And the sign is pretty damn good too." One commenter, Ken Mac, demanded: "This mystery must be revealed. Where are the musicians?"

Continuing south on Manhattan Avenue, I confront an imposing structure, St. Anthony of Padua's Roman Catholic Church, which was established as a parish way back in 1858. It is a tall, imposing red brick and white limestone structure, with white terra cotta facing, in the Gothic Revival style. As I gaze upward from the street, I have a sense of going far back in time, to a place where there were no cars, no paved streets, just rutted roads, where people wearing handmade clothes walked the streets on a Sunday morning to see and be seen and entered the church to be at one with God. It is this sense of timelessness that attracts so many to the old churches; Brooklyn has more churches than any other borough. The churches have, however, changed over time as their clientele has shifted. While the denominational affiliation stays the same, they can sometimes become a bridge between the locals of long standing and the new arrivals.

On nearby Diamond Street, I pass by Blue Bloods Productions. There's a trailer that's been driven here all the way from Universal Studios, California. Right now they're filming *The Good Wife*. But in a week or a month it could be another series or film. Greenpoint has, in fact, become a popular location for film/TV studios, and there are quite a few scattered throughout the area.

As I walk up the block, I see that stoop culture is apparently alive and well in areas like this, consistent with their old-timey feel. People sit on the steps and give me the once-over as I pass, feeling no doubt, as I did growing up, that if I pass by "their stoop" or property they have the right to check me out. Sometimes they're drinking water, juice, or beer, and sometimes they're looking at their iPad, while grabbing some fresh air on a nice day. It's a very New York thing to do.

Continuing again on Manhattan Avenue, I enter Music Planet at number 649. It looks like any old video store with but one major difference—it has a large selection of Polish CDs and videos. There's *Star Wars* in Polish, but there are also many originals from the homeland, like *Tobie moje Serce* (You My Heart). The clerk assures me that this is the biggest such operation in the area, even as he laments the departure of so many native speakers from this place of first settlement. The store is mostly empty at 5:00 p.m. and the future does not look bright for places like this. The future and the present are quite bright for Lomzynianka Restaurant across the street at number 646. This upscale Polish eatery named after a town in Poland caters to young professionals looking to connect with the locals and is often quite crowded.

Unlike Lomzynianka, Pyza Restaurant, on Nassau Avenue, does not attract a gentrified clientele. It's a working-class Polish cafeteria that is very typical of such establishments. There are others like it along Nassau, Manhattan, and Norman Avenues. They are more authentic than Lomzynianka, both in terms of food and clientele, but they lack the outer trappings of what urban professionals expect. They're reasonably clean, but they're self-service, the sugar shakers are ordinary, the eating utensils aren't polished, the tables are very plain, the lighting is dim, and the service is, well, rather gruff, with people behind the counter who speak English haltingly, if at all. Despite the lack of amenities, they do attract some non-Polish patrons.

In truth, those who want to experience another culture fall into two types. One group wants culture lite—a good meal that happens to be Polish or Thai, a couple of signs in another language, a deli mixing sausages or bialys with more familiar fare. For them it doesn't matter whether or not it's the real deal, so long as it *feels* like it is.

The second group wants what the sociologist Sharon Zukin has called "authenticity,"[3] the genuine article. For them, Lomzynianka, despite its Polish staff, won't do. It's too dressed up. The menu seems tailor-made for tourists, the Polish customers are outnumbered by gentrifiers, and the prices are high. They want Pyza, around the corner, where *they're* outnumbered and no one pays much attention to them. The menu is on the wall in Polish and English, to accommodate the workingmen who frequent it and the occasional tourist. They have a wide selection, including goulash, chicken and pork cutlets, pierogies, stuffed cabbage, and mashed potatoes with gravy, served by the scoop. Just about everything's under ten bucks.

What accounts for this craving? For most it's an intense desire to see what it really feels like to be somewhere, even someone, else, however temporarily. It's the same as going to an ethnic music festival or street fair. And for those whose roots are Polish it's a way of coming home and feeling at home.

Two blocks away, on Nassau Street, but in the opposite direction, I enter beautiful McCarren Park. I see people of every background—black, Hispanic, white, Asian—strolling, relaxing, playing ball, supervising their children, reading, picnicking, sunning themselves—in what can only be described as a bucolic scene. Many of the groups are well integrated ethnically. It's as if a social planner or, perhaps, real estate agent, had decided to pay people of every description to show up and demonstrate how much of a melting pot New York is. But no one did anything of the sort, and that's precisely the point. In fact, most parks in the city, though not all, have this kind of mix. The reason is that New York's areas are increasingly becoming multiethnic and multiracial. Ethnically homogeneous neighborhoods are no longer the norm. This has enormous implications for attitudes, friendships, and marriages.

On Bayard Street, where it meets the Brooklyn-Queens Expressway (BQE), I come to Lentol Garden, named after former assemblyman and state senator Edward Lentol. The garden, surrounded by an eight-foot-high black steel fence, features juniper and holly trees, a Chinese dogwood, roses, tulips, black-eyed Susans, and other flora and fauna. Inviting looking, wooden benches line a landscaped path where you pass by a birdfeeder and a birdbath. I notice that one side of the park border is literally attached to the Brooklyn Queens Expressway, which runs right by here. Children play, do their artwork, and water small potted plants, scattered through the area on wooden tables, seemingly oblivious to the traffic crawling by on the visible elevated highway, a mere 50 yards away. It's an oasis in a metropolis where every inch of green space counts, even if it's hard against a major expressway.

Over on Russell Street, I stroll into Monsignor McGolrick Park. Parks aren't only about beauty, play spaces, or lakes. They have specific functions—venues for art exhibits, concerts, rallies for causes, and the like. For example, every Sunday there's a farmer's market here, run by downtoearthmarkets.com, from 11:00 a.m. to 4:00 p.m. Does it matter? Yes, different from a local grocery store, it's more likely that shopping here will become a learning experience rather than simply another chore. Parents come with their children, who discover where the produce comes from, what organic means, and why that's important.

Large, stately sycamores line some of this exquisite park's walkways. While the park has its share of vandalism, it is reasonably well maintained. It features a stately, columned brick and limestone pavilion, honoring World War I veterans of Greenpoint. A statue commemorates the Civil War battle of the *Monitor* (Union side) and the *Merrimack* (Confederacy side). The *Monitor* was actually built at Greenpoint's Continental Iron Works. It's another example of how history lessons abound in the city's parks; those willing to stop, look, and read the explanatory plaques, either to themselves or to their kids can learn a lot.

Anyone who wants to see a priceless example of what the public schools looked like one hundred years ago in New York City should look at the building on Monitor, opposite McGolrick Park—P.S. 110 at 124 Monitor Street. It has a Mansard roof, and the bricks are a rich red color, typical for public schools back then. The year of its founding, "1874" is intricately carved onto its concrete facing. The school features a French dual-language program.

A few blocks away, I come to Hausman Street, where I see an amazing sight. I've seen thousands of American flags flying in front of NYC homes, but here, almost every single house on the block has one in front of it. Why? Is this block more patriotic than any other block? As it turns out, there are seventy-three of them, some accompanied by an MIA flag as well.

I ask a middle-aged woman about it. "The flags have been here since after 9/11, honoring those who fell there, especially Catherine Fagan, who lived here. We keep them up until they get dirty and then we replace them. Most of the owners have lived here for many years and they just decided to do it."

"What are the nationalities of these people?"

"Mostly Italian, Polish, Irish, German. There's even a Muslim family and they also fly it. And you can see the World Trade Center area clearly from here." Fixing me with a determined stare, she says: "We'll never forget what happened there."

This is clearly an unusually strong commemoration of 9/11, because it's so heavily concentrated on one block. Yet in the larger sense it's not unusual in the least. If there is one thing that genuinely unites all New Yorkers it is the memory of 9/11. Besides the numbers of people directly affected, there is the fact that the burning Twin Towers were seen by hundreds of thousands of horrified spectators. From Belle Harbor to Throgs Neck, from Hunters Point to Harding Park, as well as from New Jersey to Long Island, people saw buildings filled with human beings collapse.[4] A skyline is for the most part static, and its sameness gives the viewer a sense of security. So when the skies filled with flames and smoke on that sunny September day, there was a stunning and profound change. There was a feeling of shock, awe, and even perverse wonderment. "How could such a thing happen?" People stared in amazement at the unfolding tragedy as what they heard on the radio or saw on TV came to life.

Hausman Street—an American flag for every house

And then later they told everyone who hadn't seen it what it looked like to them. Like the 1963 Kennedy assassination, to this very day people ask, "Where were you when it happened?" All this and more is why 9/11 unites New Yorkers in a powerful and enduring way.

Crossing beneath the BQE on Kingsland Avenue, I discover the One Stop Beer Shop. It's in a rapidly gentrifying area, as indicated by the box-like metal and glass structures sprouting up here, there, and everywhere. They are interspersed with one-hundred-year-old tenements in varying condition, as well as row houses.

The menu is a cut above standard "bar food," but what makes it a standout among beer joints is the variety of beers offered, seventy bottles and sixteen taps as of August 2014. No wonder *New*

York Magazine called their collection "encyclopedic." One-Stop also features an unusual zigzag-shaped bar that encourages social interaction even beyond the usual convivial atmosphere that prevails in such establishments.

The back of their business card has small boxes numbered from 1 to 40, and every time you buy a beer a number is punched. When you hit 40 you're a member of the Beer Society. The special patch bestowed on you, with your name on it, is posted on the wall. Members of the Beer Society receive invitations to tasting events and are given discounts. To keep you focused on the goal of becoming a member of the society, and, perhaps, pleasantly inebriated, a pint on the house is yours for every four beers consumed. One Stop's specialties are craft beers like Stone Levitation Amber, Old Rasputin Stout, Mama Mia Pizza Beer, Two Bro Cane and Ebel, and Mad River Jamaica Red Ale.

I complete my walk on Beadel Street. The streets in this area, on either side of the BQE, would be great for a student or artist looking for cheap digs. People who can afford better, do not, as a rule, opt for a place that is noisy 24/7 and faces a wall or a busy highway. And the homes on quieter, adjacent blocks like Anthony, Richardson, and Lombardy Streets would be great for young, middle-class families. Between Vandervoort and Porter Avenues, Beadel is a tree-lined block, with very old, two-story, brick homes, each with slanted cellar doors reminiscent of a long-forgotten era. As I stroll down I'm reminded of an old children's song from those years:

I don't wanna play in your yard
I don't like you anymore
You'll be sorry when you see me
Sliding down my cellar door
You can holler up my rain barrel
You can climb my apple tree
But I won't play in your yard
'Cause you won't be good to me.

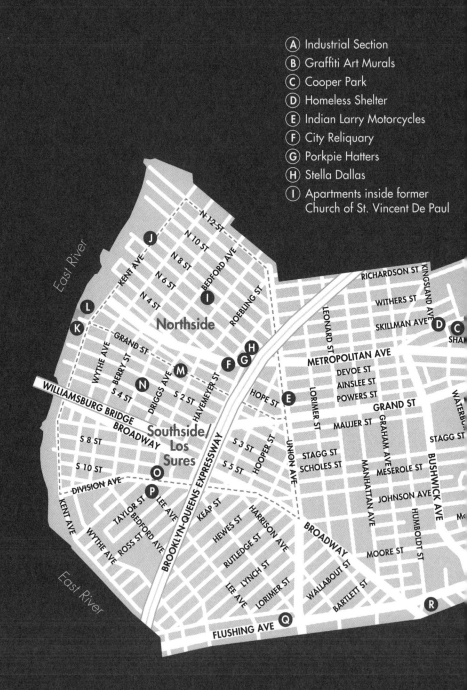

(A) Industrial Section
(B) Graffiti Art Murals
(C) Cooper Park
(D) Homeless Shelter
(E) Indian Larry Motorcycles
(F) City Reliquary
(G) Porkpie Hatters
(H) Stella Dallas
(I) Apartments inside former
    Church of St. Vincent De Paul

East River

RICHARDSON ST
KINGSLAND AVE
WITHERS ST
SKILLMAN AVE
SHA

N 12 ST
N 10 ST
N 8 ST
N 6 ST
N 4 ST
KENT AVE
BEDFORD AVE
ROEBLING ST
LEONARD ST

Northside

METROPOLITAN AVE
DEVOE ST
AINSLEE ST
POWERS ST
GRAND ST
MAUJER ST
GRAHAM AVE
STAGG ST
MANHATTAN AVE
MESEROLE ST
BUSHWICK AVE
WATERB
STAGG ST
JOHNSON AVE
HUMBOLDT ST
Mo
SCHOLES ST
LORIMER ST
UNION AVE

GRAND ST
WYTHE AVE
BERRY ST
S 4 ST
DRIGGS AVE
S 2 ST
HAVEMEYER ST
HOPE ST

WILLIAMSBURG BRIDGE

BROADWAY
S 8 ST
S 10 ST
DIVISION AVE

Southside/
Los
Sures

BROOKLYN-QUEENS EXPRESSWAY
S 3 ST
S 5 ST
HOOPER ST

KENT AVE
WYTHE AVE
ROSS ST
BEDFORD AVE
TAYLOR ST
LEE AVE
KEAP ST
HEWES ST
RUTLEDGE ST
HARRISON AVE
LEE AVE
LYNCH ST
LORIMER ST
WALLABOUT ST
BARTLETT ST
MOORE ST
BROADWAY

East River

FLUSHING AVE

J
L
K
I
M
N
F
G
H
E
D
C
O
P
Q
R

WILLIAMSBURG

WILLIAMSBURG'S OVERALL BOUNDARIES, GENERALLY, ARE N. 15TH AND N. 12TH Streets, plus Bayard and Richardson Streets to the north; the Queens line to the east, Flushing Avenue to the south, and Kent Avenue to the west. These borders, however, contain four quite distinct, geographic communities— gentrifiers, artists and musicians, Hasidim, and Puerto Ricans. In the nineteenth century it was a largely industrial section, with foundries, breweries, sugar refineries, and shipyards; there was also a resort area for the wealthy. In the early twentieth century it became a melting-pot community of Poles, Italians, Jews, and other groups. Later on, the area deteriorated, and by the 1990s, most of it was considered quite dangerous. However, it has since enjoyed a major rebirth, in the northern, and lately, eastern sections, with apartment prices now skyrocketing. It is perhaps the largest rejuvenated neighborhood in New York and one with easy access to Manhattan. It is emblematic of why Brooklyn is now seen as the hottest borough.

The northern section, known as "Northside," is the portion that has gentrified the most, almost to the point where it resembles SoHo or Chelsea. The border of this area now spreads into the southern portion, which was once almost completely Puerto Rican and known by its residents as *Los Sures*. South and east of *Los Sures* is the Hasidic section, which is home, primarily, to members of the Satmar sect of Hasidim. The Hasidic section is not gentrifying at all, for this group is determined to maintain it as a separate enclave and has economic resources and clout with local politicians to ensure that it stays that way. The eastern section, which contains an industrial zone, is now becoming an alternative to gentrifiers priced out of the north. It also has a sizeable number of artists and musicians who live and work in lofts and basements that were once warehouses and factories.

While these are distinct communities, it is more interesting, even exciting, to see them as a microcosm of what the Big Apple really is, an incredibly diverse collection of communities where completely different types of people share space with one another, occasionally clashing when defending their interests, but mostly coexisting peacefully. We begin our tour in East Williamsburg, also known as Industrial Bushwick.[5]

Williamsburg's industrial area is a perfect place to discover what the city looked like in the early twentieth century, when heavy industry and manufacturing dominated—streets like Waterbury, Stagg, Morgan, Ten Eyck, Gardiner, Scholes, and Meadows, among others. I begin my trip walking up Randolph Street toward Stewart Avenue. As I wander this part of East Williamsburg (view the map for its boundaries), I can see the old smokestacks, the hulks of now silent factories, some being converted into condos, others reborn into new businesses. Although greatly diminished in number, there are still factories here, and they serve an important purpose. Without them, food, now prepared and bottled here, would take a lot longer to get to the city. The same is true for building materials, polishing, buffing, painting, metal recycling, towing, auto collision repairs, couches, beds, ladders, leather jackets, shirts, musical

Meserole and Waterbury Streets—where graffiti art rules

instruments, and other products. And when I look around and see the shimmering and glorious Manhattan skyline so close and yet still at a distance, I can, nevertheless, feel the connection to it.

Leaving this area, I head over to the intersection of Meserole and Waterbury Streets in East Williamsburg, where there are some astounding artistic displays. Those in the know come from all over the world with cameras to view and photograph the murals, many created by well-known graffiti artists like Shepard Fairey, Dasic Fernandez, Werc, Icy and Sot, and Giant Robot. The murals change quite frequently, but they are almost always interesting. Whenever I go, I stop in to have a cup of coffee at the Newtown Café on Waterbury, which has an excellent view of the artworks.

Heading north on Waterbury, I enter the small, yet still substantial, Cooper Park. I look around and see groups of Hispanic people cooking meat and fish on the nine barbecue grills. Nearby, people play tennis on courts without nets. Every Sunday from April through October, local farmers sell their products at a farmer's market. One stand sells not only popsicles but also *pupsicles*. Indeed, I see a dog, with the help of her owner, selecting a watermelon-flavored one. She licks it with great relish. I learn that humans are also allowed to buy these one dollar pupsicles. A gimmick, but it draws people in.

Next, I head west one block and notice, just off to my right, a cluster of old, gray, brick buildings. It's a homeless shelter on the site of the old Greenpoint Hospital, just off Kingsland Avenue. Shelters are often flashpoints for controversy, as many residents worry about panhandling and crime. One man has lived two blocks from it for three years but had no idea it was even there. Another person says that as far as he knows, no one from the shelter has ever bothered anyone. People here have babies, they're reasonably well off, but the proximity to the shelter doesn't seem to be a factor in their decision making. The guards look surprised when I ask them about it. "Yes, it's a shelter, but it's not a jail or even a work-release program. So what's the big deal?" One man in his thirties said he'd heard of people being harassed, but he's not concerned. "If you're safe and you're smart, you won't have any problems, just like anyplace else. I first came to New York from Maine ten years ago. I lived in Bushwick, Bed-Stuy; never had any problems." The reality is that in densely populated parts of the city, people are just more accepting, sometimes even resigned, to its imperfections. In more sprawling and homogeneous Marine Park or Bergen Beach, a shelter or group home might cause a fuss, but not in polyglot Williamsburg.

Two blocks away, I strike up a conversation with a medium-height young man in his thirties, wearing a faded polo shirt, jeans shorts, and sneakers. Tim lives in a late nineteenth-century yellow brick row house. Hailing from Oregon, he works as a gym trainer.

Creativity is everywhere; too bad you can't always own it

His girlfriend, a New Yorker, works in marketing for a major publisher.

"What's it like to live here?" I ask.

"It's unique."

"Unique?"

"The landlord made it all very hip and urban. He pulled up all the flooring, scraped all the flooring so you could still see the original paint from the 1900s, as well as the door jambs, and he left all the metal catches that were there before. Then he put in modern stainless steel appliances, granite kitchen counters." This is what the younger people like, preserving the old while putting in the new.

"What would it cost to buy one of these?"

"Probably a million. He got it five or six years ago for about 600 thousand. The owner is charging $1,500 for a room. And there are six rooms here, plus a common space. And we have a one bedroom upstairs. We have an outdoor space, which is really cool, and we're near the L train. There's great demand here. I haven't seen anything for sale on this block in two years. Greenpoint's also getting taken over. The Hasids are starting to buy all these buildings and kicking people out. Knockin' em down and building new ones. I don't know about the legality of all this, but people have been doin' it forever."

Tim tells me that there are still many Poles and Italians living on the block. He doesn't mind living with them. They're not his type but he likes the fact that they're here. "They give the block character," he notes. He's also keenly aware that he's the new guy on the block. Who's he to resent anyone?

"How do you feel about not being in the center of everything, like in North Williamsburg?"

"I like it better here. It's quieter. Besides they all come here to these bars because they're divey and cheaper, places like 'The Boulevard.'" In others words, the digs in North Williamsburg might be more upscale, but they still want to spend time in his part of the 'hood.

"Why do you think the people from the nearby projects don't bother you?"

"Because we wave and smile at each other. We're from the same neighborhood. I go to the same bodegas they do, you know. They might do their thing elsewhere, but not here, where they live."

There's some truth to this last comment too, I'll admit. But, as I've discovered, another important factor that he hasn't elaborated on is that residents who "do their thing," meaning illegal activities, clearly understand that messing with the gentrifiers will bring heat on them, and they don't want that. It's also an example of the lack of real meaningful contact between these disparate groups. This is side-by-side living, but not integration in any sense. Neither he nor most other gentrifiers mix socially with the poorer residents who preceded them.

Nearby, where Maspeth and Metropolitan Avenues come together, I head west to Union Street where I stop in at a motorcycle shop known as Indian Larry Motorcycles, one of the best known in the country. Indian Larry, born Lawrence DeSmedt in New York, was a famous builder of choppers, losing his life at age fifty-five in a motorcycle accident. His nickname came from a chopper brand that he rode, though his face looked like the one on an old Indian head nickel. His creations were featured on the Discovery Channel and in *Easy Rider Magazine*, and he won all sorts of awards and was therefore widely known to bike enthusiasts. Inside are beautiful bikes, including two very expensive choppers with stupendous, intricate designs that sell for $350K and $750K. The second one, featured in the Neiman Marcus Christmas catalog, is known as "Wild Child."

Returning to Metropolitan, I turn left, walk under the BQE and enter the City Reliquary. It's a not-for-profit civic organization and community museum, specializing in artifacts and memorabilia about New York City. The choices are eclectic, based not on significance, it would seem, but more on whether the president of the organization, Dave Herman, found them both interesting and available. There are so many that only a fraction of them can be mentioned here. There's an exhibit about baseball great and former Brooklyn Dodgers player Jackie Robinson, mostly photos. A large collection of miniature Statues of Liberty, several actual subway doors, stones from the Waldorf Astoria and from the St. Moritz Hotel, and, unrelated to New York, collections of oil cans and pencil sharpeners all contribute to a sense that this is a place where the unusual rules the day.

I walk into Porkpie Hatters, at 441 Metropolitan, which has a large array of hats of all sorts, including some that one might associate with "hipster culture." Engaging the salesperson/manager in a conversation about that, I get an earful about the term *hipster*, as he sees it: "I don't even know what hipster means anymore. No one says: 'I'm a hipster,' but the most hipster thing in the world is to deny being a hipster."

Indeed, there are many definitions of hipster. The online *Urban Dictionary* has at least seven, and since New York City, especially Williamsburg, is seen as a center for such people, it's worth noting a little bit of what they say, to wit: "a subculture of young people who value independent thinking, counter-culture, progressive politics, an appreciation of art and indie-rock, creativity, intelligence, and witty banter." That might do it, but then again, who knows? Perhaps it's also worth quoting Stormageddon, Dark Lord of All, who noted in *Urban Dictionary* that: "Hipsters can't be defined because then they'd fit into a category, and thus be too mainstream."

Walking along Havemeyer Street, I strike up a conversation with Angelo, an eighty-seven-year old Italian man. Short, with a stocky build, steel gray thinning hair, and leathered, darkish skin, he greets me effusively when I say hello, as though I were an old friend.

"How do you feel about the neighborhood gentrifying?"

"I don't like it one bit. Agh, these yuppies. They're like gypsies in the house. You're the landlord, but if you're not there, you're livin' in Bellmore (a far-away, Long Island community), maybe, six of dem come in."

"Six of them? I thought they were all rich."

"No, no. You're not there. They all come into this one bedroom and six a dem chip in to pay $1,800 or whatever. And in and out. All different kinds a shit. And next door to my house."

It's clear that he doesn't like the fact that the newcomers are doubling and tripling up instead of renting an entire apartment like a couple. But, as we see, it goes deeper than that. It's really a clash of values that's sometimes manifested by offensive behavior, as least as he sees it, even more a trampling on communal institutions, which matters a great deal to him. Here's what he says: "For all this time, the church here has been ringing the bell on Sunday morning to tell the people to go to services. But no, this yuppie shit has no respect. They made the church stop ringin' the bell so that they could sleep. Can you imagine that? There was a time here years ago, when we had the Mafia, they would never get away with that. They would grab 'em by the collar and tell 'em: 'Don't you dare say anything about that!'"

What's really going on here? Why such hostility? It's because when Angelo observes these young, often well-heeled newcomers, eating in their restaurants and cafés, partying in each other's homes, wearing outfits that he wouldn't be caught dead in, using iPhones whose workings remain a mystery to him, he feels rejected. To them, it appears, his way of life is irrelevant, archaic even.

The saints he reveres, whose iconic presence spans both continents and generations, the ones whose miracles saved communities from disasters known only to their members, mean nothing to the hipsters and yuppies he passes on the street and who largely ignore his presence. At best, the annual feasts organized and attended by Angelo's friends and, hopefully, his own children, seem quaint, old-school relics that nevertheless convey a certain authenticity that entitles the new arrivals to contend they have reclaimed the city, even as they remake it to suit their own needs and values. Listen to the words of Chris Tocco, an actor whose name suggests his own Italian Catholic roots: "It was a tiny parade and they shut down Graham Avenue. There was one float and a horrible marching band. It was very ironic. The Latino parades are more festive." That's the verdict. Priority should be given to those with better music. For Tocco it's all about entertainment and not at all about tradition. The rejection of what *was* is given voice by Jon McGrath, twenty-seven, who observed, "It seems very old-school. It's kind of like a vestige of the old neighborhoods of Brooklyn."[6]

The newer classes also want to feel they're living in a place with real history, but one tailored to their needs—quaint and authentic, yet not challenging their lifestyles. One new resident, Jack Szarapka, ran a popular Williamsburg place called Second Stop Café, but before he did so, he thought of creating a juice bar and calling it St. Francis Xavier Juice Bar. After all, he'd gotten a statue of the saint. Would that have been seen as irreverent by the older crowd? Maybe, but to him it was probably a way of connecting to the past.

When Angelo reflects on the irreverence of the new generation that now lives in the area, he invokes the Mafia as the solution. He knows about their depredations, their well-deserved reputation for lawlessness. But he also remembers them as enforcers of tradition and respect for it. He points to an older home, a tidy two-story clapboard affair with yellowish aluminum siding, and a neat lawn, on which rests a blue and white statue of the Virgin Mary. "This they wanna knock down and put in a new ugly building with glass and metal that looks like a box."

Angelo is also expressing his frustration at a new way of life that he knows he can never be part of. And when he talks about their efforts to stop the church bells from ringing, his voice rising, filled with anger, his ire is focused not only upon their insensitivity to the old ways but also to their meaning: the calls for prayer are not important, and most of all, need not be heeded. This chasm between him and them is sometimes highlighted even more when he discovers that these young professionals are themselves from working-class backgrounds, even Italian perhaps.

My conversation with Angelo is by no means limited to Williamsburg. It could just as easily have taken place in Cobble Hill, Prospect Heights, Carroll Gardens, or in Astoria, and Hunters Point, in fact, in dozens of communities throughout the city.

The "trendy" hipster part of Williamsburg is in an area called Northside, stretching from N. 1st to N. 11th Street and from

Havemeyer to Kent Street, on the water. Its nerve center is Bedford and N. 7th Street, where the L train steadily disgorges a broad mix of mostly young tourists from every corner of the globe, Wall Street hedge fund moguls, and hipsters.

To stroll these blocks by day is to experience New York in its most gentrified state, with block after block of sleek new buildings, some utilitarian, others with tasteful brick/terracotta designs, and some that would look perfectly at home on East End or West End Avenues. Still, some tenements remain standing, their presence a reminder of what once was and will never again return, their days numbered as they wait for the wrecking ball wielded by the latest developer. There are boutiques here of every kind—hats, dresses, pocketbooks, vintage clothing, lingerie—and suitable for every taste, but always the unusual and exotic is stressed, even flaunted, in the show windows.

To travel down these streets by night is to see a totally different scene, a vibrant area filled with laughing, loudly conversing people back from a day's work and out for a night of dining, imbibing, and having fun. What's "in" is constantly changing, but the clubs, with long lines, bouncers, flashing lights, are a constant, and there seems to be no end to the demand. People wait patiently, trooping up the stairs into a scene of strobe lights, closely packed dance floors, and music at decibel levels that bring to mind the refrain, "If it's too loud you're too old."[7]

On N. 6th Street, near Havemeyer, I take a look at Stella Dallas and recognize it immediately as one of many vintage shops in the area. For those unfamiliar with the term's precise meaning here, "vintage" is to young people what "used" clothing is to the older generation. Does this mean that it's just a polite term for stuff from Goodwill? Yes and no, at least at Stella Dallas (the name of a 1937 film starring Barbara Stanwyck). They have one of the largest collections of such clothing, and it ranges from very ordinary fare to really great finds.

It's a very large, long store, filled from ceiling to floor with a gigantic selection of men's and women's clothing. Besides the usual clientele, Stella caters to filmmakers and TV producers looking for things that have a genuine old-timey look, which they usually rent for use in a film or TV episode.

There are sundresses, party dresses, shearling coats, bomber jackets, and fringed cowboy jackets; sweaters, mink stoles, the kind your grandmother wore in the 1950s, selling for $120; hundreds of T-shirts from the past with logos ranging from "Dallas Cowboys" to "U.S. Route One," to "Saturday Nite Fiedler," that is, Arthur Fiedler of Boston Pops fame. Another reads: "Firemen Never Die. Their Flames Just Go Out." There are old shoes and boots of every description and color—suede, saddle, wing tip, golf shoes. There's also a huge section devoted to military outfits and uniforms.

What's the deal here?, I think to myself. They're taking a previous generation's castaways and charging real money for them. Perhaps it's a form of time travel. Buy a hippie outfit and you're transported back to the sixties. Want to go to the fifties? Get a Howdy Doody doll, or a cowboy shirt with Hopalong Cassidy on it. Find an old toaster that still works. For some, the time period and memorabilia are irrelevant. They just like the way it looks and feels. Something funky to wear to a costume party or to dance in. Caveat emptor, as they say. The market determines the need, as well as the price.

Farther up on 6th Street stands a beautiful old Catholic church, its tall spires seemingly looking down reproachfully at the shops and the passing crowds of revelers. St. Vincent de Paul served the community for 145 years before being sold in 2011 to a private developer. No longer a church, it's been "converted" into forty lofts, renting in 2014 from between $4,500 to $5,500 a unit. As I enter I peer down a very long narrow corridor, perhaps a city block long, on each side of which are apartments. Inside the apartments, the gothic look has been preserved, with beams crisscrossing through the living room and balcony, along with exposed old brickwork.

On Kent and Grand Streets, there's a mural painted by a local group, El Puente, made up of mostly young local students and artists. The mural, about a city block long, records the community's history. Forebears of members of the community came to Puerto Rico from Spain and worked in the sugarcane fields. The mural reads: "Welcome to La Communidad of Los Sures, the south side of Williamsburg, where we take you on a journey that builds bridges to our rich history and culture." Eventually, centuries later, Puerto Ricans came to the United States, and a large number moved into Williamsburg. The mural depicts the historical stages of this journey. Community members reflect on it: "My dream for *Los Sures* is that we start waking up and empowering ourselves to do better and hold on to whatever little bit that we have." An elderly man shown in the mural, with white curly hair, says: "I miss my sugar house. I'm glad I was part of history working in the factory." There's a photo of him at work. His wife is depicted seated on a sofa in their apartment. Kids are shown enjoying the water from a fire hydrant. Women, their hair in rollers, are seated under lamps. A young girl is blowing bubbles. The words read: "I feel most comfortable when I see people in *Los Sures* in front of their homes."

I meet Charlie Ames, who has come here with his wife and a home health aide to eat lunch in a small urban oasis—Grand Ferry Park, built with the help of El Puente. He's an elderly man who walks slowly with a cane. A retired high school teacher whose father graduated from Harvard and taught at Stony Brook, he tells me. "The Domino Sugar factory site is right here, behind the mural." Charlie gives me a bit of "inside" info: "See that lady in the mural? They made a mistake in configuring the mural and had an empty space. So they put in this woman who's not part of the community. She collects the garbage in the park. But so what? She looks good in it." He sits at a wooden picnic table and invites me to share his food, which he has brought from home. Coming here is a daily activity, enabling him and his wife to eat and enjoy a spectacular vista of the New York skyline on the other side of the river, as boats of all types slowly glide by. As I face Manhattan it's possible to take in a panoramic view that includes the CitiCorp, Chrysler, and Empire State buildings, the projects, the new WTC, and the three bridges—Manhattan, Brooklyn, and Williamsburg. Couples are sitting on the big rocks, enjoying their lunch. Terrific views, from a cozy, nongentrified park.

Leaving the park, I take Grand Street and pass by the Caribbean Social Club near Driggs Avenue, informally known as Tonita's, after the woman who owns it. Walk by quickly and you could miss it. There's just a Corona Extra sign in a window covered partially with lace curtains. I look inside and see a pool table in a cluttered but homey setting. Men, most of them Puerto Rican, are playing dominoes at a table nearby and watching a boxing match, and some couples might be dancing to salsa music.[8]

On Bedford Avenue and S. 3rd Street, my attention is drawn to a very strange, almost haunting green, white, and brown wall mural. It's a creation of the artist Mike Makatron. There's a snail, and ascending along its spiral shell is a black iron railing, as though it were a walking path. At the top there's a large fire hydrant with Makatron's name on it and the initials, NYC. At the bottom in front of the snail, I see a WALK/DON'T WALK sign, and a one way sign. Stabbed into the ground at crazy angles are cigarette butts. There's a motorcycle behind it and the word "Everfresh" on a chainsaw. That's the Melbourne-based studio to which Mike belongs, one that specializes, among other things, in very bright colors. I ask a young Asian man, who turns out to be a recently arrived Californian, what he thinks about the mural. "I love it," is his response. "It's so New York, the style, the vibe. I wouldn't see this kind of thing in Los Angeles."

I head south to Hasidic Williamsburg and pay a brief visit to the venerable Gottlieb's Deli, located at 352 Roebling. Forget Katz's, Carnegie, and Second Avenue Deli icons. For truly authentic Jewish, kosher food from the old country, this insider joint is the best—and inexpensive too.

I stroll down Lee Avenue, the community's main shopping drag. A posted dress code outside a Hasidic-owned take-out food shop warns, "No sleeveless, no shorts, no low-cut necklines allowed in this store." I wonder if these rules are enforced, since the outsiders most apt to violate them would be shocked that they can't dress as they please. A sign in another store window at 173A Lee Avenue orders, "Stockings whose color closely resembles the skin are not to be worn."

There are dozens of schools, synagogues, and catering halls jammed into this crowded area, one that has one of the highest birth rates in the United States. I pass by a red brick building that was once a public school. Today, it's a Hasidic elementary school for boys only, as the sexes are segregated for education. The yard is crowded and the boys are playing punch ball as bearded teachers in long black coats keep a watchful eye on their charges. Synagogues in the neighborhood vary in size from large brick structures with grand entryways flanked by lighted globes—whose soft glow light up the marble staircases for the worshipers who come here four or five times daily to pray and study the Talmud, as prescribed by law—to simple one room affairs on the first floor of brownstones.

In the streets during the daylight hours, women wearing wigs, topped by pillbox-shaped hats, covered from head to toe, though not the face, wheel baby carriages, while their older children tag along, running before, along, and behind their mothers, lingering before toy store displays, pizza shops, and bakeries, clamoring for cars, fire trucks, and board games with Yiddish instructions, pizza, doughnuts, and *kokosh*, a Hungarian cake, filled with rich chocolate.

The walls of apartment buildings are plastered with articles about local community issues, upcoming biblical marathons to be held in Madison Square Garden or Citi-Field that will be attended by thousands of men. To me it feels as though the villages of nineteenth-century Hungary have been vaulted via a time machine into the twenty-first century, where modern culture and technology have been adapted to meet the needs of the community—McDonald's is now McDovids, there's Shalom Kosher Pizza, DVDs are sanitized to keep the outside world at bay, cell phones have built-in devices to prevent Internet access, and on and on.

But, as in the rest of the city, no community, no matter how insular, can completely wall itself off from the world. This comes into sharp focus when I reach Flushing Avenue at the end of Lee Avenue and make a left. The street seems to divide the Hasidic neighborhood of Williamsburg from that of mostly black Bedford-Stuyvesant. I stand on Flushing and see how it starkly sets off two distinct communities. On the south side is the New York City Housing Authority's (NYCHA) Marcy Houses, low-income projects, predominantly black, where the rapper Jay-Z (the J and Z subway lines ran nearby) grew up. Here black kids shoot hoops in the park while adults sit on nearby park benches, engaged in casual conversation or simply relaxing. On the north side of Flushing Avenue is the Hasidic community.[9]

The recently built red brick apartment buildings have terraces where I can see youngsters, wearing large black skullcaps and with side curls dangling by their ears, standing and animatedly talking and laughing. Some are intently watching the basketball game in progress. Do they harbor a secret desire to join the game? What a chasm between the two sides of the street, both culturally and economically. They're in different universes. The Hasidim live in privately built apartment residences and those in the Marcy Houses are in a low-income development. We know from what has happened in Crown Heights that Hasidic Jews and blacks can get along fairly well. But these are the very insular Satmar Hasidim, not the Lubavitcher, whose turf is Crown Heights. The Satmar are not into outreach.

As I wind down my journey through this kaleidoscope-like, incredibly varied section of Brooklyn on Humboldt Street near Flushing Avenue, I come across the Sumner Hotel, a modern, Comfort Inn–type place that attracts tourists from around the world. These motels are present in many outlying areas, like Fourth Avenue in Brooklyn's Gowanus neighborhood. But this one is hard up against the not always safe NYCHA Bushwick Houses. In the end, this is typical of many neighborhoods. It's almost impossible to live in a large city and construct a protective bubble where you will not see extreme poverty or great wealth, where everyone will feel comfortable with everyone else. The city cannot be controlled that way, but that's exactly what makes it so fascinating.

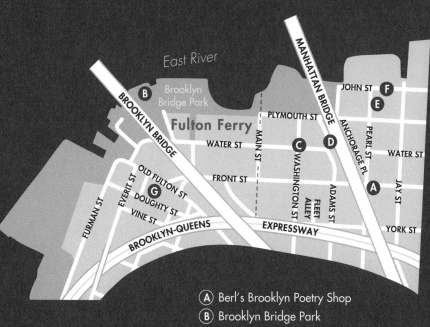

East River

Brooklyn Bridge Park

Fulton Ferry

BROOKLYN BRIDGE

MANHATTAN BRIDGE

JOHN ST

PLYMOUTH ST

WATER ST

MAIN ST

FRONT ST

WASHINGTON ST

ANCHORAGE PL

PEARL ST

WATER ST

JAY ST

FLEET ALLEY

ADAMS ST

YORK ST

OLD FULTON ST

EVERIT ST

DOUGHTY ST

VINE ST

FURMAN ST

BROOKLYN-QUEENS   EXPRESSWAY

(A) Berl's Brooklyn Poetry Shop
(B) Brooklyn Bridge Park
(C) Vista of Empire State Building
(D) "Watergate"
(E) Recycle a Bicycle
(F) Media Center
(G) Eagle Warehouse & Storage Company

DUMBO

DUMBO (DOWN UNDER THE MANHATTAN BRIDGE OVERPASS) is a neighborhood that treasures and promotes authenticity. In the nineteenth century, it was home to factories that produced boxes, steel wool, paint, shoes, tin cans, and kerosene. In the 1920s industry began moving elsewhere in the city and the country, attracted by less expensive locations. Industry also began to decline generally, and the Depression dealt a severe blow to the area. By the 1940s, most of the factories had become warehouses or office buildings. Finally, the construction of the BQE further contributed to a sense of isolation. In the 1970s artists began living here in empty warehouses and factories. This history, and the cobbled streets, gave it a certain cachet. And despite the fact that there are other areas, like Red Hook, that also have authenticity by way of factories, very old houses, and cobblestone streets, DUMBO has become a much "hotter" place. Why?

First, developer David Walentas purchased land and buildings here, creating a buzz, and thereby attracting other investors. It's also far easier to get to, using the F or A trains, than Red Hook, which has no subway. Plus, the shiny Manhattan skyscrapers across the river and the projects and remaining tenements along the waterfront make for a fascinating juxtaposition between the old and the new—one can see all of Gotham's history with one glance. Many of its old factory buildings have been converted into luxury or middle-class apartments while retaining the outer factory-facade look. DUMBO is bounded by the East River on the north, Jay Street on the east, York Street on the south, and Furman Street on the west.

DUMBO began changing over from a fairly nondescript area in 2008. Today, it contains a plethora of eateries, boutiques, upscale supermarkets, and pharmacies, here called "apothecaries." There's a small place on Front Street known as Berl's Brooklyn Poetry Shop whose owners claim it's the only store in New York City devoted solely to poetry. Running a business of this sort is no easy feat, as works of poetry are almost impossible to profitably publish. They sell books, sponsor readings and other events, and partner with many small presses in Brooklyn and around the world. It's certainly a fitting venue; the shop is minutes away from where Walt Whitman once worked and hung out.

Places like Berl's are important not only to their customers but also to the community as a whole. Even if people don't take advantage of what these places offer, they're part of how a community projects itself to the outside world. People take pride in telling others, "We have a poetry shop, an art gallery, a great restaurant," and such. It's like people who say: "I love living in (or near) the city. There's the ballet, the opera, Carnegie Hall, the Met." Never mind that they rarely go to those places. They are there and can be easily accessed. These places also make the area seem more desirable.

I head over to Brooklyn Bridge Park. Close to Brooklyn Heights, it's a beautifully landscaped park that provides an opportunity to see Brooklyn's diversity on full display. Adults of all ages and teenagers vie for space on benches and in the grass as bicyclists and roller-bladers speed past. An occasional Hasidic or traditional Muslim family enjoys an outing as a Czech documentary film crew points its cameras at the space across the water where the orginal World Trade Center once stood. For the Muslims and Hasidim, this is an ideal location—beautiful views, basketball courts, a place for kids to play, and more. Members of these groups do not go to movies or theaters, nightclubs, cafés, dance halls; the park provides their entertainment. Carnival music accompanies a brightly lit carousel whose riders include Asian couples seemingly in love and small Hispanic children accompanied by adults. There's even a wedding party being filmed against the Lower Manhattan skyline. And why not? The park has new and creatively designed landscapes that feature flower beds, lawns, and winding paths along the waterfront.[10] On nearby Main

Street, posters are mounted on a faded, multicolored brick wall in preparation for an upcoming DUMBO Arts Festival.

The views from under the bridge toward Manhattan are stupendous. Walking east along Water Street, I discover, where it crosses with Washington Street, a great view of Manhattan. It's encapsulated within a stunning vista of the Empire State Building that appears to be positioned just underneath the bridge when it's actually miles away.

Nearby, in an archway under the bridge, is a blue painted, pixelated, and wavy metal gate meant to look like waves in the ocean and dubbed "Watergate." The artist, Casey Opstad, says that the work was inspired by the powerful role of water in shaping the area. It's definitely worth seeing.

A sign above a storefront on Pearl Street reads: "Recycle a Bicycle." It's another one-of-a kind nonprofit enterprise. They take donated bicycles and rehabilitate them, partnering with public schools and providing environmental education for youth. The proprietor tells me that this not-for-profit program has so far rehabbed about 1,200 bikes. They teach kids about the importance of cycling and how to repair and maintain bicycles. The kids learn how to build bikes and also participate in charitable events and programs. Recycle a Bicycle is the only nonprofit in the city that does this; they have a branch in the East Village as well. It's places like this that reflect the values of many of the young people who've settled in DUMBO—combining entrepreneurship with a genuine concern for others less fortunate.

My last stop is at the Media Center on John Street. A "hook" of some sort can often help a business succeed, and the Media Center has one. It's overseen by the Independent Filmmaker Project, which, in turn, is funded by the city's Economic Development Corporation. And the hook is its claim to be the only workspace devoted to creative artists and writers who are combining storytelling with technological resources. In the big spacious area classes are offered on how to edit a documentary or narrative and seminars are held on

Brooklyn living—Manhattan viewing

filmmaking. Wi-fi, printing facilities, and a café are available, all for a membership of about $140 a month. A dedicated workspace costs $450 a month. The goal is to provide a home for people interested in "story and tech"—a film, book, or website.

To the west of DUMBO lies a tiny neighborhood, no more than a few blocks, known as Fulton Ferry. It has old buildings, though there is quite a bit of the new too. I walk down Old Fulton Street and see the bronze-lettered sign framing a building's archway entrance; it reads, "Eagle Warehouse & Storage." Inside this now co-op residential building, a friendly concierge greets me and rhapsodizes about the "stunning" views of the Brooklyn Bridge and Manhattan skyline. Farther along there are some old buildings, a couple of restaurants, and a pier. Soon this will all be gone, landmarked, or adapted, replaced in large part by the march of the condos and co-ops.

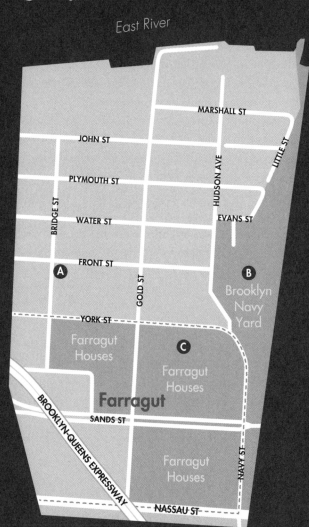

Ⓐ Los Papi's Restaurant
Ⓑ Navy Yard commandant's residence
Ⓒ Farragut Houses

East River

MARSHALL ST

JOHN ST

PLYMOUTH ST

WATER ST

FRONT ST

Ⓐ

YORK ST

Farragut
Houses

Farragut

SANDS ST

BROOKLYN-QUEENS EXPRESSWAY

NASSAU ST

BRIDGE ST

GOLD ST

HUDSON AVE

EVANS ST

LITTLE ST

Ⓑ

Brooklyn
Navy
Yard

Ⓒ

Farragut
Houses

Farragut
Houses

NAVY ST

VINEGAR HILL

VINEGAR HILL, ONCE A PLACE WHERE THE WORKING CLASSES LIVED,
and where brothels and gambling houses flourished, stands in sharp
contrast to DUMBO. It's very quiet and quaint, no trains rumbling
overhead, with small houses and modest-sized apartment buildings. It has an almost rural feel. There's one clear reminder, however,
of where the residents live. A Con Ed power plant near the waterfront, complete with smokestacks reminiscent of earlier days, over-
looks the area. As one resident of Plymouth Street described it: "It's
country living across the street from a power plant." Its boundaries
are the East River to the north, the Brooklyn Navy Yard grounds
to the east, Nassau Street to the south, and Jay Street to the west.

The original inhabitants of this area were the Canarsee Indians,
who lived here and throughout downtown Brooklyn. Vinegar Hill
was first settled by Irish immigrants, and its name dates back to a
battle fought during the Irish Rebellion of 1798. Industry did not
come to the enclave until after World War II, when the Brillo steel
wool factory and other companies set up shop here.

While walking along Bridge Street, I come across two Spanish caf-
eterias that offer an assortment of rice, beans, chicken, and beef. I
enter one of them, Los Papi's, a place that's been around for thirty
years, and I am struck by the number of young gentrifiers sitting at
the tables, relaxing, working on their laptops.

Longtime residents in gentrifying areas often complain about the
impossibility of getting coffee for less than three bucks, but that's
not the case here, where a cheeseburger is $2.50 and a mushroom
omelet with cheese, potatoes, and toast is $5.00. Places like these
only disappear in the last stages of gentrification, but during the
transformation they remain, and the gentrifiers happily patronize
them, mingling with those they're gradually replacing as they enjoy

Naval commandant's house—one of a kind

chicharrones (fried pork rinds), bacalao (dried or salted codfish), and a variety of quesadillas. Gentrification in nearby DUMBO has been going on for at least seven years, and these joints continue to flourish. There's no telling when this will change—perhaps the space will be torn down by a buyer, the seller may be holding out for a better price, but regardless, right now, it's a bargain!

A few blocks east, at 24 Evans Street, I discover a real treasure—a large, beautiful home that was a residence for Brooklyn Navy Yard commandants. Built in 1806 in the Federal style, it features a lovely wraparound porch, an observation deck, and a greenhouse. Reportedly, the oval dining room is the same size as the Oval Office, which is not implausible, since the architect may well have been Charles

Bullfinch, noted for his buildings in the nation's capitol. Perhaps its most famous occupant was Commodore Matthew Perry, who lived there from 1841 to 1843. Today's occupant is a private individual, a physician on the faculty of Rockefeller University. It all sounds enticing, but visitors aren't allowed beyond the gate or inside, so a sidewalk or aerial view courtesy of Brownstoner.com will have to suffice.

It's well worth ambling along the streets in this immediate vicinity—Harrison, Little, Marshall, Gold, Navy. The houses are charming; I hear the birds sing and dream of the days when carriages transported people along the cobblestone roads.

But then I get a reality check as I leave Vinegar Hill along York Street and pass by the Farragut Houses, a project run by the New York City Housing Authority. It's public housing, but less grim than many other such places.

I ask a NYCHA employee: "Is crime an issue here for gentrifiers?"

"Not really. There's drug dealing and weed smoking going on here on a regular basis in the projects, but the people know if they commit crimes they're gonna get caught because of the cameras and the undercover cops. So there's very little of it."

People judge the area to be safe. One late afternoon, I walked by a brick apartment building a block from the Farragut Houses and stopped to talk with a forty-something woman dressed in black jeans and a beige acrylic sweater. "I've lived here for ten years and it's fine," she tells me. "I've also got two kids. There's a boundary here that isn't crossed." Savvy gentrifiers do take into account the fact that a nearby public housing project could be a crime problem, but that fact is weighed against the positive aspects of the neighborhood. Everywhere in the city there are gentrifying areas that have public housing projects in the neighborhood or just beyond the borders, a block or two away. Sometimes the project is part of the border. But good housing near places of work is in short supply. As more and more gentrifiers move in, their numbers create safety, and the police step up their efforts to patrol and protect.

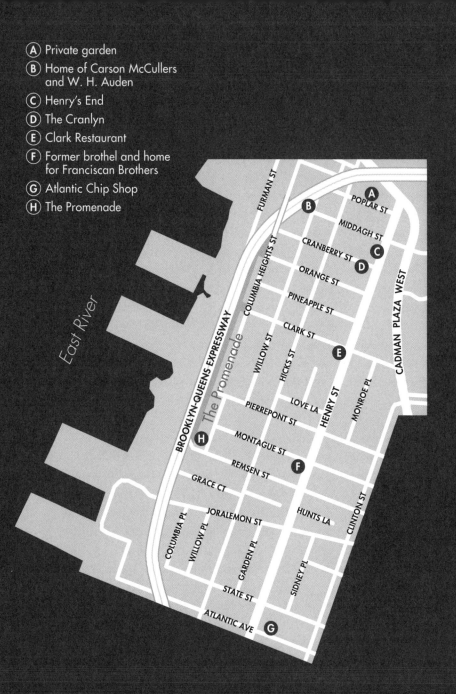

- (A) Private garden
- (B) Home of Carson McCullers and W. H. Auden
- (C) Henry's End
- (D) The Cranlyn
- (E) Clark Restaurant
- (F) Former brothel and home for Franciscan Brothers
- (G) Atlantic Chip Shop
- (H) The Promenade

East River

The Promenade

BROOKLYN-QUEENS EXPRESSWAY

FURMAN ST

COLUMBIA HEIGHTS ST

POPLAR ST

MIDDAGH ST

CRANBERRY ST

ORANGE ST

PINEAPPLE ST

CLARK ST

WILLOW ST

HICKS ST

LOVE LA

HENRY ST

MONROE PL

CADMAN PLAZA WEST

PIERREPONT ST

MONTAGUE ST

REMSEN ST

GRACE CT

JORALEMON ST

HUNTS LA

CLINTON ST

COLUMBIA PL

WILLOW PL

GARDEN PL

SIDNEY PL

STATE ST

ATLANTIC AVE

BROOKLYN HEIGHTS

BROOKLYN HEIGHTS IS THE BOROUGH'S PREMIER NEIGHBORHOOD,
and was the same well before the twentieth century. It's also been
home to rich and famous types like Norman Mailer. The neighborhood has many beautiful brownstones and luxury apartment
buildings. (The best source for seeing and photographing the
hundreds of buildings here is the American Institute of Architects [AIA] Guide.) Brooklyn Heights played an important role
in some of the most critical battles of the Revolutionary War. Despite its beauty and rich history, the neighborhood has had its ups
and downs. When the subway was extended to Brooklyn in 1908,
middle-class people replaced many of the wealthy residents. Artists and writers found the area appealing as well. Beginning in the
Depression, the neighborhood deteriorated. A positive step was
the construction in 1950 of the beautiful Promenade (also called
Esplanade, though most Brooklynites refer to it as "the Promenade") along the East River. In the 1970s, Brooklyn Heights
began to gentrify and today is considered to be one of the city's
most desirable communities.

Brooklyn Heights has convenient transportation to Manhattan,
both public and private. The boundaries are the Brooklyn-Queens
Expressway (BQE) on the north, Cadman Plaza and Clinton Street
on the east, Atlantic Avenue on the south, and the BQE and Promenade on the west. The food shopping is excellent, from traditional
supermarkets to Sahadi's, on Atlantic Avenue, a Brooklyn version
of Zabars with an emphasis on Middle Eastern foods and an outstanding deli section.

As my focus here is on the unknown, I begin with a fabulous private
garden, a full acre, on the north side of the one-block-long Poplar
Street. It's a quiet block with quaint gas lamps, an uncommon sight

in New York. It's only possible to catch a glimpse of the garden from the street, and it may look like nothing more than a narrow walkway. But there's much more to see. While officially open only to residents of the two apartment complexes on either side of it, access, if you're lucky, can be gained by hailing someone inside who just might let you in, as the residents are very proud of this Shangri-La in the heart of the city.

Whether or not to let people in is a dilemma for New Yorkers in general. Fortunately, I have a friend, Bill, who lives in one of the buildings, and he opens up the gate to give me a tour of the garden. In Central Park or on Riverside Drive or in exclusive areas like Manhattan's Sutton Place, not much can be done to prevent someone from enjoying the space. But in private places like this garden, residents control the area. Yet their pride in what they have may make them eager to obtain the positive reinforcement that admiration from outsiders brings. Satisfying this need, however, can threaten their privacy and their control over what they have created.

We walk down a narrow concrete path lined with shrubs, large bushes, trees, plants, and flowers of every shade, shape, and size, many of them rare specimens. Among them are weeping Alaskan cedars, orange trees, a rare Japanese Igiri tree, smoke trees (from afar they actually look like smoke), a Chinese golden chain tree, and many more. Bill asserts that it's "the most diverse private garden in the city of New York. Here's a kiwi plant that's not supposed to grow in this climate, but with hard work and luck we got it to take root." The garden has been tended for the last twenty-two years by a group of people dedicated to making it flourish. There are benches for contemplation and relaxation and an eating area with tables and a grill.

As we pass a hookah pipe, next to a coleus plant, Bill laughs and says: "I think I'm going to put a collection of hookah pipes here," a testament to how you can do whatever you want with a private garden. "It's hard work to do this. You've got to *understand* a garden to make it work. Over the last twenty years my friend and I replanted almost everything. I'm always planting stuff. There are hundreds of varieties in this garden. And I'm not a snob. If I see curious visitors going by and they look all right, I'll invite them in."

To say that Bill is passionate about his hobby would be an understatement, as he continues ticking off the names of whatever we see. This is the kind of thing that makes a block come together. The residents of these two buildings, plus all their friends, now have something special that they, and generally, only they, can enjoy. It's a sort of hideaway that's both real and that makes for interesting dinner talk: "We have this gorgeous garden oasis tucked away right next to where we live," and so on. Those who grow up here will always remember it fondly. Of course, it's not equivalent in beauty and range to Central Park but the difference is it's their very own park.

As we leave the garden, we are greeted on the street by a well-dressed teenager who asks us for "some change," reminding me that public space is ever present, even in the city's most exclusive precincts. I watch as he asks others, with varying results, including the owner of a private home. She sends him on his way with an admonition not to beg from people. What's rarely discussed or even noted is the risk such responses can incur. Perhaps she will anger this young man and cause him to attack her as his pent-up frustration at being rejected by others explodes into rage. Or, as happened here, he'll just move on. These are dilemmas that New Yorkers face almost daily. Should they turn down a panhandler asking for change even though they know they have two hundred dollars in their pocket? Dare they tell a subway rider occupying two seats to move over?

Bill and I head over to Columbia Heights Street, which runs parallel to the East River. It's one of the nicest streets in the neighborhood, quiet with more than a few stunning brownstones. Much of the property here is owned by the Jehovah's Witnesses organization. Bill has lived in Brooklyn Heights for many years and

Columbia Heights Street—Brooklyn in all its complexity

greets people as we walk, saying: "I know everybody here." We cross Middagh Street, home to some famous authors, including Carson McCullers and W. H. Auden, both of whom lived at one time or another at number 7. In fact, writers and other notables who've resided in Brooklyn Heights over the years are a veritable "Who's Who." They include Truman Capote, Harry Chapin, Henry Ward Beecher, Mary Tyler Moore, Paul Giamatti, Sarah Jessica Parker, Arthur Miller, Walt Whitman, and Thomas Wolfe. It has also been home for decades to a substantial gay population. Just about every building here is landmarked. In fact, Brooklyn Heights became New York City's first historic district back in 1965.

My friend takes his leave, and I walk over to Henry Street, stopping in at Henry's End, founded in 1973 and owned by Mark Lahm. It has a first-rate selection of wines and has been recognized by *Wine Spectator*. Most unusual is its Seasonal Wild Game Festival menu featuring exotic dishes such as New Orleans turtle soup, elk sausage, "rabbit strudel," wild Scottish red-legged partridge, and a combination dish consisting of elk chop, wild boar belly, and alligator-Andouille sausage. It also boasts a 25, out of a possible 30, Zagat rating.

"The Cranlyn," on Cranberry Street, is an outstanding example of art deco architecture. Designed by Hyman Isaac Feldman, architect for literally thousands of art deco structures, it has all the bells and whistles that this style is known for, from the intricate brickwork, to the elevator doors, which feature a beautiful multicolored art deco panel under which are six delicately drawn scrolls, to the lobby floors—chevrons, pyramids, diamonds, birds, sunrays, and various geometric lines.

The Clark Restaurant is a bit farther up on Henry, at the corner of Clark Street. It's actually a homey-looking Greek diner-type place. Many of the locals gather here for breakfast on Saturday and Sunday, and the food is reportedly pretty good. Every community has such places, ones that retain their clientele even as Father Time marches on. Clark Street is also where the old Hotel St. George used to be until it closed in 1995. I remember as a kid how friends from Brooklyn talked about how much they loved the swimming pool, once the largest indoor saltwater pool in the country. This staid neighborhood has even had some notoriety, as Clark Street was once home to a strip club, called Wildfire, which flourished during the 1980s and was actually a location that appears in *The Godfather*.

I'm brought up short as I approach 82 Pierrepont Street, an unusual creation if ever there was one. Built in 1888 for industrialist Herman Behr, this large structure went through several incarnations, serving as a brothel and, in a later period, as a home for the Franciscan brothers. But what's most noteworthy is the home's architectural style. Some experts believe it to be one of the best residential examples in New York of Romanesque Revival. It's a reddish brick and terra cotta, multistory building with very real-looking lions, lizards, and dragons that fairly leap out at me as I try gamely to stare them down. There are towers, stone staircases, balconies, bay windows, tall chimneys, all of which are united in a unique and unforgettable mélange. While not open to the public, the inside of the home is similarly remarkable, with marble, mahogany, oak, and intricate carvings throughout.

There's a British-styled pub called the Atlantic Chip Shop, at 129 Atlantic Avenue, which offers "killer fish and chips" and "seriously deep fried candy bars." Inside, there's a mixed clientele, some British, others decidedly not, with an English soccer game on the tube. Bits and pieces of British culture and history—darts, concerts, major English sports figures and rock groups, commemorative plates of Princess Diana—line the walls to give British patrons a feeling of being back home. Often, these nationality-themed places are ethnic markers that tell the visitor who resides in a particular area.

I end my walk at the Promenade, which can be accessed at the end of Montague Street. It's a spectacular pedestrian walkway along the water with beautiful gardens and some of the best views of the Manhattan skyline, just across the East River. Strollers or bench sitters on the Promenade can take in the same scene. They can, in addition, purchase charcoal drawings or paintings featuring the skyscrapers, bridges, and the river. As I walk, I pass several groups of children on class outings and people having a quick lunch as they enjoy the late October warmth. This is the life.

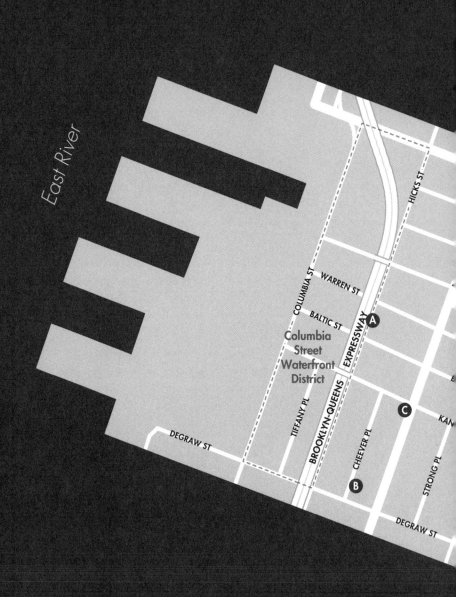

East River

HICKS ST

COLUMBIA ST

WARREN ST

BALTIC ST

EXPRESSWAY

Ⓐ

Columbia
Street
Waterfront
District

TIFFANY PL

BROOKLYN-QUEENS

Ⓒ

KAN

CHEEVER PL

STRONG PL

DEGRAW ST

Ⓑ

DEGRAW ST

COBBLE HILL

COBBLE HILL IS A BEAUTIFUL, POSTAGE-STAMP-SIZE NEIGHBORHOOD spanning two miles. It runs from Atlantic Avenue on the north, Court Street on the east, DeGraw Street on the south, to Columbia Street on the west. Its beautiful stock of brownstones and row houses were built in the mid-nineteenth century, and it has always been a well-to-do neighborhood, becoming even more desirable in the 1980s. Declared a historic district in 1969, it fought successfully against public housing. It has beautiful tree-lined streets with townhouses, apartment buildings, and some more modest two family brick houses of a type commonly found in other neighborhoods of Brooklyn. There's a compact commercial area along Court Street, with a variety of shops and even a movie theater, Cobble Hill Cinemas. While it doesn't have the promenade along the water, it has an even more small-town feel than Brooklyn Heights. The streets are quieter, there's no serious business district in its midst, no courthouses, Department of Education headquarters, or the like. This has made it one of Brooklyn's most desirable communities.

In the 1870s, a sturdy, well-designed group of buildings were constructed for lower-income residents on Hicks Street between Warren and Baltic Streets. About 140 years later, we see that they have withstood the test of time. In their renovated state, with beautiful brick exteriors and inner walkways, they are for sale, with an ad outside the building proclaiming, "Landmark Condos for Sale." Known as the Columbia-Hicks Buildings, they are an excellent example of how well-built housing can be renovated and improved to provide mixed-income housing, containing both open market and affordable housing.

As almost everyone knows, New York City is a major venue for filmmakers, and those looking for elegant townhouses to use as settings in their films can usually find them with the help of location scouts. Cobble Hill is a place where those townhouses can be found, as I learn from a conversation with Raphael Linder, a Brooklyn College graduate and software engineer. He made his home at 53 Cheever Place available for a film: "They used my home for a 2015 film starring Robert De Niro, Anne Hathaway, and Rene Russo, called *The Intern*. I moved to Montague Street in Brooklyn Heights for several weeks and, of course, they paid for everything, including the moving expenses."

"Was it worth all that trouble?"

"Well, it was a major inconvenience. On the other hand, you can make anywhere from $20,000 to maybe $90,000, depending on the length of time and other factors. Plus, there's the excitement of it being in a film seen by millions of people."

"How did your neighbors feel about it?"

"Some didn't like all the activity and commotion. Eventually the trucks had to park over on Hicks Street, but most didn't object, especially since some of them were used as extras and were paid for it."

"How long have you lived here?"

"About thirty years. I'm considered a newcomer," he says, laughing. "It's a great place to live in."

Raphael does not at all mind my taking a photo of his home and indicates a desire to be photographed in front of it. And why not? After all, he agreed to far greater exposure in letting the film company do its thing. Not everyone likes this idea, however. It's clear that it depends to a degree on whether your neighborhood is crowded, how individuals view the whole idea, and whether money and recognition are issues.

A neighborhood's status is also raised when sitcoms or films are made in it. Most people seem to like the idea that their block is "film-worthy" as long as the filmmakers are considerate of the residents. But not everyone is enamored when cameras surround their area. Architecture professor Michael Sorkin criticizes the tendency toward the "Disneyfication" of the city, turning it into a set rather than a setting, and complains about the inconvenience caused to locals. "The inauthenticity is galling," he writes, "but so is the inescapability of performing in a drama of somebody else's devising, whether it means being charmed by architectural mendacity or just crossing the street when the production assistant asks you to."[11]

Those living in the more undesirable parts of the city are less likely to feel this way. They have bigger issues to contend with, like crime and poverty. I was with my students on a class tour when the Denzel Washington film *American Gangster* was being filmed in Harlem along Malcolm X Boulevard. No one—not the students or nearby Harlemites—seemed to mind. To the contrary, they were thrilled by the fact that a major studio was using the area as a setting.

Another way in which areas acquire cachet is when famous people are associated with them. A good case in point is 426 Henry Street, a four-story brick Greek Revival structure, nice but not especially distinctive. Its claim to fame is that it was formerly home to Jennie Jerome, Winston Churchill's mother. There's a plaque outside recognizing this fact, but Jenny was actually born in another Cobble Hill home, at 197 Amity Street. Regardless, Churchill visited the Henry Street home in 1953, at age seventy-four, amid some fanfare

Cobble Hill Park—from wedding photos to toddler heaven

by appreciative locals. Standing outside the house, he said: "I am most grateful to those who have put up this tablet in commemoration of my mother."[12]

A neighborhood also becomes especially attractive when it is a site for wedding photos, as I observed while walking down a beautiful, one-block street, Verandah Place. Cobble Hill has other such small streets, lined with carriage houses dating back to the nineteenth century. Verandah also looks out onto Cobble Hill Park, a beautiful half-block space where children play in sandlots and toss footballs around, while adults sunbathe, sit on benches, or walk their dogs.

On the corner of Court and Kane Streets is the Kane Street Synagogue, Brooklyn's oldest continuously functioning Jewish house of worship. Founded in 1856, it has undergone various incarnations, from traditional, to Reform, to Conservative-Egalitarian, serving congregants from all over north Brooklyn. Music history buffs might be interested to know this is where Aaron Copland was bar-mitzvahed.

There are many nice restaurants in Cobble Hill. For those who like their dining experience to include a touch of history, Sam's, on Court Street, near Baltic Street, serves mostly inexpensive Italian food. The setting features red and white checked tablecloths and matching red leather booths; it takes you back to the post–World War II period. The place has been around for more than ninety years, and I found it fun to hang out with the old-time Italians who eat there regularly.

Finally, a neighborhood's stores provide a clue to its demographics. Cobble Hill has six toy stores (as of 2015), quite a few for an area this small. One of these establishments is Mini Max Toys and Cuts, at 152 Atlantic Avenue, owned by four mothers. It's a rather unique place that offers haircuts for kids and also toys. This makes a lot of sense since small children often dislike having their hair cut, and the toys available offer a ready-made carrot and stick opportunity. A further attraction is the option to sit in either a mini fire truck or mini yellow cab while being sheared, after which the reward is a lollipop or balloon. The kids can also wear a cape and watch DVDs. Indicative of the tony character of this neighborhood, there's not only story time on Wednesdays but also *French* story time every Friday.

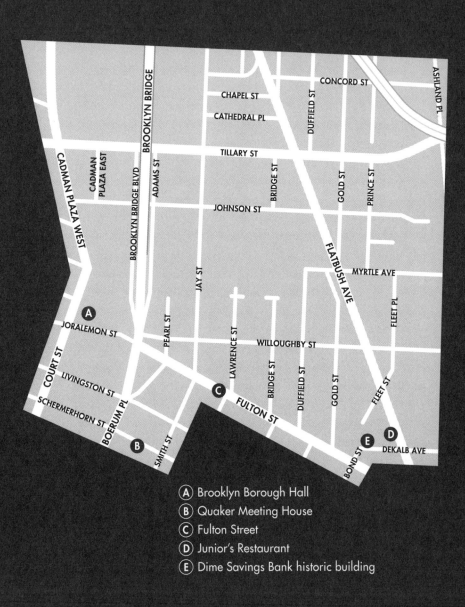

Ⓐ Brooklyn Borough Hall
Ⓑ Quaker Meeting House
Ⓒ Fulton Street
Ⓓ Junior's Restaurant
Ⓔ Dime Savings Bank historic building

DOWNTOWN BROOKLYN

DUMBO/VINEGAR HILL, FULTON FERRY, BROOKLYN HEIGHTS, Cobble Hill, and Boerum Hill all surround a small, somewhat amorphous area known as Downtown Brooklyn. Roughly speaking, its borders are Nassau Street to the north, Navy Street and Ashland Place to the east, DeKalb Avenue and Fulton and Schermerhorn Streets at various points to the south, and Cadman Plaza West and Clinton Street to the west. For much of the nineteenth century the area was dominated by refineries and factories. In the twentieth century it became more commercial. Among the most important buildings from a historical standpoint are Brooklyn Borough Hall, dating back to 1849, on Joralemon Street and the Quaker Friends Meeting House on Schermerhorn Street.

The residents of the surrounding communities shop in its retail outlets and, like the rest of the borough's inhabitants, use its courts and other municipal buildings. The Department of Education is headquartered here, and there are several private and public colleges, including Long Island University and CUNY's New York City College of Technology. The area also features Fulton Street, which anchors a section that has many inexpensive retail outlets. There's also Junior's, with its famous cheesecake, at DeKalb Avenue and Flatbush, as well as the still beautiful landmarked Dime Savings Bank building next door with the giant liberty head decorative dimes inside, but these will best serve the cause of nostalgia. With the coming of the Barclays Center as a hub and the continuing presence of Macy's, the area is changing. New gleaming towers of residential/commercial buildings now dominate the landscape on and around Flatbush Avenue for those who can afford the price tag. After all, downtown Manhattan is no more than a five- or ten-minute ride across the Manhattan or Brooklyn Bridge. One very ambitious project is a seventy-three-story proposed residential

Dime Savings Bank—complete with Mercury-head dimes inside

skyscraper on 9 DeKalb Avenue, near Flatbush Avenue, twice the height of any existing Brooklyn building.

When completely refurbished, this will be another "in," high-priced neighborhood. One structure worth seeing is the Romanesque Revival building at 271–301 Cadman Plaza (east side), currently home to a post office, the US Bankruptcy Court, and the Brooklyn Book Festival, New York's biggest free literary event. The fact that all this is nearby is yet another advantage of living in these abovementioned neighborhoods.

BOERUM HILL

CARROLL GARDENS

RED HOOK

GOWANUS

PARK SLOPE

WINDSOR TERRACE

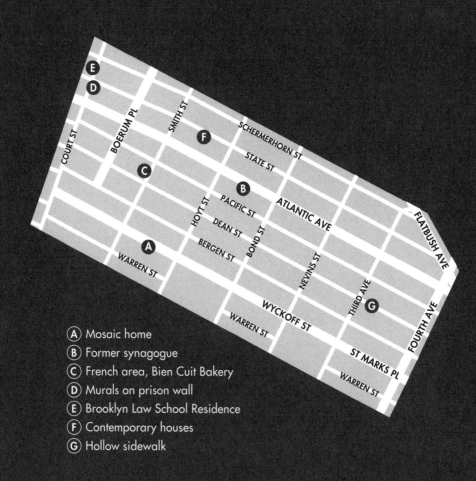

(A) Mosaic home
(B) Former synagogue
(C) French area, Bien Cuit Bakery
(D) Murals on prison wall
(E) Brooklyn Law School Residence
(F) Contemporary houses
(G) Hollow sidewalk

BOERUM HILL

BOERUM HILL IS A SMALL NEIGHBORHOOD EAST OF COBBLE HILL, south of Downtown Brooklyn, and north of Carroll Gardens and Gowanus. Its boundaries are Schermerhorn Street on the north, to Fourth Avenue on the east, St. Marks Place and Warren Street on the south, and Court Street on the west. In the 1920s, the area was home to many Irish families, and by the 1950s, a substantial number of Puerto Ricans had moved in, attracted to low rents and easy transportation to work. From the 1960s to the early 1980s the area was in decline. An outstanding novel by Jonathan Lethem, *The Fortress of Solitude*, tells the story of what it was like then and how it gradually gentrified.

Today it's an upscale community, but Gowanus Houses and Wyckoff Gardens, two public housing projects with a total of 1,600 apartments, are a stark reminder of how poverty remains an issue in the city for many struggling families. The surrounding area is filled with brownstones, mostly three stories high, built in the nineteenth century. These have been renovated by an ethnically diverse mix of younger middle-class newcomers.

Quite a few streets, like Bergen and Dean, are wider than others in Brooklyn, but the tall houses are fairly close to the sidewalk, giving the visitor a feeling of walking through an urban canyon. Boerum Hill is similar to Cobble Hill and Brooklyn Heights, but does not have the polish of those areas, a trait that some would label as "fancy." Its houses are not as ornate structurally and the run-down homes interspersed among those in better condition remind me that it's still a work in progress. Yet the total effect, augmented by many trees, is one of serenity and raw urban beauty, and it's well worth an extended stroll.

As I make my way through this area, one remarkable, nay, unique, row house, at 108 Wyckoff Street, stands out from the rest. The entire first floor is covered with a dazzling, riotous mosaic of bright colors—red, blue, yellow, purple, black, pink, orange, and green. It's literally encrusted with tiles, beads, shells, buttons, and mirrors, mostly small, of all shapes and sizes. They cover the walls, iron bars, gate, ground, and even a pipe coming out of the ground. These are all arranged in an incredibly complex series of designs featuring people and angels, some of them silhouetted in windows; of animals, street scenes, flowers, trees, butterflies, the sun, and all manner of shapes, some of which cannot be readily identified or categorized. Even a small evergreen tree is included in this display, festooned with what looks like Mardi Gras beads.

My wife and I, even my dog, gaze in wonderment at all this. If there is anything like this in the city, I have not seen it in my travels through its streets. Almost as if on cue, the door slowly opens and the woman who created all this steps out and greets us with a cheery hello. Her name is Susan Gardner, a college professor of art, and she is the artist. Her usual professional work is painting, but this is her personal creation. She is of medium stature, with wild curly black hair and small even features, her sparkling eyes framed by dark-rimmed glasses. She doesn't look particularly artsy to me, but then I notice the colorful tattoos on her wrists. A long-time resident of Boerum Hill, she has been working on this mosaic for well over a decade.

"I started this after 9/11 because I didn't want to be inside, in my studio; it was just too depressing. This is my only project of this sort. And the weather was really nice, notwithstanding the tragedy. The neighborhood was really gentrifying but we couldn't afford to refurbish it. So I thought I'd do some of my own refurbishing. And I thought, I'm really tired of everyone stripping the paint off their houses. I guess it was a rebellion of sorts. The house was built in the 1850s, one of the first 'high rises,' three stories actually, among the farms. These were tenements. Today, they call them brownstones."

"How did you conceive of this idea?"

Artistic individuality with a real flair

"I didn't," she says, laughing. "It just happened."

"What's the adhesive material made of?"

"It's a concrete caulk and I had no idea of whether it would stick, but here it is, doing just fine after 13 years."

"Is it ever defaced?"

"Well, just the kids. They sometimes take pieces off, mostly the little animals. And I just replace them."

"Are these just buttons you collected?"

"No. Someone just gave me a box of them."

"And these are people of color that you decided to portray?"

"The kids ask me sometimes: 'What color are these people?' And I just say: 'They're all colors.'"

"Are you planning on doing the upper floors?"

"At one time I thought of it. But I got up on a tall ladder and looked down and I thought. 'Lady, you're crazy.' And that was that. If I get a small cherry-picker I might go up again." But then, reflecting on that, she seems to dismiss it. "I don't know. I have enough to do down here."

Susan is a native New Yorker; she grew up on the Upper West Side and then lived in SoHo before it was SoHo. The area was known more commonly as a neighborhood with light manufacturing, printing plants, storage, and loft housing for penurious artists, students, and others. Her project reflects a common desire of people everywhere to do something meaningful and leave their mark in this world. But there's more to it here.

Susan began doing this after 9/11, clearly feeling that she had to do something to alleviate her feelings of despair. And when she comments on the weather, she reminds us that this was a tragedy with a powerful outdoor component—witnessed by so many.

It's also important to remember that the gentrifiers don't necessarily displace the poor because there's a sizeable group of people who have owned their homes for decades and feel organically rooted in the community. They watched it grow, contract, and morph into something quite different from before. And they're still here.

At 368 Atlantic Avenue, I stop to glance at what was once a combination Jewish afternoon school and synagogue. Talmud Torah Beth Jacob Joseph (the name of a prominent, early twentieth century American rabbinical leader of East European Jewry) was established in 1917, though the building itself, an eclectic, well-preserved mix of Moorish and Gothic architectural styles, dates back to the mid-nineteenth century. Unlike many old synagogues throughout the city that have sunk into decrepitude, the Hebrew lettering, Stars of David, and exterior moldings are well preserved, even though the structure isn't landmarked.

On the day after Christmas, it's not surprising that the lamppost in front of the building is decorated in red and green. This, and the many Muslim-owned shops on the avenue that has been a major Arab stronghold, remind me of how the city is shared by those of so many faiths. For many years, the former synagogue was home to a highly regarded antiques shop, Time Traders. Today, it's the Deity Event Space, a great name for what was once a religious institution. Not surprisingly, besides weddings, and other parties, quite a few Bar and Bat Mitzvahs are held here. From what I hear, they do a pretty nice job of it, and their "chocolate fountain" dessert is supposedly outstanding.

There's also a French presence in Boerum Hill, with several French-inspired food shops and restaurants, including a great bakery, Bien Cuit, on Smith Street, between Pacific and Dean Streets. Each year, on July 14, there's a Bastille Day celebration on Smith, which includes a pétanque tournament. This game is similar to the Italian and British games, respectively, of bocce and bowls, all of which derive from sports popular in ancient Roman times. There's even a French/English bilingual program in a local public school. Why did this "French concentration" happen in Boerum Hill? It's hard to say for sure, but in all likelihood it's part of what sociologists (and others!) call "a snowball effect." One comes for whatever reason and, "*voilà!*" you have a trend!

On the corner of Atlantic Avenue and Brooklyn Bridge Boulevard (a multilane continuation of Court Street), there's a line of people waiting in front of a building. I ask a police officer standing nearby what they're doing, and he tells me they're visiting friends and kin incarcerated in the Brooklyn Detention Complex. I continue asking him about the prison, and he never inquires as to my reasons for the questions. This is typical of New Yorkers in general. They don't find it unusual for people to query strangers. I'm rarely asked if I'm a reporter or anything else. It does help, of course, if you're polite, look respectable and smile a lot. On the back of the building, on State Street, there are some beautiful murals along its white brick wall, supported by a not-for-profit group, Groundswell, which partnered with the prison to create this mural. One mural features the Brooklyn Bridge and a Manhattan skyline with some young people and an elderly man standing in front of it, all with a look of sadness or worry on their faces. This was done by teenagers possibly thinking about the prison, whose barbed-wire topping hangs over these depictions at several points. The exhortations urge passersby to exhibit "Responsibility," "Respect," to show "Love." Other paintings, circular in form, are Tibetan mandalas, geometric designs representing the universe in Buddhist and Hindu symbolism. These lotus flower designs have pretty patterns that seem to visually become absorbed within themselves as one looks at them. Keys meant to symbolize opportunity through opening doors might also remind the viewer of the loss of freedom the prison represents.

I think of prisons I've seen elsewhere in the state—Otisville, Greenhaven, Woodbourne. They're usually stand-alones. But in the city, with the exception of Riker's Island, that's not possible. Density requires that a prison be in the neighborhood, not on the edge. The locals aren't happy about it, yet there are expensive brownstones, and apartment high rises across the street. Appropriately enough, though, a handsome residence for Brooklyn Law School students is located diagonally across the avenue. Well, I think to myself, these two entities have a symbiotic relationship, and so the location makes sense. Inside the residence, there's a blue neon sign honoring a famous TV correspondent and muckraker. "Geraldo Rivera 1969," it reads in bright, blue script lettering, the year he graduated.

Finally, State Street, between Hoyt and Smith Streets, is an almost perfect example of how new contemporary-style townhouses can be aligned with old buildings to maintain a street's essential character. Both varieties are of the same height, with similar windows in design and number, and approximately the same number of stairs leading to the row house entrances. The newer exteriors are brick and conform to the sandstone colors of the original homes. It's not that you can't tell the old from the new. It's that geometrically at least, they harmonize rather well. Many of the historic homes are landmarked. Whether or not one likes the look is ultimately a matter of taste. Some of the people I asked as they walked by thought they were great, while others said they were terrible. Regardless, four million plus is a hefty price for them, even if one can afford it.

Finally, at 314 Dean Street just east of Third Avenue, I come across a sign in front of an apartment building that says "Caution: Hollow Sidewalk. Trucks Keep Off." Imagine what would happen if a truck didn't do that. The sidewalk would collapse. These signs are serious, and the sidewalk is hollow because the ground beneath it may have contained a basement or storage area that was never filled in. The city is responsible for maintaining the sidewalks but not what's under them. These signs are more common in SoHo, which was once a manufacturing district. When the 1911 Triangle Shirtwaist Factory Fire occurred (146 workers perished), quite a few of those who jumped from the building fell through the pavement into basements.

Despite its relatively small size, Boerum Hill is an interesting and fun place to wander through. It has great variety, both in terms of its ethnic and racial makeup and its different types of housing. In fact, it's a very representative example of the borough as a whole.

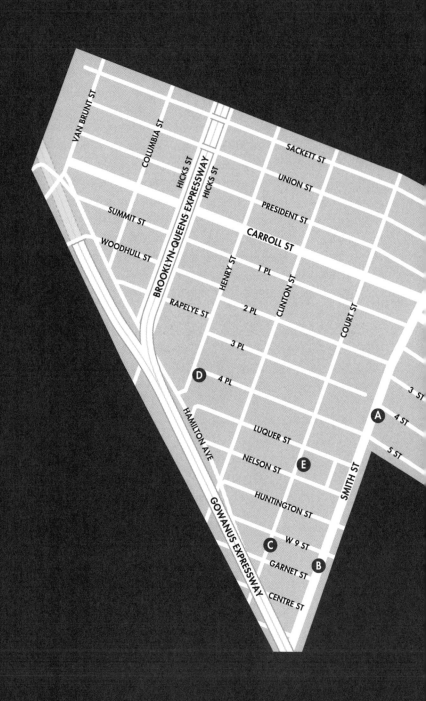

CARROLL GARDENS

CARROLL GARDENS WAS SO NAMED IN THE 1960S; it was always a special area, albeit unnamed, within the boundaries of what was called South Brooklyn in the mid-nineteenth century. It's named after Charles Carroll, a native of Annapolis, Maryland, and the only Roman Catholic to have signed the Declaration of Independence. The neighborhood was Irish until the late nineteenth century when Italian immigrants who worked on the nearby docks began moving in, followed later by more Italians employed at the Brooklyn Navy Yard. The neighborhood gradually became mostly Italian as the Irish moved out. It has long been associated with the Mafia, though not as closely as other areas like Bensonhurst and Bath Beach. Yet Al Capone did marry Mae Josephine Coughlin, in 1918, at St. Mary's Star of the Sea Church on Court Street. The neighborhood began gentrifying a bit in the 1960s, and the process greatly accelerated in the 1990s. Today the area is less than a quarter Italian, but that decline is obscured by the many Italian food stores, butcher shops, eateries, and pizzerias.

'ST

HOYT ST

Ⓐ HBH Gourmet Sandwiches
& Smoked Meats
Ⓑ Scenic view of old Brooklyn
Ⓒ Treats Truck Stop
Ⓓ Maglia Rosa
Ⓔ St. Mary's Star of the Sea,
church where Al Capone was married

Carroll Gardens' boundaries are DeGraw Street on the north, Hoyt and Smith Streets on the east, the Gowanus Expressway on the south, and Van Brunt Street on the west. The main commercial streets are Smith and Court, and the community can be easily reached by the F and G trains. Between roughly Carroll Street and Fourth Place from north to south and between Henry and Hoyt Streets, from west to east, are hundreds of gracious historic brownstones, and the streets are mostly one way and quiet. The brownstones are distinct from elsewhere because of their large front gardens, featuring old trees and roses, many of them with Virgin Mary statues. Every Halloween, Christmas, and Easter, residents of First Place erect holiday displays that attract visitors from, as they say, "near and far." Real estate prices continue to rise in what has become one of the most desirable neighborhoods of the borough. As I look around I can easily imagine myself in some midsize town in eastern Pennsylvania or upstate New York, old and preserved, but with a little bit of a gritty feel, especially with the working-class types walking by.

While walking along Smith Street, the main commercial drag in this quaint neighborhood, I ask Angela, a youngish store owner, about the area. She says: "Cobble Hill, Carroll Gardens, and Boerum Hill are quite similar. Red Hook is different. It's on the water, very industrial, and you can't get there by subway. The old brownstones here are multifamily, but many people with money have fixed them up and turned them into single-family homes. We have Prospect Park and some small parks. You wouldn't go here ten to fifteen years ago; there was a lot of crime. Today, it's a family-oriented area. Bushwick is a lot trendier, but not quite as nice. That's where I live. It's a more Hispanic area and it's loud, but I like loud."

Although adjacent and similar, Carroll Gardens has a very different feel from Cobble Hill, which lacks the large, well-tended plots that grace many of Carroll Gardens' front yards. Carroll Gardens lacks the highly gentrified feel of Cobble Hill, and it has more diverse ethnic groups. Cobble Hill also doesn't have the feel of southern Carroll Gardens, which is a bit rough at the edges. As for Boerum Hill, that neighborhood has some pretty dominant public housing projects and fewer green spaces, but most important it's right near downtown Brooklyn and the main thoroughfare of Atlantic Avenue, which is also true of Cobble Hill.

Angela's comment that "we have Prospect Park" is interesting. It's technically correct, but it's a ten- to twelve-block walk away, unlike Park Slope, Prospect Heights, Windsor Terrace, and other neighborhoods that actually border the park. But anything that reflects well on an area is likely to be emphasized, even if it's a bit of a stretch. It does have Carroll Park, a lovely space between President and Carroll Streets, with playgrounds, bocce and basketball courts, the Soldier and Sailors World War I monument, and cast iron gates.

My next conversation is with a spry, elderly man, wearing jeans, a plaid shirt, and a windbreaker, who has lived in the area for decades. Vic knows the area well and when I encounter him, he's looking at home prices in a storefront window of a realty office. It turns out he owns a house and wants to figure out what it's worth, a common pastime in this city.

"There used to be Mafia with their clubs here in the '90s," Vic offers up, speaking in a gravelly voice, with a heavy Brooklyn accent. "But you know who really changed this area? The gays, here and in Brooklyn Heights, Cobble Hill, and Boerum Hill. It was a very ethnically mixed area. Once the gays came in, the houses got fixed up and the values increased."

"Did you like that?"

"Well, I'm married to a lovely woman. But I always felt it was the straights that were violent, because they were beating up the gays, which they weren't doing to the local hoods, the gangs, the real bad guys." This being St. Patrick's Day, I compliment him on his green windbreaker, mindful that on this day in New York, everyone's Irish. His rejoinder is true to form: "Thank you. When I was growing up everyone mistook me for Irish on account of my blue eyes, but actually I'm Jewish. But because of that I'm *simpatico* to the Irish."

The Irish and Jews often had conflicts in New York City neighborhoods, as recounted in Pete Hamill's excellent novel, *Snow in August*, but, I guess, if you have blue eyes and people think you're Irish in a positive way, it can change your perspective even if you're Jewish. More intriguing are Vic's comments about gay New Yorkers, repeated to a stranger without hesitation and reflecting how accepted gay people are today compared to just twenty years ago.

My next stop is HBH Gourmet Sandwiches & Smoked Meats at 407 Smith Street. It replaced a kosher restaurant, Olga's on Smith, that couldn't make it because there are very few Orthodox Jews living here. It's also located away from the main commercial area, among a modest section of residential buildings with only a few business establishments scattered here and there. HBH is a most interesting place. The fare is eclectic and original, but leans toward barbecue—pulled pork and beef—pastrami, and chicken with walnut curry. It's all reasonably priced. There's a "Stoner Delight," consisting of crushed peanuts, sliced banana, and Nutella on pretzel bread. There's also a dish called "Redneck Wedding," a mix of various meats. I ask a young woman eating her pulled pork sandwich how it tastes. Her description: "As you start eating, it has that curry taste and suddenly it punches you in the back of your throat and it's tangy and sweet and unforgettable. I'm Korean and we love pork and barbecue."

As I sit at the counter made up of little ceramic tiles and chat with the owner, Ukrainian-born Dimitri Kirichin, my attention is drawn to a most amazing collection of porcelain, ceramic, wood, and metal pigs of all shapes and sizes, perhaps thirty of them. They're all different and unique. And in the bathroom I see another five pigs under a sign "Don't Hog the Bathroom."

Dimitri tells me that he started the collection on a whim, wondering what he was going to do with the empty shelves on the wall, when a friend gave him a ceramic pig. It soon grew into a collection when he told friends that he collects them. "I told my friends no more pigs. I have no room." Next to the piggies, there's a large painting of what looks like an abstract version of low-rise buildings. There's soft lighting throughout the place, dark-colored streamers hanging from the ceiling, and soft jazz playing in the background.

As I take a last look, I realize that HBH is typical of many places that can be found in areas like Williamsburg, Greenpoint, and Bushwick. There's a bar, tables, and a menu on a signboard. And the look is one that incorporates various elements that, more often than not, reflect the idiosyncratic preferences of the proprietor. Instead of pigs, there are clocks, or scarves hanging from a wall. The laptop population coexists with the hipsters talking in a corner and the occasional tourists who wander in. In essence it's a combination of friendliness and nonchalance. Unlike more formal places or chain stores, there's no key for the often slightly funky looking restroom, and no one ever challenges my right to use it even if I haven't bought anything. If I want to chat with whoever's behind the counter, it's not a problem, but I rarely get a cheery hello when I walk in.

As I head toward the southern end of Smith Street, near where it crosses Garnet Street, I look up and see the subway as it curves gently around toward the Smith-9th Street station. Taking stock of my surroundings I'm suddenly gripped by a feeling that I have gone back in time—the small shingled houses, narrow streets where the sun never penetrates, the metal undergirding supporting the tracks high up, the silver subway cars framed against a cobalt blue sky serving as a backdrop for cumulus clouds floating through the air. I stare at the elevated station off to my left, seemingly precariously balanced atop a jumble of twisted metal sheathed in what looks like silver foil and realize that I have wandered into the guts of this great city, a land where construction is never finished, where all-nite delis run by Yemenis are all that's there, and where people hurry through, but rarely tarry.

As I begin trekking up Court Street, the quiet, less commercial end, I come across the Treats Truck Shop. It's the base for a couple of trucks that sell cookies, brownies, and coffee around the city, and the chocolate chip cookies are really tasty. The manager, JT, is studying business at Brooklyn College; he lets me have some free cookies while I'm charging up my phone. It's a fitting end to a great day.

Returning for another walk a few days later, I notice that the neighborhood is quite integrated—a quarter of the population is black, Asian, and Hispanic. But more importantly, I can see people of different races having coffee and dinner together, interacting on the street, telling each other stories about what happened with this or that individual, what their neighbors said about the local meeting they attended, who's going to what school, and the like.

Carroll Gardens, in general, is a place with a small-town feel. When I say hello, people respond naturally. They don't seem at all surprised at my greeting. Maybe that's why it seems to have a ton of coffee shops, another natural, often leisurely, venue for people. It seems there's at least one on every commercial block, and many have two or three per block, sometimes within ten yards of each other. In fact, Yelp lists thirty-three coffee shops in this 3/10ths of a square mile area. I enter Maglia Rosa on Fourth Place and Henry Street on a cold and windy afternoon in late March 2015. Manuel, the young Italian owner, greets me with a big smile. He's only been open about four months. "What makes your place special?" I ask.

"First, we serve great coffee, but it's also a bike shop." Pointing to the bikes attached to the wall behind the bar and elsewhere, he continues. "We make custom bikes here. Bike people like coffee. These bikes are very expensive. They start at about $5,000 and go up to about $15,000."

"When I was a kid, I had a Schwinn, for which I saved up. And I thought it was a fancy bicycle. But these prices sound really high. What makes a bicycle worth so much?"

Bicycles and coffee to revel in—the perfect blend at Maglia Rosa

"Mostly it's the frame—steel, titanium, carbon. And it's not mass-produced, like the Chinese do. Each one is made individually."

"How does it affect the rider?"

"Well, it's like driving a Chevy or driving a Porsche. Imagine if you're gonna spend hours riding, making the same movements over and over. If that frame is wrong, you're gonna get hurt. Your knees are gonna ache, or your back, or neck. If a person is a serious rider, they're ready to pay. And for some people it becomes like an obsession."

It's a very nice-looking, clean place, attractively furnished. What's noteworthy is the combination of two types of stores, an increasingly typical pattern observed in many parts of the city. The premise is that one attracts the other, and it must be working.

"Citizens of Pozzallo Way" is the name tacked onto Henry Street between Sackett and Union Streets. Honoring individuals, hometowns, and organizations with street names, plazas, or vest-pocket parks is something that has proliferated in the city in recent years, and the naming generally requires community board approval. In this way people who sponsor the street names, plazas, or vest-pocket parks have a way of insuring that passersby will notice the names of the honorees. But most important, their memories will be perpetuated for future generations by those who cared about them. In this case, it was Mayor Bill de Blasio, then a city councilman, who endorsed the street renaming. People have been coming to the Society of the Citizens of Pozzallo Club since 1919, sipping espresso, playing cards and *tombola* (bingo), and talking about the old days in the Sicilian fishing village that once numbered 30,000 souls.

An article about the society that appeared on a blog, called *Voices of New York*, in February 2013 began with: "We're leftovers," said Joe Igneri, the self-proclaimed babysitter of the members of the Society. "Leftovers." One of the more visceral responses came from "Cp": "No one has to baby-sit the Society of Pozzallo . . . We are not leftovers; our roots are here; we are the true families. Some left, some stayed. Sometimes leftovers taste better the next day." The point is that the locals take this kind of stuff very seriously. They don't like being tabbed losers who stayed while most departed. They take pride in what they have and they try to adapt as well. This society, a former male bastion with several hundred members, now admits women and tries to attract a younger crowd, yet another sign that New York is forever changing.

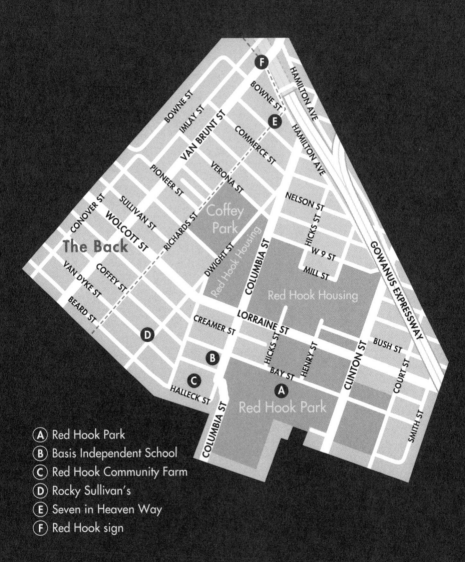

BOWNE ST
IMLAY ST
VAN BRUNT ST
BOWNE ST
HAMILTON AVE
COMMERCE ST
HAMILTON AVE
PIONEER ST
VERONA ST
NELSON ST
CONOVER ST
SULLIVAN ST
RICHARDS ST
Coffey Park
HICKS ST
GOWANUS EXPRESSWAY
WOLCOTT ST
W 9 ST
The Back
DWIGHT ST
Red Hook Housing
COLUMBIA ST
MILL ST
VAN DYKE ST
COFFEY ST
Red Hook Housing
BEARD ST
CREAMER ST
LORRAINE ST
HALLECK ST
HICKS ST
HENRY ST
BUSH ST
COLUMBIA ST
BAY ST
CLINTON ST
COURT ST
Red Hook Park
SMITH ST

Ⓐ Red Hook Park
Ⓑ Basis Independent School
Ⓒ Red Hook Community Farm
Ⓓ Rocky Sullivan's
Ⓔ Seven in Heaven Way
Ⓕ Red Hook sign

RED HOOK

COMMUNITIES LIKE COBBLE HILL, BROOKLYN HEIGHTS, and Carroll Gardens have much to admire. They are pretty, have many amenities and beautiful housing. But if you want to see a place that's really different and relatively unknown, Red Hook, so named because of its red clay earth, is a good bet. Here you'll find greater variation in income, industrial areas adjacent to residential ones, spacious parks, fine recreation centers, and, finally, a place steeped in New York lore, the setting for the classic film, *On the Waterfront*. Some of its more famous residents include Al Capone, whose career began here, Knicks star Carmelo Anthony, Norman Mailer, and Crazy Joey Gallo, a mobster I once waited on in a resort hotel.

When container shipping became popular, businesses and jobs declined and industry relocated to New Jersey and elsewhere. But in the mid-nineteenth century, Red Hook was an international shipping center. Housing was built at that time for Irish, German, and Scandinavian dock workers. Later, Italians came, as well as smaller groups from Puerto Rico and the Middle East. Today, there are still factories, but nothing like in the old days. The boundaries of Red Hook are Ferris and Conover Streets on the west and north, Hamilton Avenue and the Gowanus Expressway on the east, and Halleck and Beard Streets on the south.

There's ferry service to Manhattan, which is important because the F and G trains are a long walk or short bus ride away. In the 1990s, the area was a major center for crack use and distribution, but today it is enjoying a moderate renaissance, one that is beginning to accelerate. True, people are still apprehensive about the Red Hook Houses, Brooklyn's largest public housing project, home to some 8,000 residents, but the opportunities for finding excellent, convenient apartments and the prevailing view that it's relatively safe to live in areas with such projects is the overriding attitude today.

The area is divided into two segments. East of Richards Street is "The Front," and it includes the projects and some row houses. West of Richards, in "The Back," is an IKEA and a Fairway, row houses, made even more quaint by cobblestoned streets, and a certain rough beauty that conjures up the past. It's an isolated part of the borough, surrounded by water on three sides and the Gowanus Expressway. Red Hook's population is mostly black and Hispanic, and the white folks who live there reside mostly in The Back section.

At 58-plus acres, Red Hook Park, along Bay Street, is larger than most community parks, with ball fields, running tracks, and nice walking paths. In the summer it's the main venue for soccer games. There are also the famous *pupusa* trucks nearby, drawing thousands of visitors, as discussed by the sociologist Sharon Zukin in her book, *Naked City*.[1] Here Hispanic vendors gather and sell food to the non-Hispanic general public and, especially, to Hispanic immigrants. While they're not exactly inviting each other over for an evening of socializing, they do have contact, despite a possible language barrier, and both groups usually develop an appreciation of the other. The non-Hispanic visitors buy Spanish food and often learn about it. They hear the music and observe the immigrants interacting as families. The immigrants see the others as contributing to their own economic welfare through purchases of food. And surely some friendships develop.

Soccer is the main sports activity here in the park, and the fans' loyalties to the teams is probably as enthusiastic as that of those who followed the fortunes of the Brooklyn Dodgers until they departed for sunnier climes in 1957. The park is right by the water and has some excellent views. It also has the Sol Goldman Red Hook Recreation Center. Goldman, a Brooklyn-born son of a grocer, was a wealthy real estate developer who wanted to do something for inner-city kids. The result is a beautiful outdoor pool, a modern workout facility with all sorts of exercise machines, and a gym with a great basketball court. Teams come from all over to play competitive sports. Red Hook had a well-deserved reputation as a rough neighborhood until fifteen years ago, and it is still a bit sketchy around the projects, but nothing like what it used to be. I ask a young black woman who is an administrator at the Recreation Center: "Who comes here in the summer?"

"People come from everywhere. The yuppies from Carroll Gardens come because they don't have any big parks like this nearby except Prospect Park, but that can be farther away. The projects don't scare them because there's really not much danger here anymore. Of course I wouldn't go through the park late at night, but that's true everywhere."

It's a beautiful park if you want sports for your kids, and that seems to be what matters most. The young professionals do not have memories of what it was like in the old days because they weren't here then, and they benefit from the general and correct perception that crime in general is way down.

The projects are still poor and mostly black, but the racial hostilities of the past are pretty much absent today. The level of civility in the city is high. Why? The contact hypothesis seems to have been borne out. It's true socially and even more so professionally. Any white person walking into a black, Asian, or Hispanic church would be welcome and vice versa. A black man watching his son try out for a football team in Red Hook says: "Things are far different today from twenty years ago for two reasons—people have learned from living with each other that people from different groups aren't so bad. And there are more opportunities now for black people."

At 30 Bay Street there's an ultramodern, innovatively designed K–12 private school. Alongside the buildings are photos of the interior, and it looks magnificent—large, open, well-designed spaces with high ceilings, appealing lighting. The windows of the school are set at varying intervals of height and width, resulting in a futuristic look. And it's across from IKEA and, a little farther down, Fairway. The gentrifiers have enrolled their children in this brand new school, but the locals aren't happy. It's doubtful that even with some merit

Brooklyn's largest community garden

scholarships, many kids from the low-income Red Hook Houses will go there.

Next to the school, on Sigourney Street along Columbia Street, the Red Hook Community Farm enables more than a thousand urban teenagers annually to grow and sell flowers and produce. Unlike most community gardens in the city, which are crammed between buildings or on small corner lots, this one is gigantic, a full square block with sophisticated sheds and garden beds on what was once an asphalt playground.

A substantial population lives in the area known as "The Back." There are bars there too, like Sunny's Bar at 253 Conover Street and Rocky Sullivan's at Van Dyke and Dwight Streets. Rocky's is an authentic place with great bar food, especially grilled cheese, that even offers Irish language classes. Traditional Irish music is played every Sunday and Monday from 4:30 to 6:30 p.m. The bar caters to tourists and to members of the Irish working class that has been here for over one hundred years. It's anchored by IKEA and Fairway, which attract people from all over.

Signage on the streets here, as in the rest of Brooklyn, can sometimes make for interesting viewing. Outside The Grindhaus, a highly regarded restaurant at 275 Van Brunt Street, a hand-lettered sign slammed the departed chef: "We are closed this evening as the result of an unreliable chef. Apologies for any inconvenience. New chef starts next week." It's certainly an unusually lengthy and unconventional explanation. One of the most enjoyable aspects of walking the city block by block is the surprising number of funny signs outside stores, which often leave me chuckling to myself. Two of the many examples: "Fish and Cheeps" and "Beacon and Eggs."

A half mile away, at the intersection of Richards and Seabring Streets, I see that a portion of Richards has been renamed Seven in Heaven Way, in memory of the seven firefighters from the company, located on the corner, who perished on 9/11. I chat with a firefighter and joke about the grimy, unintentionally multicolored sofa, with a paper sign on a cushion reading, perhaps unnecessarily: FREE

SOFA. "Yes," he says, "and no charge for the bedbugs." It's that wry New York humor you get used to living here. He informs me that the area is quite safe, "not at all like 2000."

Turning right, on Van Brunt Street, I cross Bowne Street, and on the right I see a six-foot-high multicolored metal figure of a clown in front of the Apollo Metal Construction company. It's grasping a drumstick about to descend on a drum and the look on its face can best be described as that of a jolly person having a high old time. It's not attached to the ground and while a bit heavy, could be stolen in the blink of an eye. Inside the factory, a foreman tells me it was made by someone who worked there, but it's not exactly clear who. "You like it, you take it," he says, laughing, but I'm not sure he's serious or even has the right to offer it to me. Personally, I hope it stays there as it is, in a way, a symbol of New York's free-wheeling spirit. Not every sculpture is in a museum and this one's not even in a garden. It's on a public street, unattended and unguarded.

Continuing on Van Brunt between Hamilton Avenue and Summit Street, I spot a red seven-foot-high sign with the letters RED HOOK emblazoned along the brick wall of an industrial building. At night, it lights up thanks to the tiny electric bulbs along the letters; its bright red glow is a favorite among the neighbors. In front of it on the side of a bus stop an ad reads: "Welcome to NY. It's been waiting for you," signed by Taylor Swift. And so has Red Hook.

Across the street, a young, blond-haired woman clad in a sleeveless green T-shirt, despite the forty-degree weather, is in an empty fenced-in lot. She's flexing her well-muscled, tattooed arms as she uses an improvised pulley made from a parachute as an exercise machine. "Aren't you cold?" I ask her.

"Not at all," she responds cheerfully. "I do this all the time. It's my exercise routine." She's originally from a suburb outside of Philadelphia and expresses the hope of many locals that Red Hook won't lose its grittiness, it's artistic and "real" feel, as opposed to its next door gentrified neighbor, Carroll Gardens. Sure, lower rents are a factor, but so is the desire by these people to live in this kind of place.

In truth, Red Hook, with its large stock of industrial buildings, more closely resembles DUMBO in its earlier state than it does Carroll Gardens, but DUMBO has changed dramatically. Its appeal was the same, but today it is highly gentrified, a process that seems almost inevitable because of the profit motive, scarcity of space near Manhattan, and the influx of young, well-heeled professionals searching for housing with all the amenities fashionably encased in the veneer of authenticity. Strolling along these blocks it soon becomes clear, as I see factory after factory being renovated for the condo market, with apartments selling for a million plus, that in five or ten years *this* may be the next DUMBO.

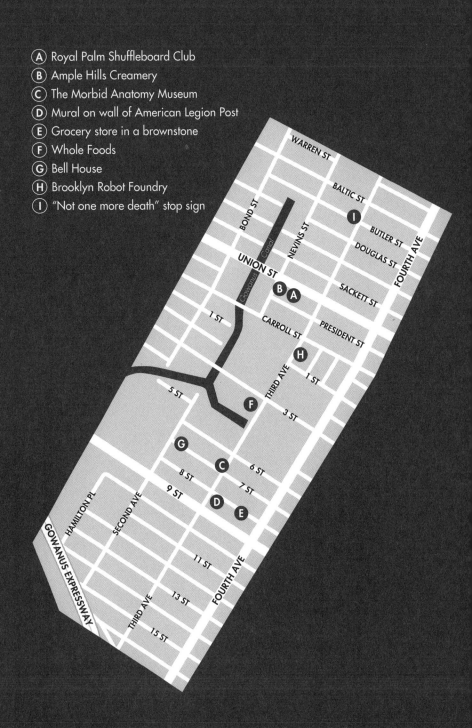

A Royal Palm Shuffleboard Club
B Ample Hills Creamery
C The Morbid Anatomy Museum
D Mural on wall of American Legion Post
E Grocery store in a brownstone
F Whole Foods
G Bell House
H Brooklyn Robot Foundry
I "Not one more death" stop sign

WARREN ST
BALTIC ST
BUTLER ST
BOND ST
NEVINS ST
DOUGLAS ST
FOURTH AVE
Gowanus Canal
UNION ST
SACKETT ST
CARROLL ST
PRESIDENT ST
1 ST
THIRD AVE
1 ST
3 ST
5 ST
6 ST
7 ST
8 ST
9 ST
HAMILTON PL
SECOND AVE
11 ST
FOURTH AVE
THIRD AVE
13 ST
15 ST
GOWANUS EXPRESSWAY

GOWANUS

GOWANUS IS AN INTERESTING NEIGHBORHOOD whose northern boundary runs along Wyckoff Street and St. Marks Place. Fourth Avenue is the eastern boundary, the Gowanus Expressway the southern, with Smith and Hoyt Streets composing the western border. The population here increased significantly with the construction of the Gowanus Canal in 1869, which required many workers. It attracted all types of industry, but with the growth of container shipping in the 1970s, the area declined. While still pretty scruffy looking, especially between 8th and 16th Streets where many small industries make and repair all manner of goods—there are window, awning, and metal fabricators, and lumber yards—change is coming rapidly. On heavily trafficked Fourth Avenue, there are highrises, usually about ten to twelve stories, with developers boasting about their "Juliet balconies" and locals complaining about their shabby construction. You might wonder why anyone wants to have a view of a busy, noisy street, but no one wonders that about SoHo or Second Avenue in Manhattan. Like everywhere else you get what you pay for, and these digs cost less than quiet brownstones on Carroll Street, and that makes sense. Regardless, if you live on Fourth Avenue you're on the border of Gowanus and Park Slope, a very desirable neighborhood. As a member of this exalted class, you can enjoy the bars and eateries of Fifth Avenue just like anyone else and wait a few years to trade up.

The area has students living on the avenues and numbered side streets, plus gentrifiers who saw a bargain, one of whom observed to me: "We flipped our Tribeca place and bought a much larger one here." Some knowledgeable folks claim that this has become the hottest real estate market in the borough because The Slope, Fort Greene, and Prospect Heights have filled up. There are also plenty of inexpensive hotels like Comfort Inn and La Quinta for tourists looking for a cheap and easily accessible launching pad to Manhattan venues. This will no doubt be a haven for the well-heeled, too, in five years or so, though not without many complaints from the local folks who see their way of life slipping away.

I begin this trip by heading over to the Royal Palm Shuffleboard Club on Union Street between Third Avenue and Nevins Street. I can't understand why shuffleboard would be so attractive; to me it seemed like one of those games at Catskill Mountains resorts that hardly anyone under sixty would be caught dead playing. But sociologists know that there's no accounting for fads unless you accept the idea that something's popular because no one thinks it would be. Perhaps it's because at a certain level we all want to be a contrarian at some point in our lives, to break out and do what we feel like doing. In any event, the Royal Palm has great food, good booze, comfortable seating, and a big feel about it right down to the spacious rest rooms.

On the corner of Nevins and Union, I discover the Ample Hills Creamery, truly something special. They have four locations, but this is where the ice cream is made, and I look through a plate glass window into the inside of the shop and watch how they do it in their spotless kitchen. I'm given a taste of their ice cream, one with bee honey, called Sweet as Honey, and it's delicious, as are the other flavors I sample, most notably Mexican Hot Chocolate, a flavor with a spicy kick that blends nicely with the creamy dark chocolate. The Creamery is staffed by genuinely friendly employees who seem to enjoy their work. "What's special about your place?" I ask Che, the manager.

"All of our ice cream is made on the premises and we use a farm, Byrne Dairy, in upstate New York for the milk, cream, and eggs, so everything is really fresh. Other places freeze stuff for quite a while before serving it, partly because it has to come from far away. We sell what we make very fast, by the next day, in fact. And what's made here goes to our other smaller locations in Brooklyn and Manhattan. Everything is organic and natural too."

I also take a quick look at the rooftop, where, from the deck, I enjoy a beautiful view of Downtown Brooklyn. A class on how to make ice cream is in session. There are students from the City As High School in Manhattan's West Village, churning away and having a lot of fun. It's a chance to be introduced to the idea of having a skill, even a craft.

I begin to chat with a young bearded man from Long Island who's taking in the clouds overhead and enjoying some ice cream with his wife and son. His account of crime and gentrification is illuminating, to say the least: "I've lived here eight years on Fifth Avenue and DeGraw Street. Way back when I first came, I had my car broken into, I had a bike stolen. The car was parked near the projects. Today, it's completely different. If someone walked around here and wanted to sell drugs on a street corner, the police would come in thirty seconds. Why? Because I, or someone like me, would call the police. I mean, no one's gonna tolerate that today. I saw a guy poppin' a tire off a car and I thought I'd call the police and at least give some ID on this guy. But no, the police were here in sixty seconds. There's a lot of police, a lot of undercover cops. And I do think the people in the projects know they'll have trouble."

So we see that residents, or at least this fellow, have an expectation that the police will protect them from harm. And this guy seems to be correct in his assumption. It also exemplifies the idea of living in a community where people look out for each other, a long way from the idea of the cold hard city where people fear one another and avoid contact.

The Morbid Anatomy Museum on Third Avenue and 7th Street opened in June 2014. As I walk in they're getting ready for a fundraiser but consent to giving me a brief tour. They're into their third exhibit, "Do the Spirits Return?," which is about the life, times, and miraculous feats of Howard Thurston, a former con man who employed magic to understand, and perhaps even control, life and death. Artifacts, props, and posters elaborate on this man who was the main

Your scariest dreams explained

rival to Harry Houdini. An earlier exhibit explored the history of mourning in various societies. The museum also has a library containing thousands of books about topics like anatomical art, weird sexual practices, "oddities," medical topics, magic, and so on.

There are lectures and films about Goths, witchcraft, psychedelics, ancient phonographs, and other topics centering on the occult. I was also shown a group of really interesting preserved specimens in bottles filled with formaldehyde, such as a stingray, a hummingbird, several bats, a dragonfly, and a snake. There are also various animal bones. The museum is still evolving and establishing an identity, but it's staffed by energetic and creative young people and the future looks bright.

On the corner of 8th Street and Third Avenue, a wall mural in the small parking lot of the American Legion Post on 8th Street includes the Statue of Liberty and the emblems of the various armed forces, plus a portrait of an American eagle. A cartoon-like balloon depicts the eagle saying, "All gave some. Some gave all," meaning the ultimate sacrifice of one's life for their country. There's hardly a legion post or fire department company in the city that doesn't have a patriotic message emblazoned on its outside walls.

Farther up 8th Street between Third and Fourth Avenues, on the first floor of a three-story brick row house I see in gold letters the words "P. De Rosa, 180 1/2 Grocery" on a window with white vertical blinds on the inside. Underneath and off to the sides are neon signs, unlit, advertising Schaefer and Rheingold Extra Dry, two beers of an earlier New York. The commercial signs look out of place on this completely residential block, and I wonder why the place is there. It certainly appears closed, and I cannot see any sign indicating that it's a functioning establishment. I spot an elderly woman sitting on a stoop across the street and ask her about it.

Her answer clears it up. "The grandfather owned the store forty years ago when I moved in here, and then it was open as a store. They're an old-time Italian family, been here a hundred years, and the grandson lives there now and he keeps it that way. And every Christmas and Easter he lights up the beer signs."

I cross the street again and ring the bell, but only a dog responds, the deep bark letting me know that he or she is on duty. It is a rather unusual use of space. The grandson has maintained this permanent shrine and tribute to his grandfather and has shown filial loyalty and respect for his forebears. And his deed is known by his neighbors and all others who stop and inquire about its meaning.

On Third Avenue and about 3rd Street is a new Whole Foods market. The staff is enthusiastic and on top of everything. A sign proclaims that 250,000 bricks from a demolished building in Newark were used inside and out to build this place. Outside, in a pleasant area with benches, I practically bump into one of the largest fire hydrants I've ever seen. It's approximately 5 1/2 feet tall, pretty wide, bright red, and dedicated to supporting a shelter for animals that never kills. A large slot accepts all contributions. And if you slide open a drawer, you can take a pouch containing a dog treat. Dogs love fire hydrants, and I wonder how many have used this facility for their basic needs.

I sit on the bench and look down at the Gowanus Canal. Dirty and mud-colored as it is, with a long-term federal cleanup project underway, it's no Venice, but, as someone noted, "It's relaxing to sit and watch the water flow by." The real estate agents would no doubt enthusiastically support that and the idea that this is the next Venice.[2]

I speak with a young man, Rich, who lives in Gowanus with his three kids, and he, an expatriate from Manhattan, tells me, "This is a really fine place that will only get better. We've got Bell House, a really hot nightclub with comedy shows, bands; NPR broadcasts from there sometimes." Rich is correct. Located at 149 7th Street, the Bell House is one of the most "happening" joints in the area. There are live bands on the weekends for every (mostly young) taste, with reservations an absolute must. And they host weddings and private parties as well.

There's a store for everything in New York City, as I can see when I look at the Brooklyn Robot Foundry, at 303 Third Avenue, which beckons young mothers and fathers with its welcome phrase on the awning: "Robot Building for Kids." They offer classes and parties for little tykes, and as the kids design robots they learn about mechanics and electrical fundamentals. You can even hug the robots if you want to. It claims to be Brooklyn's only establishment dedicated to this endeavor, at least as of April 20, 2015!

On Butler Street just west of Third Avenue, I face an impressive wall memorial to children hit by cars in recent years while walking, playing, or riding on bikes. Within the shape of a red STOP sign are the words: NOT ONE MORE DEATH, a sobering reminder of how quickly a careless driver can snuff out a child's life. Throughout the borough, in fact, murals exist that not only memorialize people but also that exhort people to change, be it drugs, gun control, finishing school, caring about others. Most of them don't directly order people to do things. Rather, they convey a powerful visual message that shows the destructive effects of not doing so.

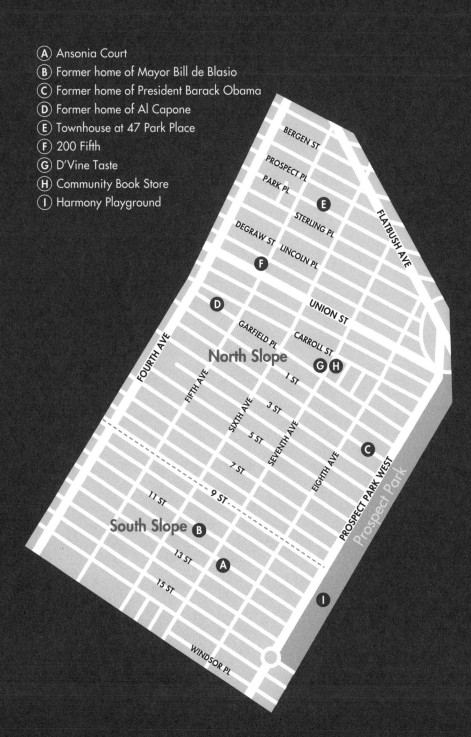

- (A) Ansonia Court
- (B) Former home of Mayor Bill de Blasio
- (C) Former home of President Barack Obama
- (D) Former home of Al Capone
- (E) Townhouse at 47 Park Place
- (F) 200 Fifth
- (G) D'Vine Taste
- (H) Community Book Store
- (I) Harmony Playground

BERGEN ST

PROSPECT PL

PARK PL

STERLING PL

DEGRAW ST LINCOLN PL

FLATBUSH AVE

UNION ST

FOURTH AVE

GARFIELD PL CARROLL ST

North Slope

1 ST

FIFTH AVE

3 ST

SIXTH AVE

5 ST

SEVENTH AVE

7 ST

EIGHTH AVE

9 ST

11 ST

South Slope

13 ST

15 ST

PROSPECT PARK WEST

Prospect Park

WINDSOR PL

PARK SLOPE

PARK SLOPE IS AN ARCHITECTURALLY ENTRANCING AREA that is much larger than Brooklyn Heights or Cobble Hill, and is equally stunning. Its boundaries are Flatbush Avenue on the northeast, Prospect Park West, running alongside Prospect Park, on the east, 17th Street on the south, and Fourth Avenue on the west. It was developed in the 1870s when mansions were built on Prospect Park West, attracting the well heeled. This mansion building was followed by apartment construction and after World War II more working-class people moved in. Ethnically, the neighborhood at this time was a mix of Irish, Italians, Jews, Puerto Ricans, and Jamaicans. Today it's a kaleidoscope of ethnic and racial groups with dozens of nationalities represented.

I would recommend walking almost every block here to take in the beauty and variety of the buildings. Among the nicest are Garfield Place, Berkeley Place, and Carroll, President, Union, 1st, and 9th Streets. It has great restaurants, the celebrated Park Slope Food Co-op, boutiques, bookstores, fine public and private schools, and, most important, Prospect Park, as well as excellent public transportation. It was ranked the number one community in Gotham by *New York Magazine* in 2010.

Park Slope wasn't always a safe area. In the 1980s it was dangerous, along with many other areas in the city, with muggings, drug dealing, and homelessness. But there were opportunities here for brave investors. Here's one person's recollection of her experiences when she and her husband moved to Park Slope in 1979:

> Eleventh Street was bad then. It was a slum. Our neighbor across the street referred to his rundown brownstone as "Jaws." The center of Park Slope was very good, from the

name streets to Eighth Street. Flatbush Avenue to Seventh Avenue was good. But from 1979 to about 1983, Fifth Avenue was a hell-hole. It was working class, though, not a really dangerous place. We were robbed several times during the years we lived there. We moved there because we wanted a house with a convenient commute. But it took too long to get to work, and the trains were not reliable then. And I had to stand forty minutes every day on the subway. And we believed Park Slope was going up. We were definitely part of the early gentrification process. But the brownstone we got was in bad shape. Every time it rained water would cascade down our walls. We had to put in a floor. It was actually homesteading, not exactly gentrification. Everyone had the same crappy brownstones. We were very proud of the gas lamp outside our house and of our little garden. And the fact was you could get a three-story house and a basement rental for a grand total of $90,000. We sold it a few years later for $180,000, so we made money on it. Carroll Gardens was also a mess then, and so was Boerum Hill, and if you walked into Prospect Park at night, you had a very good chance of getting mugged.

The dangerous days are now pretty much in the distant past; all of Park Slope is gentrified. One example is the Ansonia Clock Factory, built in the nineteenth century, at 420 12th Street. From the 1960s until the 1980s, the area around it was seen as increasingly unsafe. Today it's a premier address in Park Slope and has been renamed Ansonia Court. As Cherie Marcus, a resident who invited me into her apartment, recalled in 2014: "Our building was renovated in 1982. We have original columns, with an exposed ceiling that shows the pipes and raises the height. As you go up to the higher floors the ceilings get lower, this one being about 12–14 feet. The most unique feature is the courtyard, which used to be a loading dock." To gain entry, ask someone entering, or go with a real estate agent, or, if you dare, walk in after someone else.

"Why do people care about moving into this type of place? What's its appeal?" I ask. Cherie uses the bad old 1980s as a reference point that identifies when things began to change: "We joined the wave of newcomers moving in here during the '80s. They were mostly liberal, highly educated people, who were committed to living in the city and who liked that lifestyle. For one thing we were happy that we didn't displace anyone from their home. We were gentrifying, but we were not kicking anyone out of their place." Owing in part to the criticism leveled at gentrification by many well-off liberals and displaced residents, people who believe they are tolerant and caring often feel guilty about what happened when many poorer people were gradually pushed out when they moved into these neighborhoods. And so they develop rationales that minimize their discomfort. Cherie continues: "We also like the fact that the features aren't just ornamental, but have, in many cases been preserved as authentic parts of the building's history. As you look at the brickwork and fire escapes you see how many of the elements have been preserved. We have large windows. The highest price so far here is for a three bedroom, 1.7 million. Keep in mind that there are no elevators." All in all, it's a really attractive space. We see here how preservation isn't just something required by city agencies. It's a desired commodity, evidence that people want to be in touch with the history of where they choose to live.[3]

Today prices for brownstones in Park Slope begin at $1.5 million and go much higher. The comment that Park Slope was "not really a dangerous place" followed by "We were robbed several times" reminds me that the 1980s were a time of far lower expectations. A few robberies apparently didn't qualify as "dangerous."

Having famous people who reside in a certain neighborhood gives it cachet, and Park Slope, as in Brooklyn Heights, has that to a considerable degree. Mayor Bill de Blasio lived in the less prestigious but still nice South Slope at 442 11th Street. Today, of course, he lives in Gracie Mansion and rents out his Park Slope home. And Barack Obama lived on the fourth floor of 640 2nd Street in the mid-1980s. Others, past and present, include Steve Buscemi, Anne Hathaway, John Turturro, Pete Hamill, Jonathan Safran Foer, Jonathan Lethem, Jane Brody, Andrea Dworkin, Hugh Carey, Marty Markowitz, Charles Schumer, Bobby Fischer, and, believe it or not, Al Capone. One of eight children, whose family emigrated here from Naples, Capone lived in an apartment at 38 and quite likely 21 Garfield Place. Today it's one of the Slope's most picturesque streets, but when he lived there, it was just another tough, down-at-the-heels Brooklyn neighborhood.

As we've already seen, a neighborhood also derives status from preserving its authenticity, and that means, among other things, a certain ambience. I wonder about that as I stop and take a good look at 47 Park Place, which has a modern-looking wood facade. It's jarringly out of place on a block filled with brownstones and brick homes. The original structure housed carpentry and painting workshops. After they were demolished, the property became a brick, one-story oddity, nothing to brag about, before acquiring this new look. Some residents think the current house is ugly, while others love it, but, seen from another perspective, its uniqueness highlights, by way of contrast, the architecture that predominates here. These disputes are common to every borough—not surprising for a city that often elevates individual expression to an art form.

But a neighborhood isn't simply about bricks and mortar or which famous people lived there, or even about preserving history. It's about everyday life and how people live that life. In her witty, satirical, and, at times, scathing novel of the mores of life in Park Slope, *Prospect Park West*, Amy Sohn describes some of the prejudices of those residing there. One character in the novel reveals, among other things, that, notwithstanding the liberal mindset of the community, tolerance has its limits:

> Karen had read in *New York* magazine that houses in the [P.S.] 321 zone cost an average of $100,000 more than similarly

sized apartments in 107 but felt that was a small price to pay if it meant your kid went to a school that was 62 percent white instead of only 43. . . . The apartment was not only on a name street, which meant the northernmost, priciest area of Park Slope, but a park block. Better, it was in short walking distance of the Prospect Park Food Coop. . . . The North Slope was also closer to the central branch of the Brooklyn Public Library and the Montauk Club, where Karen already schlepped twice a week for her Weight Watchers meetings.[4]

So much about New York revolves around sports. And on a Sunday, it's possible to notice this as people everywhere are glued to the flat screens. Typical is a huge sports bar and eatery called "200 Fifth" on Fifth Avenue near Sackett Street. There are small TV screens at every table tuned to Jets or Giants football games. People are eagerly consuming burgers and fries and washing them down with beer and soda amid the loud din of fans exclaiming loudly and shouting at the screens, seemingly trying to will their teams to victory. When the home team scores, the roar of approval as the people explode in joy can be heard halfway down the block. It's a beautiful, warm, sunny day in early fall, but for these people the action is definitely inside, not outside. And I too am caught up in the excitement of being one with the crowd. These are the kinds of activities, enjoyed in local hangouts, that form the glue that holds a community together.

One of the shopping "gems" of Park Slope is D'Vine Taste at 150 Seventh Avenue, a specialty food store with really scrumptious baklava, especially the pistachio variety. The shop has been here for almost thirty-three years. The Lebanese owners are siblings; their mother is Jewish and their father Christian. In addition to their extensive Lebanese offerings, they also cater to the large Jewish population that lives here. They offer challahs, gefilte fish, potato latkes around Chanukah time, tagelach, and Israeli couscous. But mainly they carry a large assortment of specialty cheeses, high-quality olive oil, unusual beers, and homemade breads, fig cake, and their famous flatbread topped with Lebanese *za'atar*, a mix of delicious herbs.

Across the street is the Community Bookstore, a longtime fixture in this literate community. The bookstore is emblematic of a dying breed—nicely polished bookshelves, wooden floors, and an atmosphere where books are well arranged, displayed, and treated with care and love. Ezra Goldstein, the owner, tells me, "We cater to a more discerning clientele than your typical Barnes & Noble. Our people are really well-informed about books." But perhaps the owner's most important contribution beyond what he sells is the series of talks and workshops that are offered to the public, free of charge. When people venture out of their homes they are offered a chance to interact with their neighbors and become part of a larger community.

A few doors up on Seventh Avenue, I stare at a sign that reads "Norman & Jules Toy Shop, Established in 2012." It's a great place, with many unusual toys. It strikes me that in a world where so many businesses advertise how many *decades* they've been open to emphasize their success and the fact that people clearly trust them, 2012 must be an expression of optimism. In the future, in forty years, say, that sign will really mean something. But why not put it up now?

Walking up to Prospect Park, I arrive at the Harmony Playground, on Prospect Park West between 9th and 11th Streets, one of several themed play areas for children within the park. This one stresses music and features statues of musical instruments, like a harp and xylophone, that children can climb on. In the summer, water comes out of the harp, resembling what the strings would look like. I think back to how one of my children who was especially gifted in music used to be chased around our home by the piano teacher who tried to entice him to return to the piano by waving ice cream pops in his face. This seems to be a much more organic way of getting kids to relate to music—turning sculptures of instruments into a playground.

Harmony Playground—all musical prodigies and their friends welcome

Across a large meadow, I stroll into an area that makes something positive out of the devastation wrought by Hurricane Sandy. Trees felled by the hurricane have been sanded down and made into different shapes. It has become an exploration area, where children can crawl through a space cut into the trunks of trees, climb on other trees lying on the ground, and simply appreciate the many imaginative designs that have been sculpted from them. The design is fresh, low-tech, more natural and, judging from the number of children enjoying it, quite appealing. No, children will not hope for more hurricanes as a result, but imagine what the area would be like if the trees remained broken and dead on the ground.

Farther into the park, there's a huge meadow bordered by trees, where hundreds of dogs frolic and gambol off leash every day between 8:00 and 9:00 a.m. A group known as Fido offers a "Coffee Bark" on the first Saturday of each month. A table is set up with coffee, muffins, and dog biscuits. There's also a dog beach in a nearby area, where the canines can swim to their heart's content. I soon learn that doing this in November is a matter of taste. One dog, a Labrador, declines. Another, a Heinz 57 variety, gladly jumps in. This has a larger impact on the community. People who are dog lovers, and their numbers are legion, are more likely to move to communities that welcome them. A space like this can be the tipping point for deciding on which neighborhood to live in.[5]

Park Slope is a hugely attractive, full-service community. And for those able to pay the price, it's well worth it. Nonetheless, some people aren't so charitable in their evaluations of gentrification and express negative views that seem based on both perceived and real class differences. A longtime Hispanic resident of Park Slope who works as a teacher's aide in nearby Sunset Park expresses her feelings about the yuppies in her neighborhood: "They even complain that the birds make too much noise. They don't want Whole Foods to come in, because they buy everything from farmers. And they want to ban cars in all of Park Slope. They should go back to the Midwest, or wherever they came from. You know how I know this? I go on the Park Slope blog." Is she stereotyping? Quite possibly, since she acknowledges having no friends from this group. Regardless, it's certainly something to think about.

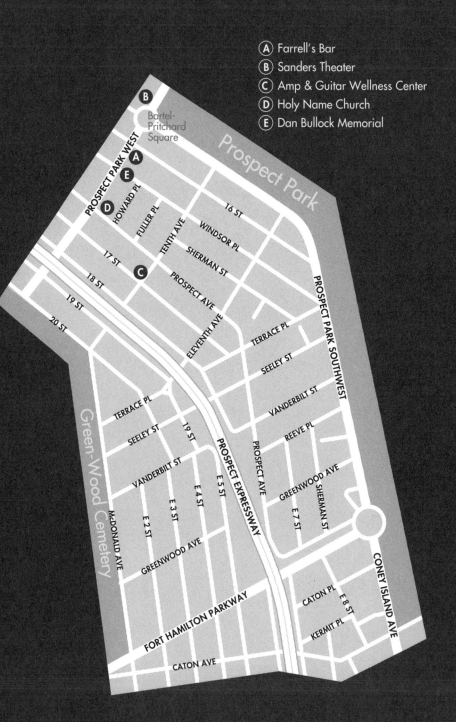

WINDSOR TERRACE

WINDSOR TERRACE WAS ONCE A FARM OWNED BY JOHN VANDERBILT.
It became a residential area in the mid-nineteenth century. Irish,
Poles, Italians, and Germans settled here. Today, it's much more
diverse, with Greeks, Jews, Hispanics, and Asians moving in with
their families. It also boasts some famous literary people who resided here at various times, including Pete and Dennis Hamill, Paul
Auster, and Isaac Asimov, who lived at 174 Windsor Place.

This is a quiet, not especially well-known community, with excellent housing—brick row homes, brownstones, Queen Annes,
Italianates, colonials; most are in very good condition. There are
apartment buildings, too, though none are higher than ten stories.
People here look out for each other, and members of the community organizations are strong advocates for the residents. Natural
boundaries, namely, Green-Wood Cemetery and Prospect Park, and
a paucity of through streets, further reduce the likelihood that it will
ever become an impersonal space. The formal boundaries of the area
are Prospect Park West on the north, Prospect Park Southwest and
Coney Island Avenue on the east, Caton Avenue on the south, and
McDonald Avenue on the west.

The main, though small, commercial drags are on Prospect Park
West, which still retains a feeling of quaintness, and Fort Hamilton Parkway, where more trendy shops have sprouted up in recent
years. Perhaps the most beautiful street in this section of Brooklyn is
Sherman Street, with its many gorgeous brownstones. And be sure
to take a look at the stately Romanesque Revival firehouse at 1309
Prospect Avenue, built in 1896. In those days this was a popular
style for firehouses. The engines were horse-drawn and there were
no work shifts, like today. Firefighters typically worked twenty-four
hours a day, six days a week.

I'm standing in a historic bar called Farrell's, open since 1933. It's noon on a Thursday and the bar on Prospect Park West, at the corner of 16th Street, is filled with old-timers drinking beer, talking, and watching the Mets, who are off to a great start, having won ten games in a row. (They went on to the World Series that year.) Everything seems typical, I think, as I drink my own beer, except for the three gentlemen standing around a wooden counter off to the side. They are in their forties, and one is wearing a smallish velvet skullcap. Most important, they're in real estate and their conversation is all about what's selling for what in the neighborhood.

They are standing under a glass-framed American flag, which is accompanied by a description of its history. The flag flew over Iraq during the operation known as Southern Watch, and was flown by Air Force Captain Ellen McKinnon, who came from this patriotic community.[6]

Windsor Terrace is surrounded by other areas in advanced states of gentrification, and is following the same pattern. That's why the bartender says to me, "This used to be all Irish a couple of years ago, but now everybody's moving in here." He remembers the old days when Pete Hamill's brother used to come in here. Is this a bad thing? What's wrong with a new culture being established here? Isn't that the way of the world? Certainly it is in a metropolis where change is a predictable occurrence. The insular community that flourished here for generations is being affected, as the people no longer feel comfortable because those other people—Jews, Asians, Greeks—are now their neighbors.

In truth, the ways of the past are rarely completely erased. Sometimes they even become enshrined by those wishing to preserve them. And yet, when I walk around in 2015 I can see the changing of the guard unfold before my very eyes, along with the feeling of longing for the past, of hoping that the spires of the local churches will always tower over the neat lawns and carefully tended frame or brick houses in which generations of the faithful were raised, right through the high crime decades of the 1970s, '80s, and '90s. Perhaps, they think, it will somehow survive the shifting winds, even as they know it won't. And the feeling of sadness and resentment among the inhabitants is real and palpable. Yes, their modest homes will fetch a good price, but at what cost? Yet how can they stay when they themselves are aging? The answer is they can't, and they don't. This pattern happens in many places, but its emotional impact is most clearly appreciated when the changing of the guard is actually happening before one's eyes.

Even I feel nostalgic for the old-time places I never knew, like the Sanders Theater off Bartel-Pritchard Square with its war memorial. Hamill's mother worked there for years as a cashier, a time when work that made a person happy wasn't a priority. Today the theater has a new name, The Pavilion, and ten films are showing simultaneously, something that was incomprehensible in the 1940s of Hamill's rough and tumble childhood. And that sign, "Now featuring reclining seating"! How futuristic from the standpoint of the old folks still alive.

Pete Hamill is a great writer and essayist who has penned many fascinating, unforgettable novels about New York and, especially his community, the South Slope, and nearby Windsor Terrace. To read him is to enter the unique culture of the Irish in America, as well as that of other ethnic and racial groups. And when I do read his works, I start to comprehend what is being lost here and in so many of Gotham's neighborhoods. Farrell's was one of his father's favorite haunts. Here's a snippet from his absorbing and richly textured memoir, *A Drinking Life*:

> On Sundays the family sometimes went visiting. That's what it was called: visiting. You went to someone's house and brought along cold cuts or Italian bread or beer and entertained each other. . . . After Mass, the whole family would walk down to Fifth Avenue, still dressed in Sunday best, and

get on the trolley and rattle out to Bay Ridge to see Uncle Tommy or Uncle Davey, Aunt Louie or Aunt Nellie, and all my cousins. We couldn't play in the street because we were in our good clothes; but visiting wasn't play to us, it was a show. There would be food and drink and singing in the parlor. . . . I would be forced to draw in a state of anxiety that was worse than fighting Frankie Nocera [a local bully]. I gave them Dick Tracy. Or Flattop. Or Batman.[7]

At Tenth Avenue and 17th Street, I stop in to visit Jeff Bloch's Amp and Guitar Wellness Center. "Have you ever been asked why you call this a wellness center, as if it was a doctor's office?"

"Yeah, about 10,000 times," says a man enjoying a quiet lunch with another man. They are both gray haired, and I feel as though I have interrupted them, especially because I'm the only visitor in this quiet place dedicated to the sale of musical instruments. "Playing music is what makes you well, not necessarily doctors."

"So this area is changing over, it seems."

"No, it's already changed."

"Well, not Farrell's." He agrees but assures me it's an illusion: "They come from all over, but everybody's selling out here. It's now very expensive. It's quiet now because everybody's at work. But even at night it's not like Bay Ridge nightlife. When we opened here sixteen years ago there were junkies and drunks. But now it's nice and some of the drunks woke up and wanted to sell. Of course, like everywhere else, most of the people were hard-working and the area was always pretty nice." Our little talk confirms what's happening here.

I peek into Holy Name Church on Prospect Park West on a Sunday morning and see that it's half-filled for an English mass. The crowd seems to be ethnically mixed, not like the old days when it was predominantly Irish. There are masses in Spanish too. The church has been beautifully maintained. A parishioner can now do

Howard Place—how things looked in the old days—sometimes you can go home again

online giving, and there are many activities for the worshipers: the annual card party, Weight Watchers, and art shows—all things that bind a community together.

Around the corner, I go up Howard Place with its long row of identical brick homes, all more than a century old. The block used to be almost exclusively Irish, but that's changing as gentrifiers snap up houses at nearly $2 million each. Turning left onto Windsor Place, near the F and G lines subway stop, I stare at three plastic-covered sheets of paper, one on each tree, that commemorate soldiers who died in Vietnam, some with roots in the community. One, in particular, catches and holds my attention. It's about a fifteen-year-old, Dan Bullock. This must be really unusual, I surmise, and indeed, it is. A marine serving in Vietnam, he was the youngest soldier to die since World War I; he altered his birth date to accomplish this feat. Bullock, an African American, was raised in North Carolina and moved to Brooklyn at age twelve, living in Williamsburg, on Lee Avenue. Is it important that this tree carry his name? After all, a one-block stretch of Lee Avenue is named in his memory, and there's a small photoengraving of him on the rarely visited Vietnam Veterans' Memorial in Lower Manhattan. It *is* important, so that this man, who died in battle for his country, be remembered as much as possible. Although many disagreed with that war, this man was a fifteen-year-old foot soldier, not a policy maker.

I chat with three elderly local residents who tell me about Windsor Terrace. One of them, a woman with dyed raven-black hair and still-sparkling blue eyes, tells me with a smile: "You should see Green-Wood Cemetery. It's funny to say this, but it's a real attraction because all these famous people are buried there."

"What's the neighborhood like?"

"It's changing. It used to be really friendly, small town, with everyone knowing each other. It was a blue-collar working-class community. It's transitioned because it's very accessible to the city. My father bought his house in 1962 for $29,000 and now it's worth 2 million dollars."

"You know what they call us?" The other one chimes in, "The Leftovers."

"That's not a nice thing to say," I volunteer.

"Well," says the first, "they now say we're a community of winners. We're in the big time. Before we were blue collar—city cops, firemen, like that. But we don't care what the houses are worth. We're not movin' and the house is gonna be inherited by our children and that's all that matters; which is good, because our kids could never afford to buy a house here."

These people recognize reality. Their time has come and gone. But the neighborhood is still safe, and they still have their own delis, eateries, good public schools for their grandchildren, and the church. They're happy about the convenience, the subway, a half hour to midtown Manhattan, Prospect Park, the botanical gardens, and the newcomers, while not their type, aren't bothering them. This compact, quiet area will continue to attract the gentrifiers.

FORT GREENE

CLINTON HILL

PROSPECT HEIGHTS

BEDFORD-STUYVESANT

CROWN HEIGHTS

PROSPECT LEFFERTS GARDENS

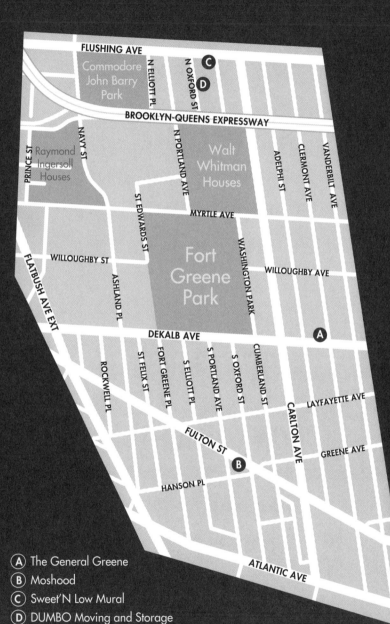

FLUSHING AVE

Commodore
John Barry
Park

N ELLIOTT PL

N OXFORD ST

C

D

BROOKLYN-QUEENS EXPRESSWAY

PRINCE ST

Raymond
Ingersoll
Houses

NAVY ST

ST EDWARDS ST

N PORTLAND AVE

Walt
Whitman
Houses

ADELPHI ST

CLERMONT AVE

VANDERBILT AVE

MYRTLE AVE

WILLOUGHBY ST

ASHLAND PL

Fort
Greene
Park

WASHINGTON PARK

WILLOUGHBY AVE

FLATBUSH AVE EXT

DEKALB AVE

A

ROCKWELL PL

ST FELIX ST

FORT GREENE PL

S ELLIOTT PL

S PORTLAND AVE

S OXFORD ST

CUMBERLAND ST

CARLTON AVE

LAYFAYETTE AVE

GREENE AVE

FULTON ST

B

HANSON PL

ATLANTIC AVE

A The General Greene
B Moshood
C Sweet'N Low Mural
D DUMBO Moving and Storage

FORT GREENE

FORT GREENE'S BOUNDARIES ARE NASSAU STREET and Flushing Avenue on the north, Vanderbilt Avenue on the east, Atlantic Avenue on the south, and roughly, Flatbush Avenue Extension and Prince Street on the west. One of its several important areas is the recently expanded commercial center around Flatbush and Atlantic Avenues, home of the Barclays Center. Here you'll see Best Buy, Marshall's, Victoria's Secret, Target, a Pathmark Supercenter, and much more. The center has changed the face of all of Brooklyn, greatly contributing to its reputation as "the hottest borough," but a neighborhood like Fort Greene is even more affected because the center's location on the southern edge of the neighborhood places it *within* the community—walking distance for most of its residents.

Another very important institution, one that's been in Fort Greene for a long time, is the Brooklyn Academy of Music, *the place*, especially in this borough, for music, theater, film, opera, and everything related to music, serving both the community and the entire city. Founded in 1861, it has been at this location, 30 Lafayette Avenue, near Ashland Place and Fulton Street, since 1908 and has a well-deserved reputation as a premier urban venue for cutting-edge entertainment. Along with the reopened King Theater and the planned restoration to its earlier glory of the famed Paramount Theater, it's clear that this revitalization of the area will be long-lasting.[1] Fort Greene also hosts a major arts festival every June that attracts about 40,000 visitors.

Fort Greene had many residents who worked at the Brooklyn Navy Yard, which closed in 1966. The city bought the Navy Yard and built an industrial park on the site. The community worked hard to make the area safer, and in the 1970s people began buying up the still-attractive brownstones, yet the area around the projects remained dangerous. Slowly, however, things got better, as they did elsewhere in the borough. Today the industrial park is thriving, but most significantly, Fort Greene is in the midst of a major building boom of luxury apartments. These literally tower over the neighborhood and are located in Fort Greene and also Downtown Brooklyn. The thousands of apartment residents these will attract, many of them affluent, will transform this area. Upscale shops, restaurants, movie theaters, wine bars, and such have now joined the many stores, delis, and ethnic restaurants that currently line Myrtle Avenue and Fulton Street, and only the strong will survive. The row houses that have multiple dwellings will be converted into elegant homes or torn down in favor of the glass and steel apartment buildings that presently dominate many parts of Greenpoint, Williamsburg, and other areas.

As is the case elsewhere, the Whitman-Ingersoll, NYCHA, buildings will remain, less crime ridden than fifteen years ago, but a reminder, nonetheless, of the poverty that still exists in New York City. I often wonder what better-off people think about when they walk by the projects. Do they just ignore the implications of inequality? Do they feel a need to support affordable housing of a better kind? Do they ever wonder what the inhabitants think *about them* as they pass through?

Then there are the graceful, well-tended brownstones that prevail on tree-lined Adelphi Street, Clermont Avenue, and other nearby blocks. This community has always had a beautiful core, with a substantial black middle-class presence, even throughout the crime-ridden 1980s and '90s. These give the neighborhood the same charm that typifies portions of Clinton Hill, Boerum Hill, and Bedford-Stuyvesant, all nearby.[2]

I come across the General Greene on the corner of DeKalb and Clermont Avenues, a down-home eatery with a fine wine list and an eclectic menu of burgers, buttermilk fried chicken, Ukrainian soup, steak, mussels, and such. Proudly stating that it was founded back in 2008, it caters to a gentrified crowd of mostly younger folks. Restaurants like this send a clear signal to would-be residents about who already lives here. I engage in some light-hearted banter with the waitress. Knowing full well that Fort Greene derives its name from Revolutionary War General Nathanael Greene, who was headquartered in this area, I nevertheless say: "This general must have been quite an impressive guy to have a restaurant named after him."

"Oh yes," she responds with a smile. "And he's still here."

"I guess he's not here right now."

"No. He's down in the basement."

"Wrapped in formaldehyde, I suppose."

"Yes. Exactly!" she says, laughing.

This kind of banter with a slight edge is typical of "New Yorkese," a style of conversation that, if nothing else, helps make the day go by pleasantly.

Continuing up Fulton Street toward Flatbush Avenue, I see restaurants of all types: Ethiopian, Cuban, Turkish, Japanese, African again, and two German biergartens, with traditional wooden benches and a large selection of beers. Why these two exist a block apart is a bit of a mystery. Perhaps they will attract basketball fans and others who want a little fun after they've been to an event at Barclays.

This is what happens in places where residential and commercial areas commingle. A little bit of everything can be found. Across from one of the biergartens, I enter Moshood, an African-style clothing store at 698 Fulton. As I walk in, the middle-aged man who works there is eating what he tells me is a traditional African dish. He greets me effusively, saying his clothes are "made for *you*. Please come back and bring your wife." Moshood is a well-known designer of African clothes from Nigeria, and his fans include Wesley Snipes and other celebrities. The store's slogan is "Wear Moshood, Wear Yourself."

Clearly, Fort Greene is a suitable neighborhood for gentrifiers. But that term doesn't adequately describe the different subgroups, ethnically, religiously, and culturally, that encompass it. Let's take one such case—nonobservant Jews, who, in fact, live everywhere in the city, perhaps a half a million strong. Often they reject formal affiliation. When that happens, those wanting to identify as Jews must find other ways to connect. And they do. Here's one account by Steve Sachs, a forty-five-year-old magazine executive who lives with his wife in Fort Greene: "There aren't Jewish institutions in Fort Greene or very close by. We joined a synagogue in Park Slope, but we wanted to find other families and just create some kind of community here. And we created, about a year and a half ago, a monthly potluck dinner. We thought we'd get maybe two or three families, and the first time we did it we had about forty people here between kids and adults, and we were stunned! At the end of the evening we said, 'Would people like to get together again?' People said yes."[3]

This is typical of how young people, wary of organized religion, find ways to express themselves. What's interesting is that they too center it on a ritual, the potluck dinner. This can't compare to the hundreds of practices the Orthodox follow, but one ritual tends to give birth to others related to it; for example, there might be (and perhaps is by now) a discussion of Judaism while eating. In a sense, this example demonstrates how religious or cultural identity isn't necessarily dying among the young; rather, it's changing and evolving into new forms.

A small area north of Park Avenue extends for only one block to Flushing Avenue, where it bumps up against the property of the Brooklyn Navy Yard. On the west, it begins at Navy Street, and its eastern boundary is Vanderbilt Avenue. After the American Revolution, the shipyard, also known as the US Navy Yard, built merchant ships. At its peak, in World War II, more than 70,000 people worked there. Today, under the ownership of the city, it's an industrial park, home to a commercial farm, Steiner Studios, other businesses, and a workplace for artists.

One typical block, North Elliot Place, has old red-brick row houses, some of which are home to families of former Navy Yard workers; others contain artists and gentrifiers who like the quietness of the area or are unable to afford places nearer the livelier center of Fort Greene. A mailman named Don tells me: "The area's a lot better than it was before. I've been covering this neighborhood for 25 years. It was so bad twenty years ago that even me, a black man, was worried about walking here. It's just not about color, but safety. The corner project is now a co-op. Yeah, there's still Whitman, but you got projects everywhere. And the park's got good programs and they even have a dog run."

"Wow!"

"It's changed, man. Many of the poor folks and criminals left."

"Where did they go?"

"Far Rockaway, I imagine."

"Why there?"

"That's cold country. People don't wanna live there. People think it's beautiful, but in the winter, the subways freeze up outdoors and nobody can go anywhere." Don notes how things improved, and in what is perhaps an unconscious attempt to reduce any racial distance he tells me that even as a black man he wasn't safe here. Or maybe he's just stating a fact. In truth, blacks are far more likely to be victims of black criminals than are whites.

North Portland Avenue and Cumberland Street have similar, old two-story houses, but interspersed through these streets are small companies, supply houses, schools, and storage areas. It was also headquarters for the recently closed Sweet'N Low Company, which had been there for decades. The company had a beautiful mural on Cumberland Street painted in rich colors on its brick wall, displaying a golden ear of corn, a teacup, and bright red strawberries.

It's beginning to snow more heavily; very few people are out and about as I walk into DUMBO Moving and Storage on nearby North Oxford Street. It's called DUMBO despite its Fort Greene location because that's where they began in 2007. When I asked if it was confusing, one employee responded: "It hasn't been as far we can see. But it certainly attracts more attention, which is good for

Flushing and Cumberland—some things never change

business." The company has fifty-six trucks and numerous branches in Brooklyn, with large storage facilities in New Jersey and elsewhere. Young people dressed casually work from their laptops helping people move from and to all parts of the United States. Helping create the friendly atmosphere for the employees are Ping-Pong and pool tables. I talk to a salesman who hails from Serbia and has been in the United States for about five years. His trajectory is revealing: "I came here on a basketball scholarship at a university in South Carolina. But I got injured in my junior year, a dislocated shoulder. So they cut me from the team. I lost the scholarship, but with some loans I finished. I needed a job, so I came to DUMBO Moving."

"Do you like living in the US?"

"Yes, a lot."

"Do you have anyone in Serbia?"

"Only my father."

"How did you learn English so well?"

"I watched cartoons and movies in Serbia. I'm serious; that's how I did it." I guess not everyone goes to school to learn English.

A lanky six feet seven, with short blond hair and a pleasant demeanor, this young man has a green card and intends to become a citizen. His talents got him here and he hoped to play pro ball, but his injury forced him to enter another field. He hopes to rise to a higher position or enter a different profession. He accepts all this philosophically, saying, "I love America and New York and am going to make the best of my opportunities." I think to myself, but for fate I could have been watching him on TV.

Cold weather might be seen as an obstacle to walking, but it really isn't. I subscribe, within limits, to the Scandinavian view— "There's no such thing as bad weather, just bad clothing." If I waited for good weather, I'd lose four out of every twelve months, not a way to get things done. Moreover, in New York, people bundle up and walk around in the cold, traveling to work, shopping, and everything. If they're too cold to talk, I can always appreciate architecture, signage, and the like in any type of weather except a snowstorm. And when extremely bad weather forces me indoors, I simply walk into shops, minimalls, factories, building lobbies, and schools and talk to people there.

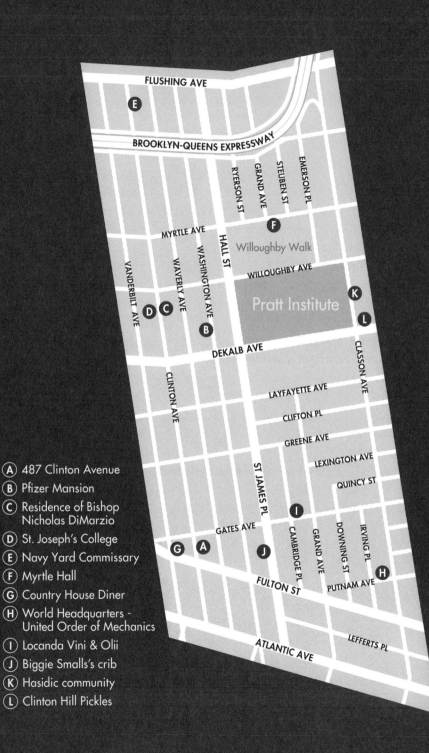

FLUSHING AVE

E

BROOKLYN-QUEENS EXPRESSWAY

RYERSON ST

GRAND AVE

STEUBEN ST

EMERSON PL

MYRTLE AVE

HALL ST

F

Willoughby Walk

WASHINGTON AVE

WAVERLY AVE

WILLOUGHBY AVE

VANDERBILT AVE

D C

K

Pratt Institute

L

B

DEKALB AVE

CLINTON AVE

LAYFAYETTE AVE

CLASSON AVE

CLIFTON PL

GREENE AVE

LEXINGTON AVE

QUINCY ST

ST JAMES PL

I

GATES AVE

CAMBRIDGE PL

GRAND AVE

DOWNING ST

IRVING PL

G A

J

H

FULTON ST

PUTNAM AVE

LEFFERTS PL

ATLANTIC AVE

Ⓐ 487 Clinton Avenue
Ⓑ Pfizer Mansion
Ⓒ Residence of Bishop
   Nicholas DiMarzio
Ⓓ St. Joseph's College
Ⓔ Navy Yard Commissary
Ⓕ Myrtle Hall
Ⓖ Country House Diner
Ⓗ World Headquarters -
   United Order of Mechanics
Ⓘ Locanda Vini & Olii
Ⓙ Biggie Smalls's crib
Ⓚ Hasidic community
Ⓛ Clinton Hill Pickles

CLINTON HILL

WHILE AT FIRST NEIGHBORHOODS SEEM TO BE SIMILAR to each other, distinctions do emerge. Compact Clinton Hill is more like Fort Greene, while adjacent Prospect Heights more closely resembles Park Slope. The former are a bit grittier, the latter a tad more staid, though there is variation within each of the areas. If architecture is your thing, Clinton Hill has many Romanesque, Victorian, and Italianate homes from yesteryear.

Clinton Hill's boundaries are Flushing Avenue on the north, Classon Avenue on the east, Atlantic Avenue on the south, and Vanderbilt Avenue on the west. The area has easy subway access and is close to the Barclays Center. While it's still a little rough around the edges, it's quite safe, and gentrification continues its march through this section of northern Brooklyn, though not as quickly as in Prospect Heights or Carroll Gardens. It has wonderful restaurants, especially if you like Italian food, and a throbbing night life for those who enjoy clubbing. It's a mixed neighborhood with all of the ethnic groups that typify today's Brooklyn.

Clinton Avenue, heading north from Fulton Avenue, is lined with many magnificent homes and churches. This is where wealthy industrial and commercial families chose to live in splendor—the Pratts, Bristols, Bedfords, Underwoods, and others. It's a wide, tree-lined street and an absolute delight to gaze upon, not at all like the streets with brownstones and row houses in Cobble Hill and Brooklyn Heights, where the houses are set more closely together and the streets are narrower.

One outstanding example is 487 Clinton, a five-story stone and brick structure that, with its tall turret, resembles a castle, and that boasts a stunning Romanesque entry. Homes like these are one-of-a-kind creations with unusual designs; they are made from stone, brick, and wood, and have tiled or slate roofs, often in striking shades of brown, red, and beige, and numerous interestingly shaped windows. Some even have spacious wraparound porches with latticed designs and wooden floors. Other homes of architectural interest are at 356, 324, 315 (a gorgeous condominium, divided into seven apartments), and especially 241, a beautiful mansion in which Brooklyn's Roman Catholic bishop, Nicholas Anthony DiMarzio, resides. Taking a short detour at this point over to Washington Avenue, I stroll by 280–282 Washington, the homes built by the Pfizer family—nineteenth-century grandeur personified. Their Otis elevator is believed to have been the first elevator in the city.[4]

Everyone needs a brief rest at some point and I'm no exception. St. Joseph's College, on Clinton, between DeKalb and Willoughby Avenues, is an excellent choice for a resting spot. I turn left in the middle of the block and in thirty seconds I'm sitting on a comfortable curved bench in a grassy, bucolic area, with a very large overhanging tree. I close my eyes, relax, and listen to the robins singing the melodies of spring. To my right on the campus is the Dillon Child Study Center, an excellent preschool founded in 1934. As I get up, I remember that Pratt Institute, which has wonderful sculptures on its campus, is located just three short blocks away on St. James Place. It's definitely worth a visit.

The blocks between Park and Flushing Avenues and from Vanderbilt Avenue on the west to Classon Avenue on the east are part of Clinton Hill, but the neighborhood is more industrial. On Clinton, near Flushing, I come across an official-looking blue sign that reads, "Navy Yard Commissary," which turns out to have nothing to do with the Navy Yard. It's a place where city-licensed pushcarts, in this case of the halal variety seen all over town, go home for the night. These "garages" are often located on the fringes of residential areas and are essential to the city's ability to provide such services. Imagine if the city didn't have these locations available to vendors. Well, there'd be a lot of hungry folks!

Fellowship and history in the black community

No community would be complete without its local characters, and I find seventy-four-year-old Bob Adams soon enough, on Waverly Avenue near Greene Avenue. He's a tall, good-looking African American gentleman with curly gray hair and a smile for everyone. He is standing in front of his garage, which houses his 1970s Lincoln Continental, and manages to say hello to at least ten people in the half hour I spend with him. They range in age, race, and gender, but their faces all visibly brighten when he greets them.

But even friendliness has its limits. I ask Bob: "What about the new gentrifiers? Are they friendly?" Bob seems momentarily taken aback by the question, almost as if he hadn't considered it.

"Well, it's funny you should ask me that because a friend of mine lives in one of those mixed housing situations, with both rich and not so rich. And he tells me that the new people with money can be somewhat snobby, you know, like keep their distance. Of course, they might not have that much in common with people who have less. That's always gonna be the case." These comments highlight once again that gentrifiers may live among the common folk, right next to them in fact, but even with well-intentioned efforts at socializing, some barriers will always remain.

I explore this issue further with artist Fred Terna, a ninety-one-year-old Holocaust survivor who lives on Washington Avenue. "I was just invited to visit Dachau by the government there, all expenses paid. I have mixed feelings about it, but I want to see it together with my son."

I ask him how he survived the camps, and he answers: "Pure luck. I have no idea how I made it; that, plus an optimistic attitude." It was that optimistic attitude that led him and his wife, Rebecca Schiffman, an obstetrician specializing in high-risk pregnancies, to purchase a home in the 1980s. "Why did you choose this area? It was a high crime location then."

"We actually wanted to be in Park Slope, but we couldn't afford it. And it was a beautiful Italianate style home that had lots of potential."

"What was it like?"

"A lot of crime. I was mugged twice. But I thought we would make it work. Like everything else in life, you do your best. We never dreamed then that it would become a really desirable and hot place."

"Since there were few people like you moving in at the time, did you become friendly with the locals?"

"To some extent, but it wasn't easy. We invited our neighbors, who were black, over a few times and they eventually reciprocated. But we never could get really friendly with them, though they were basically nice people."

These comments further illustrate the challenge. One can have the best of intentions, but sometimes ingrained prejudices remain. Things are more likely to work when each side is open to the idea of getting to know people outside their usual friendship circles. But even then it can feel like "work" for some individuals. Happily, in my experience running the City College Conflict Resolution Center, most people completely change their views once they engage with those who are from different backgrounds.

And then larger issues echo both history and reality in general. As my friend, the noted sociologist of the black community, Elijah Anderson, has argued, blacks and whites share a history beginning with slavery that is fraught with conflict. The residue is palpable and, especially among older people, many blacks just don't like whites and vice versa. Plus, having grown up in different neighborhoods, the chances that they will have anything in common, or even know anyone in common, are slender. Too often, the attitude is one of "Why bother?"[5] These are among the truest impediments to meaningful integration. Is there hope? Definitely, but it lies with members of the younger generation who have formed earlier friendships in schools, playgrounds, neighborhoods, religious and social organizations, and the like.

There has been much talk about how neighborhoods in Brooklyn have changed, but people often fail to grasp just how difficult it is on the ground for an area to turn around. It's not just about coming in and building, but also about developing relationships with other players in the community. The imagery embodied in the moniker for Myrtle Avenue during the 1980s, "Murder Avenue," lives on for those in the know. Yet an article in the *New York Times* on February 15, 2011, by Fred Bernstein, told about an eleven-year effort to revitalize the area.[6] It began with the formation of the Myrtle Avenue Revitalization Project, headed by Thomas F. Schutte, president of Pratt Institute. He had a real stake in the project, because Myrtle Avenue was the closest shopping area to the campus. Its initial efforts included sweeping streets, removing graffiti, and finding retailers to take over empty space.

In January 2011, Pratt opened the doors of Myrtle Hall, a $54 million, six-story building containing offices, classrooms, and galleries. It wasn't easy, however. The owner of the property, real estate developer Michael Orbach, had no desire to sell it to Pratt, but he and Schutte became acquainted and an unusual deal was struck. Orbach would control the first floor and basement as retail space, and Pratt would control the building's upper floors. This highlights the fact that gentrification works best when different parties work together, which requires that all interests be served.

Emerging from the C train on Clinton Avenue, I enter the Country House diner on the corner of Fulton and Vanderbilt Avenues and have a real New York experience. Needing a restroom, I order an iced coffee that I don't really want. And then, eying a croissant, I tell the heavyset man behind the counter that I've changed my mind and would like the croissant instead. I also ask to use the restroom, at which point he says to me with a smile: "You don't have to buy something if you just want to use the toilet." I insist on the croissant but add: "I guess if one minute I want a coffee and the next a dessert, I'm giving away my reason for doing so." "Yes, you did," he exclaims, laughing. Joe is a pleasant-looking man who exudes genuine warmth. His apron is stained, evidence of a hard day's work serving people. A Yankee cap is perched on his head above twinkling eyes and dark eyebrows.

Perhaps he's being nice to me because I'm like him in terms of color, age, and economic level. Then again, perhaps he'd be nice to anyone who didn't look like a homeless person he fears will mess up his bathroom. Observing me glancing at the sign reading: "Bathrooms for customers only," he adds, almost apologetically, "I only have this because, you know, some people come in here, they homeless and they're really gonna mess up the bathroom and then it's a big job cleaning it."

"Where are you from?" I ask, noting an accent.

"From the Middle East," he answers, adding, after some prodding, "I'm Palestinian, but you know, my family's been in New York City since the 1890s. We run this diner, which is open 24/7. When I go home, my brother takes over."

This is yet another typical version of the immigrant dream. Over and over again I hear the gratitude felt by those who immigrated to this country. He's a man in his fifties who didn't finish high school. Joe tells me in an oft-heard refrain, that in the United

States different cultures don't matter because everyone needs to get along—Jewish, Chinese, black.

"How do the gentrifiers and the locals get along here? Do they sit together in your place?" I ask.

"I see they avoid each other. They don't have anything in common. But this is a good place. We even had well-known people who came in here regularly, like Biggie Smalls. He lived around here and used to come in every day. Lil' Kim came in here too. She was an exotic dancer and a rapper too, like Biggie." This makes sense, as these two big-time players knew each other well. The meaning here is clear. If these people who could write their own ticket were customers, it must be a good place. And eating here is like rubbing shoulders with the rich and famous.

Walking up Classon, I turn left on Putnam Avenue and stare at an imposing structure with a tall, beige turret, surrounded by stone-inlaid grapes and other fruits, topped by a silver spire. A large, black-lettered sign proclaims it to be the WORLD HEADQUARTERS BUILDING OF THE INDEPENDENT UNITED ORDER OF MECHANICS—WESTERN HEMISPHERE INCORPORATED.

How many members do they really have? What does it mean to be a world headquarters? This grand-looking building, with paint peeling here and there, is still quite impressive. Its Romanesque architecture would fit in well on Washington or Clinton Avenues. Indeed, it's landmarked, like so much of Clinton Hill. Entering through the lobby, I strike up a conversation with a tall, elderly black man from the West Indies. To the side is an ad for a boxing match to be shown live in May in the organization's social hall for free. "This group was started in 1878 and people still come to meetings, though it's mostly to socialize. Originally, it was called the Lincoln Club, a place for rich white folks. Then the Mechanics Order took it over after 1940 and made it into a nice place for mechanics, a club where they could be themselves."

"Could someone like me become a member?" I ask. He looks me over appraisingly and chuckles.

"Why not?"—this said almost as a dare. He clearly doesn't think I'm serious. But frankly if I had the time, I'd join just for the experience. Apparently being a mechanic is no longer a requirement. On Gates Avenue, near Cambridge Place, I see a sign for Lewis Drug Store. As I peer through the window, I realize it's nothing of the sort. It's a Northern Italian eatery called Locanda Vini e Olii. I ask the owner why the old sign (actually it's a "restored" but very real-looking version) is still there. His answer is instructive: "This was a pharmacy before, that served the community for more than a century and we felt it would be nice for the customers to preserve the memory. So we kept a lot of the original stuff."

They certainly have, in the form of rolling ladders, drawers, cabinets, and a variety of medicines from the old days—sodium and potassium in their original bottles. Even the sign "Prescription Center" still adorns what is now a spotless, gleaming kitchen, behind a partition. There's also a very cute painting of a coat rack, with a fedora hat and a long overcoat hanging from the hooks. In addition to the pharmaceutical products, there are all sorts of odd, collectible items in the glass showcases, usually donated by customers, including a cocoa can, old Schweppes bottles, and a collection of teacups. As Logan, the manager, reminds me, reservations are definitely required for this highly rated bistro.

This is an increasingly popular trend—retaining the original signage and even interior elements, both for memory-lane lovers and to give a place that elusive feeling of authenticity. For authenticity of a different sort, I stand in front of Biggie Smalls' crib at nearby 226 St. James Place, Apartment 3L. Biggie lived here with his mother for about twenty years. Today, his place has been converted into an expensive three-bedroom dwelling.

My next experience further explains the complexity of gentrification. I'm walking on Classon Avenue, the eastern border between Clinton Hill and Bedford-Stuyvesant, when I pass a large, somewhat dull-looking apartment building that turns out to be exclusively populated by Hasidic families. I'm surprised that they live this far away from the community, which is centered in Williamsburg around Lee and Flushing Avenues. And I'm even more surprised to learn that all the blocks in between have a Hasidic presence, too, in what has been, until recently, an almost exclusively black and Hispanic section of Bed-Stuy. I approach two young Satmar Hasidic men standing outside the building and ask them why they chose this location to settle in.

"We needed space and we came here because it wasn't expensive."

"So how come you don't go further into Clinton Hill?"

"Because we can't afford it. The rich yuppies have moved in there, or you have young people from Missouri, Wisconsin, who knows where, living six people in a three bedroom place, paying $800 each. We have families with eight kids with only one breadwinner. It's economic war and we can't compete with that. And now even Bed-Stuy, which is turning white, is becoming a problem with us affording it."

This makes it clear that this is isn't simply a battle between incoming gentrifiers versus poor Hispanic and black minorities, but Hasidim as well, who find their path to expansion blocked by wealthier people. Hemmed in by rising prices, they can expand only so far.

It's appropriate, perhaps, that my next and last stop should be half a block down on the corner, at Clinton Hill Pickles on 431 DeKalb Avenue. It was started by the owners of the legendary Guss' Pickles on the Lower East Side, which served generations of mostly Jewish customers. I try a sour pickle out of the barrel and it's delicious. The Jewish man behind the counter mentions, in passing, that he's not at all observant religiously. How ironic that the Hasidim up the block are so traditional in the twenty-first century, while most of Guss' Jewish customers are not, despite the fact that both groups originally came from the same "Old Country."

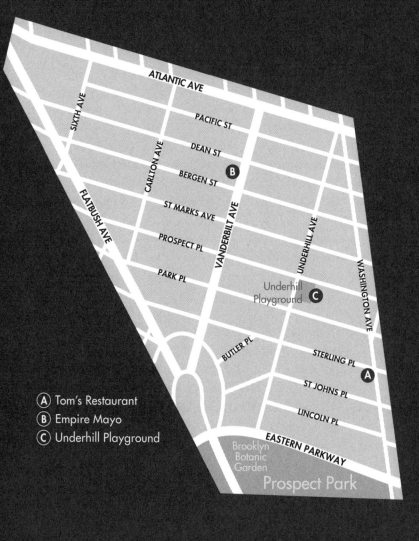

ATLANTIC AVE

SIXTH AVE

PACIFIC ST

CARLTON AVE

DEAN ST

BERGEN ST **B**

FLATBUSH AVE

ST MARKS AVE

VANDERBILT AVE

PROSPECT PL

UNDERHILL AVE

PARK PL

WASHINGTON AVE

Underhill
Playground **C**

BUTLER PL

STERLING PL

A

ST JOHNS PL

LINCOLN PL

Ⓐ Tom's Restaurant
Ⓑ Empire Mayo
Ⓒ Underhill Playground

EASTERN PARKWAY

Brooklyn
Botanic
Garden

Prospect Park

PROSPECT HEIGHTS

PROSPECT HEIGHTS IS A SMALL NEIGHBORHOOD, about half a square mile in size, that began improving economically twenty-five years ago. Nestled between the Barclays Center on the north, Prospect Park on the south with its spectacular entrance at Grand Army Plaza, and adjacent to Park Slope, it's one of Brooklyn's hot communities. The precise boundaries are Atlantic Avenue to the north, Washington Avenue to the east, Eastern Parkway to the south, and Flatbush Avenue to the west. Barclays Center is in walking distance, Manhattan is minutes away, and the Brooklyn Museum, the main branch of the Brooklyn Public Library, the Botanic Garden, and Prospect Park, with its winding lanes, leafy woods, and many recreational activities, are nearby. Housing includes brick row houses, brownstones, and old apartment buildings in good condition with large rooms, as well as the usual new glass and steel structures. Prospect Heights has one of the largest historic districts in the city. There's also ample shopping and restaurants along Flatbush, Vanderbilt, and Washington Avenues.

Like Fort Greene, it's a diverse area with a variety of ethnic and racial groups living in relative harmony. The major controversy in recent years centered on the Barclays project. Building the center required razing buildings, which some residents opposed. New restaurants are constantly opening, but the longest waits on Saturday are still for the venerable Tom's Restaurant at 782 Washington Avenue, which has been there forever, or, more precisely, since 1936; it's a real crowd pleaser among authenticity seekers.

I notice an elderly black woman on Carleton Avenue near Dean Street. She is sitting on a chair at the top of the steps in front of her graceful brownstone on a chilly, cloudy March afternoon, bundled up. Her home has a most attractive garden filled largely with evergreen species of various bushes, plants, and a few small trees. "Great job on this garden," I say by way of striking up a conversation. She thanks me and I continue: "What do you like about this neighborhood?"

"I love the history of the place. George Washington was here and the Revolution happened here. I have done the research on this neighborhood."

"I bet if you lived in South Carolina or in Queens you wouldn't get this kind of history," I say.

"Well there's history everywhere, but not one with George Washington marching around and the Revolution and all."

We learn here that people live in a neighborhood not only because of money, safety, or even beauty, but also because of its history. For in so doing, they become a living part of that history. It makes them feel proud to be residing in a place where important events occurred. This is its cachet, not unlike a white store owner in nearby Bedford-Stuyvesant who informed me how important it was to her that the location may have been a stop on the Underground Railroad in the days of slavery.

"How do you feel about the Barclays Center nearby?" I ask.

"Well there's good and bad. It made the neighborhood safer, it brought better services, like more stores, and property values went up."

"I bet you could sell your house for at least a million."

"A million? Try like three million."

"Would you sell it?"

"Heck no, I like it here. I've lived here since 1951. Bought it for $17,000. I love this house. I wouldn't go anywhere," she reflects. "We got it cheap because the white folks here were running away."

How ironic, I think. In those days of blockbusting, whites fled at the first sign of blacks moving into their neighborhoods. Panicked, they sold their homes at bargain rates and departed for white areas in Brooklyn or Queens, or the suburbs. There they remained, raising their children. And now we have come full circle. Today, these children are part of the movement back to the city, which now includes Brooklyn, where they pay millions to live in homes that could have been the ones they grew up in and which their parents or grandparents might well have given them.

But this is only part of the story. In those days, many of the blacks and Puerto Ricans who came into these areas were poor, unemployed, and uneducated. Largely because of a lack of opportunity, crime increased, and these communities became undesirable. After the crack epidemic of the 1980s subsided, crime dropped precipitously and more resources were devoted to helping the city's poor; things then began to change.

On Flatbush Avenue, I pass Sharlene's, a local bar. A sign on a chalkboard reads: "Sharlene's Cranky Hour—All Drinks Full Price, 7 pm to 4 am." I walk into the place and ask why the sign is there. "If you have to ask, that's a problem," is the answer. I laugh and reassure the bartender that I have indeed heard of happy hour. The sign certainly achieves its goal of attracting attention.

Vanderbilt Avenue, a main shopping thoroughfare, gives the walker a snapshot of transition and change. There are dive bars, some bodegas, storefront churches, and one or two soul food joints from back in the day. But the trend is clearly toward the new urban classes, with all manner of boutiques and small plate, nouvelle cuisine eateries. Contemporary ethnic restaurants like Zaytoun's offer, among other items, "pitza," a pizza made with pita dough. In addition, there's the Little Cupcake Bake Shop and a bookstore called Unnameable Books. And, tucked away, at 564 Vanderbilt, is Empire Mayo. Empire may conjure up the idea of something grand, and this hole-in-the-wall place is anything but that. But it's a grand place nonetheless, the only shop in the city, and, some claim, the world, devoted exclusively to mayonnaise.

I'm used to Hellman's Best but game for anything, so I walked in and a young woman named Crystal, a student at Kingsborough Community College, invited me to sample the product. She offered a tray of different flavors to sample—with a bunch of tiny

Mayonnaise heaven for those who love it

plastic spoons to use, one each for each bottle. The flavors sounded intriguing—smoked paprika, rosemary, red chili, lime pickle, sriracha (red chili and garlic), white truffle (a top seller), and others—and indeed they were intriguing. One of Empire Mayo's customers is Dean & DeLuca, the well-known purveyors of fine food. I asked to use the restroom and there I saw a poster advertising a 1952 Warner Brothers film called *The Iron Mistress*, described as a "fiery southwestern adventure in Technicolor," and starring Alan Ladd and Virginia Mayo, "the shameless belle of Natchez, Mississippi." What a happy coincidence for the store! I suggested to Crystal that the poster belonged in the window and could attract passersby into the shop. She agreed. Stay tuned.

This is an area with a mix of black residents and the newer gen-trifying arrivals who include other blacks, Asians, whites, and a small number of Hispanics. And I see this mix as I stride by the Underhill Playground, near Prospect Place on Underhill Avenue. There's a significant change from 2010 to now, 2015. On my first trip, the playground was a model of integration, with a roughly equal number of white and black parents/grandparents and caregivers supervising the children as they played in the sandbox, climbed various types of equipment, or just raced around. I wondered then if the integration also extended to play dates at each other's homes. Now, in 2015, the ratio of white to black in the playground is about eighty to twenty, a clear indicator of how gentrified, and not integrated, the area has become.

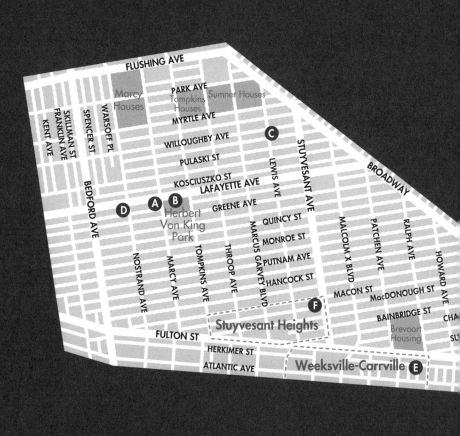

BEDFORD-STUYVESANT

A Hattie Carthan Community Center
B Herbert Von King Park
C Former site of St. John's College
D Bedford-Nostrand Wines
E Weeksville-Carrville Section
F Akwaabe Mansion

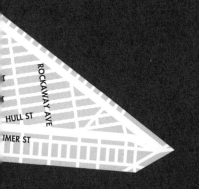

ROCKAWAY AVE

HULL ST

IMER ST

BEDFORD-STUYVESANT, ALSO KNOWN AS BED-STUY, is one of Brooklyn's most important neighborhoods, rich in culture and history, politically significant, and home at one time or another to well-known people of various backgrounds. Bed-Stuy has always meant a great deal to the black community that settled there in the mid-nineteenth century and whose members constituted a majority of its population from the early 1940s on. It's bounded by Flushing Avenue on the north, Broadway on the east, Atlantic Avenue on the south, and Classon Avenue on the west. The main commercial streets are Nostrand Avenue, Fulton Street, Franklin and Bedford Avenues, and Broadway. It has one of the largest collections of brownstones in the city, plus a large historic district.

As is the case in many of the other neighborhoods in Brooklyn, the latest challenge facing this evolving community is gentrification. The white population may by now be one-third of the total, with accurate figures hard to come by because it is rapidly shifting. Opinion in the black community is divided on how to deal with this issue. Displacement of poor residents, the importance of preserving Bed-Stuy's rich cultural heritage, home-owners' desire to make a profit on their investment, a feeling that gentrification makes the area safer for all but that it also causes the police to unnecessarily crack down on minor offenses, are all relevant and debatable issues. And as newcomers continue to pour in, their sometimes-differing views on these matters need to be taken into account. None of these issues should dissuade anyone from visiting, especially in the daytime, as the area, like New York City as a whole, is fairly safe. The crime rate is higher than other areas but the chances of something happening to an individual are very low, provided you are reasonably careful and alert. It would be a shame to tour Brooklyn and pass up this beautiful part of town, with its often stunning churches, private homes, and fine parks.

I start my day in a bodega on Nostrand Avenue, purchasing some Tic Tacs and using that as an excuse to leave both the book I'm carrying and the paid-for Tic Tacs as "hostages" until I return from my walk, thus freeing my hands. It's my usual M.O. and it has always worked, but this time it has a more interesting outcome. I'm a quarter of the way down Lafayette Avenue when I hear someone yelling: "Hey you, mister!" I turn and see a short black-haired man gesticulating at me; so I wait, wondering what he wants. As he approaches, he's waving some money in the air. Well, I think, I haven't won the lottery, so what's it all about?

"You dropped your money on the floor when you left the store. Here it is. It's thirty dollars."

"Thanks so much," I say gratefully. "Let me give you something."

"No, no," he responds. "You don't have to do that. I just don't want anyone losing this money in my place. I'm the owner." A man waiting for the bus chimes in: "He's a really nice guy." I agree and ask the proprietor: "Where are you from?"

"Dominican Republic."

"I am so impressed with what you did. That's a lot of money. It's people like you that make this such a great city." He says, "*De nada* (It was nothing)," and I can see in his eyes that he means it. Where does this integrity and modesty come from? Is it upbringing? Is it self-taught? Whenever something like this happens, I feel like doing something to encourage it, a reward. It's not the first time this has occurred to me in the city. I suddenly remember a woman, in a Dominican bodega too, in Washington Heights, who returned fifty cents to me after I gave her a buck for a bottle of water. This may not seem like a big deal, but in the poorer communities it is. Sure, this city has its share of violence, which is what grabs the headlines, but the vast majority of people in this world are nice and decent, wanting to do the right thing.

This is brought home to me in a different way at my next stop, a beautiful community garden on Marcy Avenue near Clifton Place, one of the largest I've ever seen. It's the Hattie Carthan Community Garden, and it's devoted to keeping alive the agricultural aspects of Brooklyn's history. That's why there are lots of vegetables, with neat identifying labels, being grown here—tomatoes, okra, collard greens, broccoli, eggplant, Swiss chard, cauliflower, and so on, as well as trees. Hattie Carthan was a community leader and activist who chaired the Bedford-Stuyvesant Beautification Committee, made up of over one hundred block associations.

Today, the garden is managed by the New York City Department of Parks. There are about six hundred gardens in Brooklyn alone. I speak with one of the people who sets up gardens like this, a young, earnest NYU grad who majored in politics: "I could get hungry just from looking at what you're growing. But what does this accomplish in terms of the neighborhood?" I ask.

"Well, it gets people to respect the history and culture of the community. And it keeps young people out of trouble, by focusing them on constructive activities," the gardener responds. I reflect on this and realize that in poorer neighborhoods, this is very important.

It has not, however, attracted that much interest among the professionals moving in, according to those who work here.

Today, the garden is also having a plant sale, which has attracted a lot of people. I ask a young man wearing a red and black Bank of America T-shirt and pulling a wheelbarrow full of plants for a customer why he's doing this. "I'm a volunteer."

"What's your regular job?"

"I'm a portfolio analyst for Bank of America." He's a tall, round-faced fellow with a pleasant, open demeanor, who graduated from Fairfield University in Connecticut.

"Do you get paid for this?"

"No, but we get the day off, and do it because we want to. We don't gain anything material from it and we do it a couple of times a year. I enjoy it because I'm helping others." I ask another young fellow wearing a gray knitted kipah, and his answer is similar. I note that Bank of America gets free advertising, and he readily agrees. It's a trade-off, though no one knows how many customers they actually corral. This strikes me as a fair exchange. It keeps the costs of running the city down for the taxpayers. There's no big sign advertising Bank of America. The sign belongs to Hattie Carthan, as it should. This is all part of a program involving thousands of enterprises. I also see it as encouraging interaction between different types of communities and corporations. The reward, like in the other instances, is doing the right thing, as Spike Lee famously said.

Two minutes later, I enter beautiful Herbert Von King Park, bounded by Marcy, Tompkins, Greene, and Lafayette Avenues. A well-tended and beautifully landscaped park with ball fields, handball courts, chess tables, playgrounds, amphitheater, and a dog run, the park was designed by Frederick Law Olmsted and Calvert Vaux. One young man, Don, a computer engineer, tells me that he walks a mile each way almost every day from the Bushwick border to the park because it's the nearest dog run for his white Labrador. That will no doubt change in the future, since his part of town is also gentrifying, but Don and his fiancée are departing for Los Angeles because his computer company is asking him to transfer and he wants to live in a warmer climate.[7]

I speak with another woman in her late thirties, originally from Taiwan, who moved here recently from Colorado and Wyoming. She's walking her friendly, vocal collie dog and greets me with a cheerful hello. This is quite common in these neighborhoods as people size me up and decide if I'm one of "them" based on color, dress, and age. As she walks up the block with me, she sometimes lightly touches my arm for emphasis as she talks, indicating a level of comfort with me. And when she makes an observation that she believes might be offensive to those within earshot she lowers her voice to a conspiratorial whisper. This woman, Joan, provides a revealing glimpse into how the gentrifiers see things: "To start with, everything in these areas is block by block. One can be very different from the one next to it. Like the blocks north of here, up Marcus Garvey Boulevard, towards the projects on Myrtle Avenue, can be a bit iffy and the same is true of the ones going down Lafayette and Kosciusko Street, again by the projects. Those are the 'hoodie' areas."

"Hoodie areas," can refer to the neighborhood as a whole or to the youths with pants well below their waists who wear hooded sweatshirts, even when the weather is not that cold, and are feared by others. Gentrifiers realize, now that they actually live here, that the block matters more than the overall neighborhood. Moreover, they have acquired a new spatial map that tells them how to navigate the streets to get to their "safe" spaces. They are generally unaware that working- and middle-class blacks had to take the same precautions for decades, as the newcomers now do. And they were living here in an era when thousands were murdered annually in the city.

"Are you really afraid when you walk here?"

"Naw, it's not terrible. It's just . . . you never know. But the men around here are polite. They never really ogle you or make suggestive comments. Still, I know where I'm living because it's much harder to get sushi and other quality foods I like delivered here than it is further up, closer to Clinton Hill and Prospect Heights."

In other words, the new residents, especially in the early stages of demographic change, don't feel at home here as they would in a more economically homogeneous community. But they're willing to take the chance because in the less gentrified areas, the rents are lower, and if you're on the cusp of change, you can always hope that things will improve. Indeed, as I discover, Joan is currently unemployed and looking for a new job.

Farther down Lafayette across the Eleanor Roosevelt housing project, I talk to James, an elderly black man in his late sixties who is sitting on the stoop of a frayed brownstone with paint peeling. He has a grizzled, thin, gray-colored beard, and the lines across his face give the impression of someone who has been through a lot in his life. He's wearing a Los Angeles Clippers cap and a black, cracked leather jacket that evinces signs of age. I ask him whether or not it's safe to live directly across the street from the project, and his answer is enlightening, even as he fixes me with a wary look, probably wondering if I'm an undercover cop: "Well, it's safe now, but it wasn't ten years ago. Things have changed for the better."

"Why do you think that's so?"

"Well, because young people finally got wise and realized that there's no point doing crack and winding up in a pine box. And that goes double for the small-time dealers, who thought they could get away with pocketing some of the merchandise and then found themselves dead because they didn't realize there's a lot of powerful people behind that stuff." A black man passing by across the street shouts out a greeting, asking him how it was the other night, and James tells him it was wonderful. I look at him about to ask what that was about. He smiles and says: "That dude invited me to his house and fixed me a boilermaker; that's seven types of liquor you know, and it knocked me out." He laughs with delight as he reflects on the experience. I nod in assent and tell him I'm going to try one next chance I get. Eventually, our conversation drifts to the

A Romanesque forerunner to St. John's University

late 1960s, and he tells me about his father, who was a friend of Dr. Martin Luther King Jr. and marched with him in Alabama, where James was raised. We find common ground here as I tell him about my work with the Black Panthers. He warms to the subject and issues a careful but meaningful invitation. "If you was interested and had a couple of hours, I could tell you some things 'bout those days." He has put himself on the line, knowing that I could reject his offer. I don't want to but am not sure I'll have the time, so I tell him I'll try to come back. Perhaps I will.

At 75 Lewis Avenue between Hart Street and Willoughby Avenue, there's an amazing block-long structure. Built in the Romanesque Revival style in the 1870s, it was once the home of St. John's College, Brooklyn's Catholic answer in those days to Fordham University in the Bronx, which in those days was also called St. John's College. The Brooklyn version was a separate institution. It became known as St. John's University in 1933 and moved from Bed-Stuy to Queens in 1955. The building is completely engrossing with its dazzling reddish brick bays, bows, cupola, turrets, tower, and mansard roofs.

By the end of the day's walk, I decide to buy a gift for the bodega owner who returned my thirty dollars. I find a wine shop on
Nostrand, between Lafayette and Clifton Place, called Bedford-
Nostrand Wines. I start a very interesting conversation with a young
woman, Kilolo Strober, who sells me a bottle of wine. She knows
what she's doing, having been in the wine business for thirteen years.
An attractive African American woman with an authoritative, confi-
dent air, she speaks about the evolving community in Bed-Stuy and
how its people reflect various cultural differences. Kilolo's mother,
Jacquelyn Harris, is an urban planner for New York City. Kilolo
attended the predominantly white Calhoun School in Manhattan,
a bastion of the white upper middle class, and so she knows from
whence she speaks: "I've seen a lot of New York, a lot of different
sides of this city. And so for me when I speak about whites and
blacks, I know. So I have no problem with saying that when black
people say: 'Look at all these white people moving in,' it's not necessarily that there are so many white people that are pushing the black
people out. That is happening. But what's also happening is that our
culture is different. As black people we stay by our families, or hang
out on the stoop with friends and relatives. We cook at home, we
stay at home. We're not necessarily a group of people, even though
we have our restaurants, to be walking around and saying, 'Look at
this store or that restaurant.' Our culture per se in New York is to
stay in our neighborhood. And we'll get good take-out food and
bring it home to eat. But Caucasians, white people, they will travel,
they will go far; Asian people, 'Oh, there's food somewhere that's
good, I'm gonna go.' But that's not how we black people have lived
our lives because when we go outside, we get interrogated, we get
ostracized, we get singled out as troublemakers, like, as you can see
what's happening now in Baltimore, Staten Island, and elsewhere."

Of course, Kilolo doesn't mean all this literally; black people do
travel a lot and do eat in restaurants. But she's referring to walking
and eating habits, and she's placing them in a historical context of
oppression. However, Kilolo says that blacks are more attentive to

these differences and are beginning to change as they come into greater contact with white people. She continues in this vein: "I'm part of this new generation that's incorporating all this. 'I wanna go to this restaurant. Let's not all stay on the stoop where it's safe. Let's show our faces; let's show that we're here.' And you're starting to see more of that. But it's a process that will take time."

She's right, and her comment demonstrates that integration and cultural changes cannot be measured by friendships alone. Even without true integration, change is occurring because people who have contact observe, study, and learn from each other's actions. Kilolo has focused on one small area, but this fascinating narrative highlights how contact leads to shifts in everything—values, education, religious expression, dress—in short, everything that matters to human beings.

For those really interested in "historic preservation," a visit to the well-known Weeksville-Carrville section of Bed-Stuy is highly recommended.[8] It is bounded by Fulton Street on the north, Ralph Avenue on the east, and Troy Avenue on the west. The southern border in Bed-Stuy is Park Place, but the actual southern border of Weeksville-Carrville is East New York Avenue in Crown Heights, which lies a bit farther south. Established in the mid-1800s by African American freedmen, it was a thriving community with important organizations and its own newspaper. The area served as a safe haven for blacks fleeing Manhattan during the 1863 Draft Riots. Today it's a landmarked district with historic homes and a cultural center.

I end my walk at an inn called the Akwaaba Mansion in Bed-Stuy's historic Stuyvesant Heights area, on tree-lined MacDonough Street, near Stuyvesant Avenue. It's an 1880s historic mansion with an Afrocentric emphasis. There's the "Jumping the Broom" room and also the "Ashante." The rooms are beautifully appointed, the breakfast is southern style, and the price is half that of a Manhattan hotel. The back of the Mansion is a lovely garden for parties. Manhattan is but nineteen minutes away by subway.

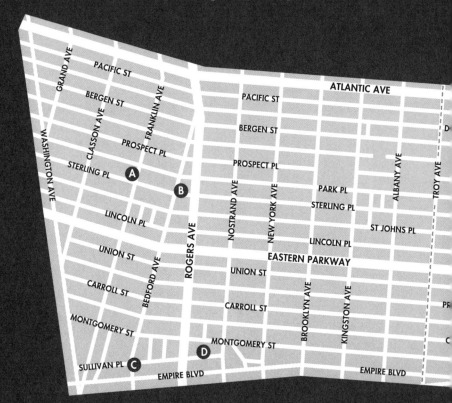

Ⓐ Chavela's
Ⓑ Former Studebaker Dealership
Ⓒ Mural
Ⓓ Dodger Playground

CROWN HEIGHTS

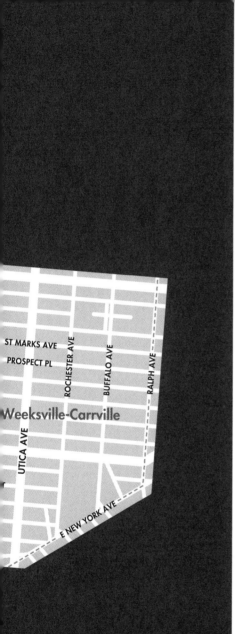

THIS IS A FASCINATING NEIGHBORHOOD bounded by Atlantic Avenue on the north, Ralph Avenue on the east, Empire Boulevard on the south, and Washington Avenue on the west. You can begin by taking a long leisurely stroll down famed Eastern Parkway, a verdant six-lane boulevard with two wide walkways with benches all along its route. It's lined with gracious apartment buildings interspersed with churches and synagogues. The world headquarters of the Lubavitcher Hasidim is located at 770 Eastern Parkway. The parkway's closest equivalent is the Grand Concourse in the Bronx. Designed by Frederick Law Olmsted, of Central Park renown, Eastern Parkway begins (or ends) at Grand Army Plaza, in the vicinity of other iconic Brooklyn sites: Prospect Park, the Brooklyn Museum, Brooklyn Public Library, and the Botanic Garden. It also includes part of Weeksville, the old African American community.

The neighborhood's two major population groups are the Hasidim and a large, generally middle class black community, most of whose members hail from the West Indies and who were already living in Crown Heights in the

1920s. The Jewish community, then primarily middle class, arrived in the 1940s, becoming more populated by Hasidim as time passed. The two groups coexist more or less peacefully, and because peace is a matter of self-interest, occasional flare-ups between the groups are quickly addressed by their respective leaders. Every year on Labor Day weekend, there's the West Indian American Day Carnival and parade with spectacular floats and displays that proceeds up Eastern Parkway, with several million participants and onlookers.[9] The main commercial streets are Nostrand, Franklin, Utica, and Kingston Avenues and there are many blocks of beautiful brownstones and other styles of homes to admire.

Crown Heights is changing demographically. Much of the western section north of Eastern Parkway has gentrified, with the usual assortment of boutiques and cafés along Classon and Franklin Avenues. I talk with an attractive young woman with long blond hair who's wheeling a baby carriage along Classon; Jan gives me her take on what's happening: "This part of the area, which is two blocks from Prospect Heights, is really gentrifying. In fact, it already has. I feel bad for some of the people, mostly black and middle class, who had to move, especially those here for thirty years, but what can you do? They took the buyout."

"Would you take a buyout?"

"No way. I live in a magnificent one-bedroom apartment and I'm rent stabilized. If I took it, I wouldn't get anything half as good for the same price." But Jan admits that if the offer was really high she'd consider it. After all, the area is very attractive in many ways: "You see it's not just the apartment, but it's become really safe. People are riding the subways at 2:00 a.m. And the more people the safer. I grew up in Chicago and it's nothing like here. Chicago is still a very dangerous, gang-controlled city. Even Santa Fe, New Mexico, where I also lived, had many places I'd never go through at night, and here it's no problem. There's restaurants and parks and it's really close to

Williamsburg and Manhattan. Did you hear? They're opening up an Apple Store in Williamsburg."

So we learn that other, more happening places in Brooklyn become part of the Big Apple draw too, not just Manhattan, and if they have an Apple Store, then I need not say more. Interestingly too, and she's not wrong, the number of people walking around increases safety, as the urban historian, Jane Jacobs, and many others, have observed.

The neighborhood still has buildings in areas not yet gentrified that are no frills with apartments available at relatively low prices, say $1,600 a month for a two-bedroom place with a balcony and a view. These would be perfect for students and artists. Contrary to expectations, management isn't necessarily drooling at the prospect of gentrifiers coming in, because for them there's a downside—high-maintenance tenants. As one owner put it: "Say, I sell you a watch for $5. You don't like it, you throw it away. If you buy it for $500, then you have expectations. It has to work perfectly. These yuppies want a lot for their money, as do the Hasidim in the neighborhood. And they're often a pain in the ass, not worth having in your building." Sure he can make money if he turns the building around with buyouts and the like, but in some cases at least, it's not worth it because the people are too demanding.

Crown Heights strikes me as a real foodie neighborhood. I stop in at Chavela's on Franklin Avenue, near Sterling Place and see that it's a place with creative decor and soft lighting that feels homey. The bar area is decorated with hundreds of beautiful tiles of many colors, and there are curios tastefully arranged throughout the place. It has a fun feel.

At 1469 Bedford Avenue, near Sterling Place, I see a pretty, white neo-Gothic building whose entire surface is covered in glazed terra-cotta. Built in 1920, it was a Studebaker car dealership. Today, it's affordable housing. The website "Brownstoner" calls it "one of Brooklyn's coolest buildings."

Mural at Nostrand and Sullivan—the black community and the police come together

On the corner of Sullivan Place and Bedford Avenue there's a mural made up of people rarely seen together—Police Chief Patrick Brennan and two other cops, whose visages look out over the street along with Nelson Mandela and former representatives Shirley Chisholm and Major Owens, both militant defenders of the black community. In this era of tense relations between the police and blacks, it's important to remember that these groups must and often do work together. They share the same turf.

Farther up Sullivan, between Nostrand and Rogers Avenues, I take a look at Dodger Playground, a tiny but beautiful space, courtesy of the New York City Parks Department. It's nestled between two small older brick apartment buildings. The children's playground is modern with beautiful equipment. There are metal stick figures of Brooklyn Dodger players as well as some statues of the stars of the glorious 1950s. Two black teenagers are playing a one-on-one game. I challenge them and they laugh saying: "You got the game after this!" I say: "Can't wait." They know I'm kidding.

I pass by a Jewish nursery in a brownstone, one of many in the area. Its next-door neighbor is a small Haitian church, also in a brownstone. According to those on the block, they get along just fine. Most of the Jews living here are followers of the Lubavitch sect, also known as Chabad, whose late leader was Rabbi Menachem Mendel Schneerson, a world-renowned, revered leader. I ask a Hasidic mother walking with her two small, blond-haired sons about getting along with other groups here. She answers freely without the wariness of those who belong to the Satmar sect in South Williamsburg. The Lubavitcher are more contemporary. Her dress is more modern, too. This woman, who has lived in the neighborhood for twenty years, is clad in a royal blue sweater, a skirt in a red and yellow floral pattern, and she is wearing makeup. "I have a neighbor who's black, single, and a bartender," Devorah tells me. "Any time I need something he'll help me. Today's generation is different on both sides. They're more open. Around the corner there's a music studio where blacks and religious Jews get together on Saturday night and jam. There's even a man named Richard Green who has worked hard for many years as a community organizer to bring the groups together, organized basketball games with teenagers and ran other activities."

"What's it like with the gentrifiers who are moving in?" I ask.

"A lot of them are coming in now. I have the feeling that some of them don't like us. They're very secular and they may not be happy that we're openly religious. We had yuppie neighbors and they clearly didn't want anything to do with us. They wouldn't say hello or anything. We finally broke the ice when they adopted a child, and I guess they were trying to teach their child to be friendly to others and so they said hello. I feel that when they're not friendly they lose something, a certain understanding about people who are different but willing to meet others. Sometimes I can't help wondering if it isn't anti-Semitic."

"But some of the gentrifiers might be Jewish themselves."

"Yes that's true, but then maybe in those cases it's a dislike of religion."

There's a lot of truth to these observations. The relationship she has with her West Indian neighbor is typical, one marked by cordiality and mutual respect. These groups don't have much in common with each other culturally, but they do believe in acting as neighbors should. It helps, too, that most are middle class and homeowners. The gentrifiers, while middle class, are secular and tend to see religious expression as old-school. Those who are Jewish may feel that their more observant brethren look down upon them, notwithstanding the almost relentless efforts by the Lubavitchers to be friendly. Organizations for Jewish gentrifiers are springing up in neighborhoods in which they live, and Crown Heights is no exception. For example, Repair the World is a national Jewish service nonprofit emphasizing justice and education. The organization's targets are Jewish millennials. The director of the project, Allie Lesovoy, has held over 350 meetings with people in the area. Chabad seems to be supportive of these efforts at outreach.

Devorah's reference to Richard Green, a black man, is spot on, as he brought the communities closer together in the wake of the Crown Heights riots twenty-five years ago, sparked by the accidental death of Gavin Cato, a young boy who was struck by an automobile driven by a Hasidic Jew. A police officer with whom I spoke said that he told people: "You got to get along with the Hasids because, you know, they can give you work when you need it."

Another Hasid, a young bearded man wearing a gray Ivy League cap, blames the media in part for tensions that do exist. "If there's any disagreement between Hasidim the papers will blow it up," he observed. "When the Gavin Cato tragedy occurred, there was rioting, but the whole city was a lot more violent then. It's also true that we live in close contact and they tend to see Jews as richer than they are. This might be true but we the Jews are not rich as a group. We also have a different lifestyle, different beliefs, a different history."[10]

"What if a black neighbor invited you over for a cup of coffee and made sure everything was kosher—paper plates, plastic knives, and the like. Would you go?"

"Definitely, though they might not think I would. I grew up in Miami Beach where things were a lot more open. It's a hot climate and you'd see women walking by in bikinis. The truth is you can't keep the outside world out anywhere, especially with the Internet."

What this discussion reveals, is that even when people want to reach out, there are obstacles. The communities have a mutual hesitancy to take a chance and risk rejection or misunderstanding. There's a history of animosity, there's little chance that they will have friends or relatives in common, and their religions are different. What they do share is socioeconomic class. In that sense secular whites and blacks are apt to have more in common, as would those who are Christians.

The ambivalence about engaging is further expressed to me by a young black man wearing a Knicks cap, sitting on the steps outside his brownstone home. He runs a music school specializing in drum instruction called the Salisbury School of Music. "Do you give lessons to the Hasidic kids on the block?" I ask.

"No, but I would like to. I don't have hardly any contact with them though they once asked me to help them carry something into their house. Frankly I'd rather wait till they come to me."

"That's not likely to happen," I counter. "If you want business you have to be the one to approach them. If you're friendly, they're likely to respond."

He seems surprised at the suggestion and says: "You know, I'm going to try that next time." He also invites me to join him in front of St. Phillips Church in Bed-Stuy on June 4, Brooklyn Day, for a parade, an invitation which I happily accept.

The Hasidim have their own parade-like events. Three times a year, on the Jewish holidays of Passover, Shavuot, and Simchat Torah, they have an outreach program. They walk, several thousand strong, in the late afternoon, along the streets of Crown Heights, their center, to the far reaches of the city, even the Bronx and Queens. They visit synagogues on these holidays and try to engage the local congregants in wild song and dance in order to raise the levels of spirituality in their temples. The event is called *tahaluchah*, meaning, literally, a walk.

Bystanders stare at them as they pass by, wondering what the young celebrants are doing but not asking, because they feel a bit intimidated and because the Lubavitcher, with their distinctive dress, do not seem very approachable. As they stride along, they frequently burst into the songs and melodies that characterize the Chabad movement. It is an impressive display of ethnic solidarity, with participants from all over the United States, Europe, Latin America, and Israel. What makes it even more remarkable is that their leader, the last Lubavitcher rebbe, has been dead for many years. As they say, "But his spirit lives on!"

Why do rituals and customs matter so much? Because they ground the community and give it the unity that occurs when many people are doing the same thing. Because the traditions are not generally known to outsiders, those who adhere to them feel somewhat unique. These perceptions are enriched when, as is often the case, the traditions go back hundreds, if not thousands, of years. Members feel they are the latest link in a long chain of events that they are duty-bound not to break.

At the corner of Union and New York Avenue I enter a Yemeni-owned deli and ask one of three teenagers minding the store how they get along with the Hasidic customers. To break the ice, I tell them I loved visiting Jordan and Egypt. Their answer is surprisingly upbeat: "We get along great here. Some of them are Arabs, Arab

Jews, and we can talk with them, even in Arabic, which is cool. This is New York City, so everybody gets along. The problem isn't the people. It's the politicians, and they mess everything up." It is a refrain I have heard many times before by members of ethnic, national, or religious groups who assert that there's no desire for such conflicts in America.

- (A) Hornsmithing craftsman
- (B) Dorsey Gallery
- (C) Statue of Liberty replica
- (D) Chester Tudor homes

PROSPECT LEFFERTS GARDENS

THIS IS A GORGEOUS NEIGHBORHOOD, and it has been so since 1905 when construction began on five hundred homes, most of them featuring white limestone. The area's boundaries are Empire Boulevard to the north, New York Avenue to the east, Clarkson Avenue to the south, and Flatbush Avenue to the west. It has remained virtually unchanged, especially the Lefferts Manor section, a designated historic district. To see these streets is to get lost in the past, in an era when change moved at a glacial pace and when beautiful, well-maintained homes, surrounded by lush greenery, gave city dwellers the illusion that they lived in the countryside. The area was also one of the first truly integrated communities, with whites, Asians, and African Americans living together amicably and serving in the various associations that successfully preserved their quality of life.

But change is coming to this part of Brooklyn, as newcomers, attracted by prices lower than those in Williamsburg or Park Slope, explore the streets and are captivated by the charm. In their wake come those who cannot afford the homes but are willing to purchase apartments. This has led to new construction of glass and steel towers, like the twenty-three-story, 230 unit building going up on Flatbush Avenue. Neighbors fought it, but they lost. A similar building is going up on Clarkson Avenue and Nostrand. The new juice bars and cafés along Flatbush compete for space with Chinese take-out shops, old style pizza joints, branches of SUBWAY and Dunkin' Donuts, mainstays of the not-so-distant past. Nostrand Avenue, too, is beginning to show signs of accommodating the demographic changes taking place.

As I walk up the steps from the Sterling Street subway stop, I think about what awaits me. This is because I never know what I'll find in a neighborhood that's new, but I do know from experience that these walks rarely disappoint.

I had always wondered how the Yemenis took over much of the grocery store business in New York City. Like Laundromats, dry cleaners, take-out shops, and shoe repair places, the businesses had the ingredients that all new, poor immigrants look for—low capital investment, a chance to employ the entire family, no requirement of fluent English, and independence from prying eyes wanting to know one's immigrant status. The work almost always involved long hours and the locations were frequently in dangerous parts of the city.

This was my lucky day. As I gave Mustafa, the Yemeni owner of a nearby grocery store, my subway-reading book and the Tic Tacs I'd purchased to hold until I returned from my walk, I noticed that he was fluent in English, especially for a middle-aged immigrant, and so I popped the question to him. And the answer was both knowledgeable and interesting: "I'm here since 1969 and I can tell you that it was a few Jewish lawyers who lent some Yemenis the money to start the businesses. True, they charged interest, 20 percent, but who else would lend us the money? We were strangers here. They held onto our passports or green cards until we paid back the loan. And once we did, we had our own businesses and so it grew. When cousins or good friends from Yemen came here we took them in and it kept going like that. Of course, we didn't charge our friends and relatives interest. We couldn't even if we wanted to." It's almost impossible to trace a pattern stretching back forty-five years to its precise origin, but he does seem to know about his community.

Mustafa is an educated man. He attended CUNY's Medgar Evers College for two years, majoring in history. Why? Because he liked it: "I lived in this area, right where the college is, and I loved learning about St. Thomas Aquinas, Churchill, Roosevelt, all the great leaders in this world and what they achieved, and also about the Chinese and the American Indians. I surely didn't need it to run this business."

Mustafa succeeds in this business because he works hard and is smart. He owns other stores too. But he also has something else—the gift of gab, the ability to make his customers smile, laugh, and feel wanted. A man who came in was short fifty cents for a five-dollar purchase. Mustafa told him to forget about it, not to worry. It's ironic, given the tensions in the Middle East, that the Yemenis may have gotten their start in this country from Jews. Mustafa does not resent them for charging interest any more than he would a bank willing to give him credit. In fact, he laughs about the idea that Jews would help Arabs make it in the United States. It's well known that once an ethnic group establishes a beachhead in a trade or profession, an opening is created for many more to follow in its path. What is far less known is how it all begins—a chance meeting, an individual decision, and others, even outsiders, willing to help make it happen.

Mustafa also defies another stereotype, and in the process demonstrates that you can never know what people have accomplished. While he may be one of a very select group of Yemeni grocery store owners who attended college, he's also a throwback to an earlier era when a liberal arts degree was something that people didn't pursue primarily for career reasons, but because they had a thirst for knowledge for its own sake, as when Mustafa says: "I loved learning about St. Thomas Aquinas . . ." Think of how much he had to struggle to study in college after working long hours in a store. It's a truly inspiring story.

Traveling down Nostrand, I meet a receptionist from Haiti who tells me what she thinks of the area: "I went away to SUNY upstate for four years and when I came back I saw that even in that short period of time things had changed. I lived then on Ocean Avenue and Lincoln Road and now it had become, oh, so like Manhattan, you know, with stores outside, really nice."

"And how did that make you feel?" I asked.

"Very good. I didn't mind at all."

"But of course the prices of apartments and store items went up a lot," I countered, wanting to see how she felt about what locals often cite as a downside.

"True, but that didn't matter much because now the area is a lot nicer looking. It was always pretty safe, but now it looks really pretty and I like that."

So we see that people have nuanced views about changes in a community, which don't all fall into one category. I did get the sense that this woman, from her dress and general demeanor, saw herself as upwardly mobile. For her, these developments may also have made her feel that her own status had improved as a result of living in a place that seems to be on the way up.

Turning right I go up Fenimore to Rogers Avenue. On the corner of Rogers I see a man filing something outside a store that at first seems to be devoted to repairing washing machines and other appliances called ADA Washer Repairs. And then I notice a sign that reads: "Hornsmithing," something I didn't know existed. Meet Winston Stiells, a hornsmith par excellence. He's an elderly man, wearing a Knicks hat with a complicated design, a light jacket, denim shirt, and jeans. He has a mid-length whitish beard that comes together near the bottom in pony-tail style. But it is his light brown eyes, so full of life and warmth, that capture my attention.

"So you're a hornsmith!" I exclaim by way of beginning a conversation. "What's that? I didn't know there was such a thing." He smiles and responds: "When people say to me, 'What does a hornsmith look like?' I say he looks like me because I believe I'm the only hornsmith in New York, if not the entire country. I like to say that." I cannot find hornsmith on the Internet, and while some items made from horns *are* available for purchase, it's a very unusual profession.

"But what do you do that makes you one?" I persist.

"Well, I make things from the horns of animals, in particular, bulls and cows. Where I come from in the Caribbean we have cows

Have you ever met a hornsmith?

that also have horns. Mostly I create birds, but I also make boats. I started doing this as a teenager back in Carriacou and people encouraged me to make things for them." Winston points to the window of his store. "Look here, I just sold one of my best creations, a small one, to a woman. Its head is turned backward as it looks somewhere."

"Where are you from?"

"Carriacou. It's an island in the Grenadines. A beautiful place. It has about 10,000 residents and I'd say I know 5,000 of them." Indeed, that's its reputation. It's also where Leonard James Paterson, father of Harlem political leader Basil Paterson came from. Basil's son, David Paterson, is a former governor of New York State. Back to the hornsmith: "How much work does it take to create a bird from a horn?"

"The last one I made took 85 hours. It's a labor of love. I don't make real big money from this. That's why I also repair washing machines. Frankly it's a form of therapy for me. When I'm carving these horns I feel so peaceful, so relaxed." The inside of Winston's shop has a sort of friendly, intimate, cluttered feeling. Yet, I see from his movements as he shows me different items that he knows where everything is. There are beads, tiny carved skulls that would fit on a key ring, paintings, and such scattered throughout the cramped space.

"Why do you only use bull and cow horns?"

"Because of the quality. They're smooth and don't crack easily."

"How do you get them?'

"Various places. For example, people mount them and then get tired of them. Someone also gave me a bunch from Haiti. I can also find them sometimes on the Internet. And then I get them from butchers locally who don't need them."

Winston is a community character. Everyone walking by, gentrifiers, elderly black matrons, young toughs from the neighborhood, knows and likes him. He can tell me who's sick on a particular block, who threw a party for their aunt, who works where. Perhaps ten people greeted him as we stood outside talking, including two small girls who told him how cute the bird in his hand looked.

Winston is also an artist who loves his work. As this area gentrifies I'd bet that he'll have many more customers because people like something that's unique. The quality of the work is not for me to judge, but it certainly looks attractive and reminds me that the days when many people did this in villages and towns are long gone. In a technological age, this man stands out.

Dorsey Gallery is also here, at 553 Rogers. The artist Otto Neals usually hangs out on Wednesdays. Neals is a well-known, largely self-taught African American artist, whose bronze figure of a boy sitting with his dog and reading a book is in Prospect Park's Imagination Park, adjacent to the park's Lincoln Road entrance. Another well-known wood carving of his graces the front of the Brooklyn Post Office.

Residents with whom I speak view Lefferts Gardens as a hidden treasure, a safe area where people look out for each other. They speak with pride about their community, hoping it won't be discovered.

At 145 Maple Street, in front of the entrance, an impressive replica of the Statue of Liberty stands over six feet high. Despite the fact that it weighs perhaps 200 pounds, the bottom has a shiny golden chain wrapped around it, secured to the house with a lock, clearly to prevent anyone from stealing it. There's something ironic about a statue that symbolizes freedom wrapped in imprisoning chains. To find these hidden gems, I try to walk every block in an area; I never know when I'll stumble across one.

A bit of trivia: Where in Brooklyn is the one-block-long Beekman Place, whose ultrachic namesake may be found in the Turtle Bay portion of Manhattan's East Side, running between 51st and 49th Streets? The answer: Just west of Maple Street off Flatbush Avenue.

I walk two blocks farther south on Flatbush and come to a street parallel to Beekman Place, Chester Court, and this one is really special. Now known as the Chester Court Historic District, the short street dead-ends into the outdoor tracks of the Q and B subway line. The eighteen Tudor Revival–style homes were built in 1911–12 and are among the earliest row houses in this style in Brooklyn and, quite possibly, New York City. They have orange clay-tile roofs, oriels, half-timber and stucco fronts, and are modeled, roughly, on homes in Chester, England, built from the sixteenth through twentieth centuries. Chester Court is also known informally as "Pomander Walk" after a romantic comedy show that opened in New York in 1910 and whose setting was a fictional small street in eighteenth-century London. The same name, Pomander, is used for a private street of Tudor homes situated between Broadway and West End Avenues in Manhattan, running from 94th to 95th Streets. Many New Yorkers have peered through the locked, barred wrought-iron doors straining to see the homes. The ones on Chester Court are accessible 24/7. Which ones are prettier? Who can say, but Chester Court is worth the trip.

BUSHWICK

CYPRESS HILLS

BROWNSVILLE

EAST NEW YORK

CANARSIE

EAST FLATBUSH

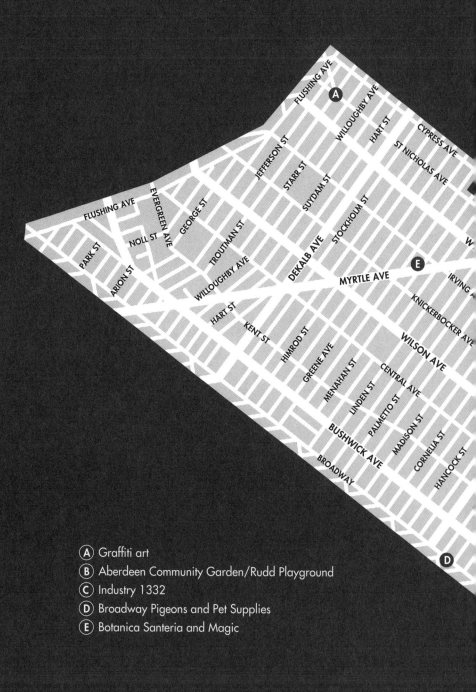

(A) Graffiti art
(B) Aberdeen Community Garden/Rudd Playground
(C) Industry 1332
(D) Broadway Pigeons and Pet Supplies
(E) Botanica Santeria and Magic

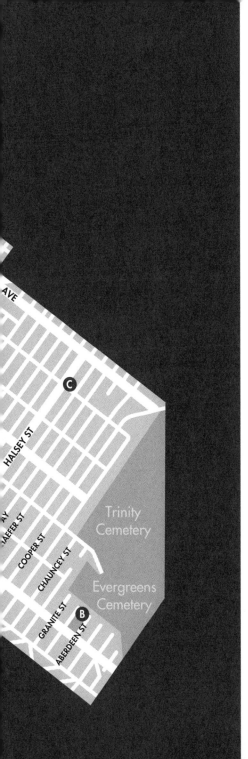

BUSHWICK

BUSHWICK IS A REALLY UNUSUAL PLACE with a rich history. In the nineteenth century it was the location of most of the city's breweries. Ethnically it was largely German, and many residents moved to the area from the overcrowded "Kleindeutschland" part of Manhattan's Lower East Side. Russians, Poles, Jews, and Irish also settled in Bushwick, and then later, in the 1930s and 1940s, large numbers of Italians arrived. They were followed in the 1950s and 1960s by African Americans and Puerto Ricans. Eventually Bushwick became a poor neighborhood, one synonymous with crime. In the 1970s and '80s, Dominicans, Ecuadorians, and Jamaicans, among others, moved in, most of them poor and newly arrived from their native lands. Recent years have witnessed another major development—the beginnings of gentrification as those unable to afford Williamsburg, Greenpoint, and other areas search for cheaper digs conveniently located near Manhattan.

Bushwick's boundaries are Flushing Avenue on the north, the Queens County line on the east (Cypress, St. Nicholas, and Wyckoff Avenues), Conway Street and the Evergreens

Cemetery on the south, and Broadway on the west. Most of Bushwick is Latino, with the largest groups made up of Puerto Ricans and Dominicans. Only a small portion of Bushwick has gentrified. There are still many artists, musicians, and hipsters there, but as prices climb and the cheap food joints and bodegas close, these groups will find another undeveloped place in which to live and work. Some of the major commercial thoroughfares are Broadway, Myrtle, Irving, Knickerbocker, and Flushing Avenues. While Bushwick has a relatively high crime rate, it has dropped, along with the general levels throughout the city.

Wanting to explore the ground zero of New York City's most fascinating graffiti art, I began walking on Troutman Street, from Cypress to Irving Avenues, then made side tours toward Flushing Avenue off St. Nicholas and Wyckoff Avenues. I was not disappointed; I saw some amazing murals, right in the shadow of a gorgeous view to the north of the Manhattan skyline. When I was there in August 2015, the murals included upside-down, gravity-defying large drips of paint—blue, red, green, pink; a huge multi-eyed monster; dozens of human skulls; an orange and yellow face of a woman with green eyes; frightful faces seemingly from horror movies; stupendous floral designs; Sluggo from the comic strips; magnificent stallions; and many others. These painted spaces are controlled by the Bushwick Collective, which decides what goes up and for how long. The Collective is an organization headed and run by businesspeople and artists who believe that street art can transform lives. They see it as a way of revitalizing the Bushwick area, and they have been able to attract artists from all over the world to tell their stories through their works. In time, other works of art will replace those described here.

Part of Bushwick is an area of gentrification; geographically, the area transformed ranges roughly from Flushing Avenue on the north to Suydam Avenue on the south, Irving Avenue on the west to Cypress Avenue on the east. These borders aren't precise and are constantly changing/expanding as more people move in and buildings are renovated. In general, the newcomers are moving from the Queens border on the west, namely, the Maspeth and Ridgewood sections, and the East Williamsburg neighborhood north of Flushing Avenue. Within this pocket are numerous new buildings, upgraded homes and row houses, and factories recast as lofts, cafés, nightclubs, supermarkets, and boutiques.[1]

I start at the southern border of Conway Street and head north along Bushwick Avenue. There's evidence from both the rehabbed older buildings and some new ones that change is taking place here. What was once a black and Hispanic area, largely comprised of working-class people, is beginning to change. More affluent and younger whites, blacks, Asians, and Hispanics are beginning to move in, two miles away from the main area near Flushing Avenue. The process, as always, is uneven, with some blocks already containing a mix of improved and not-improved housing, while other blocks remain virtually unchanged.

I walk up Aberdeen Street, which dead-ends after one block at the Evergreens Cemetery. The homes are modest one- and two-family clapboard or brick structures. At the end on the left is the Aberdeen Street Community Garden. Next to it is the beautifully refurbished Rudd Playground, with protective rubber surfaces around the playing area. There are innovative swings and other equipment, painted in bright colors, a basketball court, a spray shower, and a turtle sculpture. What's most appealing is that it's tucked away on a side street and has shade trees.

I speak with Letitia, an older black woman who's lived on the street for more than fifty years: "How's the block?" I ask.

"Pretty good, but a woman who lives across the street from the community garden took the keys and locked it up."

"But it's not her garden. How could she do that?"

"That's what we're trying to figure out. Anyway, they reopened it now and we'll see what happens. Our main problem here is with the raccoons." These are the kinds of things I can only learn when I

What's it like to always be in the shade?

ask. The streets are teeming with life, and disagreements and squabbles are part of it. A block is the sum total of all its residents, and things are usually done through consensus, but, as I see here, not necessarily.

Farther down is Granite Street, which also dead-ends at the cemetery. The houses here are better kept. Well-tended, leafy trees line the block. Some of the homes are built in a Romanesque style. A man tells me this block and the surrounding streets are safe. On the corner of Bushwick Avenue, one builder is rehabbing a five-story walk-up tenement. The construction foreman tells me it's being built for the gentrifiers. As of now, however, there are still many artists and musicians living here. The part of Bushwick that's on the northern Ridgewood border, referred to by locals as "Bushwood," is similar.

Heading up Halsey Street, I cross Irving Avenue and notice a beautiful mural along the side of a tapas bar, called Industry 1332. The restaurant is at least one and a half miles south of the gentrified area, and I'm wondering if it's doing any business in what appears to be a poor, predominantly Hispanic area. Speaking with the bartender, I learn more: "This place was started by two Hispanics who grew up in the neighborhood. We just opened two months ago, but we're doing fine." I'm inclined to agree since at 5:30 there are quite a few people there, including professionals wearing what looks like business attire, as well as interestingly dressed hipsters. The place is spacious, looks beautiful, with brick walls, attractive wooden menus that hang in a long row on the wall, and good food. This place would fit perfectly in Chelsea, North Williamsburg, or SoHo. The immediate area is one of those "fits and starts" gentrification examples, almost like a crossword puzzle in progress where some words have been filled in and the rest of the squares are empty, but won't be for long.

Another "fits and starts" example makes its appearance at 358 Grove Street. It's a twelve-story brick building, the only one of its kind on the block, offering one, two, and three bedroom apartments, with central air conditioning, stainless steel appliances, marble countertops, great views, and a train station just a block away. Planet Fitness is also around the corner on Wyckoff Avenue. Completed in 2007, the apartments will undoubtedly increase in value, though right now the area's still a bit gritty.

Bushwick Avenue is lined for two miles with nice brownstones, though some are suffering from neglect. One block over, parallel to Bushwick Avenue, on Broadway, is a completely different story. The street consists largely of fast food joints, storefront medical offices, tiny churches, bars, bodegas. It's noisy and dark, as the J, Z, and M trains rattle by overhead. I see a promising-looking place at 1622 Broadway. The sign on the pea green awning reads: "Broadway Pigeons & Pet Supplies." A PhD graduate from my program, Colin

Broadway Pigeons and Pet Supplies—a home for every type of pigeon

Jerolmack, wrote his doctoral dissertation on the pigeons; Bushwick was the setting for his research, and his project was published as a book, *The Global Pigeon*, so I'm intrigued. I speak with Tony Graham, who's in the store, hanging out on his day off, and who's friendly with the store's owner. A forty-six-year-old year old black man, wearing a Yankee cap, clad in a navy blue shirt and pants, Tony knows all about pigeons and loves them. He also knows about Jerolmack's work: "It all originated with the Italians who lived here a long time and they taught it to the younger Afro-Americans and Puerto Ricans, mostly. And there are still a couple of Italians doin' it. I've been doin' it since I was fourteen." Tony invites me to come to the back where the pigeons are kept.

Almost all of the business is devoted to pigeons. The owners raise and sell them and one of the employees, Lisa, a young outgoing woman with an easy laugh, points out that different breeds require different foods: "For example, some pigeons have short beaks that can't eat big corn. They eat popcorn or no corn. In the summer they don't like corn but in the winter they do because it gives them heat."

Tony shows me the pigeons: "We get 'em in all different colors—blue, black, yellow, and in all different types, from different countries. These here are called 'tipplers,' on account of their flight path."

"What's the fun in all this?"

"Seeing them fly, training them, and catching other peoples' birds. That's the name of the game."

Lisa continues: "The whole thing is catching the birds. It's called 'catch and keep.' One pigeon gets the other one to follow him home. And when you catch one, you don't give it back. But it's all in good fun."

Tony shows me another type: "You see these blue homing pigeons? They can fly 500 miles at one time. Those birds over there, on the other hand, like to go up high and then come down, but they don't go very far. The ones in this cage are Polish birds, and there are some folks in Greenpoint that fly them. These ones are called English tumblers. They do flips in the air. These are kind of orange because they breed red with yellow." As he talks, patiently teaching me about the pigeons, their habits, their owners, I realize that this is a whole other world, with its own rules, customs, and community, united by the fact that these pigeon-folks are doing something they love. Tony reminds me of Allan, a Marine Park owner of World Class Aquarium, who is in love with the fish in his store. Tony has two children of his own, so I ask him: "Are your kids into this?"

"You bet. My oldest is fourteen and when he comes home, he goes up to the roof and takes care of the pigeons. This keeps him outta trouble, away from drugs and gangs."

"How long's he been doing this?"

"Since he was nine years old, for six years. And you know what? He wants to fly himself. He wants to go into the air force and be an airplane pilot. That's his goal. And I'm grateful for it."

"Wow, that's amazing! What about your other son?"

"He's eight and soon I'm gonna be introducin' him. But right now he's still into video games."

Tony, like the others, has found his muse, so to speak. This is what infuses his life with meaning. He has something special and has successfully transmitted his passion to his oldest son, and perhaps the same passion will ignite in his eight-year-old one day. Is his son's choice of aviation as a career coincidental? Possibly, but it would seem to me that it's unlikely, given all the other career paths out there.

This heavily Hispanic neighborhood has more than a few *botanicas*, stores catering to the Hispanic community that sell herbs, potions, and charms of a spiritual and religious nature. I see such a place just off Myrtle Avenue, on Menahan Street, called Botanica Santeria and Magic, and I walk into a dimly lit shop. Spanish-language music is playing. There are bottles of liquid for everything—for casting spells, curing illness. There are various magic and numerology books that promise to reveal the secrets of the rich and famous. I also find a copy of a novel, *Let Me Whisper in Your Ear* by Mary Jane Clark, a mystery about a boy who has been missing for thirty years, who was last seen on the site where New Jersey's Palisades Amusement Park once stood. It's here because *botanica* customers come to the shop to try to find out how to solve problems through magic. This story fascinates them—who did it, how did the boy disappear, and how can one one use magic to get the perpetrator?

Safe is, as always, a relative term. I ask a woman in Bushwick how safe the area is. "Oh it's pretty safe anywhere in Bushwick." "So, can you walk here at night?" "Oh God, no. Certainly not late at night." So then, why does she feel it's "safe"? Because eighteen years ago you couldn't feel safe in Bushwick even in broad daylight.

Occasions like Mother's Day help cement the social glue that holds communities together. Walking the streets of Bushwick one Mother's Day, I saw many parties. Houses were festooned with balloons, many of them silvery heart-shaped ones, proclaiming, "Happy Mother's Day!" In an area like this where many face significant challenges in everyday life, people welcome the opportunity to be happy about something. I passed by a two-story, newish brick dwelling where a crowd of Hispanic people, probably family members, had gathered. The music was loud, the atmosphere convivial. Parked in front of the house, looking incongruous in this impoverished part of Brooklyn, was a bright red, gleaming Rolls Royce. A rich relative? A rental? A lottery winner? Who knows?

Ⓐ Vienna Flats
Ⓑ Gran Mar de Plata
Ⓒ P.S. 65
Ⓓ Andre Charles's home

CYPRESS HILLS

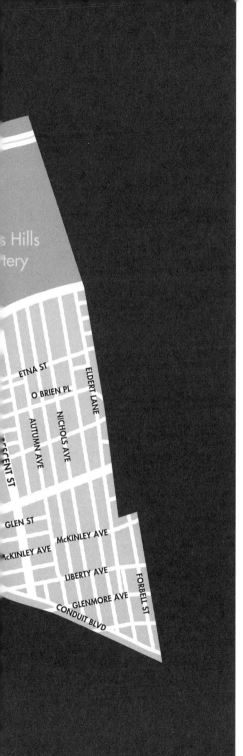

CYPRESS HILLS IS A NEIGHBORHOOD in eastern Brooklyn that borders Queens. Its boundaries are the Jackie Robinson Parkway to the north, Eldert Lane and Forbell Street to the east, Atlantic and North Conduit Avenues to the south, and to the west, the point where Fulton, Jamaica, Williams, and Broadway all meet. Today, the population is mostly Hispanic, black, and Asian, with some whites. The ethnicity of the neighborhood shifted in the 1950s and 1960s as Irish, Poles, Germans, and Italians moved out. This is a residential community, and the only really commercial streets are Fulton, Atlantic, and Liberty Avenues. Fulton Avenue is the main commercial thoroughfare of Cypress Hills; it's the place for all purchases—groceries, clothing, jewelry—and also where the restaurants and medical offices are. The J train traverses it overhead. This line provides excellent links, starting from the Wall Street area on one end and linking up with AirTrain JFK on the other.

The area contains literally thousands of two- and three-story row houses, bay and bow styles, with the yellow, orange, and beige brick hues also seen in Bushwick and in Ridgewood, Queens. Walk along Ridgewood Avenue starting at Linwood Street and ending at Crescent Street, turning left and/or right at any of the cross streets and you'll see them.

Like some other neighborhoods, Cypress Hills struggles to thrive because it borders a really gritty area, in this case, East New York, just across Atlantic Avenue.

The Highland Park area, near the Queens border, features many graceful homes along Highland Boulevard and more modest, but still nice, houses on adjacent Sunnyside Avenue. City Line, which is on the southern side of Atlantic Avenue, lies between Euclid Avenue and Forbell Street and has always been regarded as a distinct community. In recent years it has become a Bangladeshi enclave with mosques and specialty shops. The Bangladeshis have also spearheaded an annual festival in which other ethnic and racial groups participate.

At 190 Jerome Street, at the corner of Atlantic, there's an unusual, recently painted building. One portion has an oriel structure in a shiny burgundy color with bow windows. At the very top are the words, in large, raised, wooden letters: VIENNA FLATS. It has been known as such as far back as the 1940s, if not before. The rest of the building is mauve colored. The windows have attractive pediments and pilasters surrounding them, and the building has been refurbished inside and out.

On the corner of Fulton and Logan Streets, I step into Gran Mar de Plata. The place has live Latin music on the weekends and serves Hispanic and American food at reasonable prices. It's large, with flickering colored lights that make a dim interior seem romantic. The ceiling, walls, and pipes are covered with fabric in various shades. There are fake gnarled trees and branches, along with hanging lanterns. A patron gets the impression he or she is wandering through a forest. When in the area and in need of a place that's open all night, Gran Mar de Plata serves decent Spanish food and has live music and dancing on the weekends.

Cypress Hills, with its old two-story brick, shingle, or clapboard homes, and with the occasional Tudor motif, as I see on Chestnut Street, reminds me of a neighborhood of fifty years ago. The single air conditioning units visible in many of the houses also remind me that there was a time, before central air, when a house or apartment had only one room with an air conditioner and people crowded into that little cold and heavenly space, savoring the contrast between it and the rest of the house or apartment. Ah—to put your face in front of that box, to feel the blast of cool air blowing from the vents, was heaven on earth!

Here's an example of how technology has changed lifestyles over the last thirty-five years. Today, few people go anywhere without an iPhone's maps to direct them, block by block. And they don't even have to go to the place if they just want to see what it looks like. They can just look at Google's street view. I meet a man who's nostalgic about Highland Park, where he lived until age eight, when the family left for the greener, safer pastures of Whitestone, Queens: "I remember the house very well. I have great memories of it because my grandparents lived there and the backyard was big and beautiful and green, with grapes, vines, olive trees and all that 'guinzo' stuff that my grandfather brought over from the old country."

"Have you ever gone back since then?" I ask.

"Just once or twice. It would be, how should I put it, too depressing to see how the house went down. It's a pretty rough area now, mostly Hispanic, and back then it was almost 100 percent Italian."

"But wait," he says. "I can get it for you." He finds it on his cell phone. Together we look at a picture of the house, and the whole block no less, Sunnyside Court. He looks at it fondly. In the picture the roughness of the neighborhood is not a factor. In short, with technology you can go home again, without having to encounter the new reality, a changed block with none of the old bunch hanging out.

I spot an old, small public school, behind two Corinthian pillars on Richmond Street, between Ridgewood and Fulton Avenues. It's

35 Richmond Street—an artist takes his stand

P.S. 65, with the distinct shade of red brick that means it's really old—and quaint too. The plaque above the entrance says the school was built in 1889, over 120 years ago. It is the proud "home of the Golden Lions." Immediately to the right of the building, a lonely pair of kids' sneakers dangles. On the stairs, where feet climb every day to presumably new heights, are various exhortations, "Work hard to be nice," followed by "It takes hard work to achieve," then "Raise the bar," and finally, "We are climbing the mountain to college." And a mountain it is, indeed, in a place like Cypress Hills. This is a charter school, and people say the parents and students have great pride in the school. The teachers with whom I spoke briefly love teaching there.

At 35 Richmond Street near Jamaica Avenue, there's a most interesting home framed in front by a tall white picket fence. The public property square of greenery between the house and the street is decorated with flowers, two very thick giant pencils made of wood, and a tiny bungalow. A sign reads: "Beware of the graffiti artist." Gargoyles stare intently at me from the second floor, by the window. The house belongs to Andre Charles, an early graffiti artist who became a leader of the movement in the 1980s. Among his many accomplishments are memorial murals of Tupac Shakur, Mother Teresa, and Princess Diana; a long involvement with Urban Works, which brought art into the nightclub scene; and a working relationship with Donna Karan and DKNY. In front of the home, near the curb, are two multicolored plastic benches framing the patch of green grass, with an emphatic request in front of a tree: PICK UP YOUR DOG'S SHIT.

There are many well-known people living in Manhattan, but I don't always know when I walk by their apartments. Here, you see the person's private home, it's artistically vibrant, and it's marked in such a way that it's clear that someone special lives in it.

I finish my walk in Highland Park, the area adjacent to Queens. A good number of its steeply sloped hills have remarkable panoramic views of all of Brooklyn, as well as Jamaica Bay and the distant Rockaways, in Queens. Highland Park's barbecue areas attract throngs of people on the weekends from both Brooklyn and Queens. The park also features farm gardens for kids and lots of sports facilities. Some of the landscaped green areas are a great place to lie down in the grass and reflect on the glories of nature.

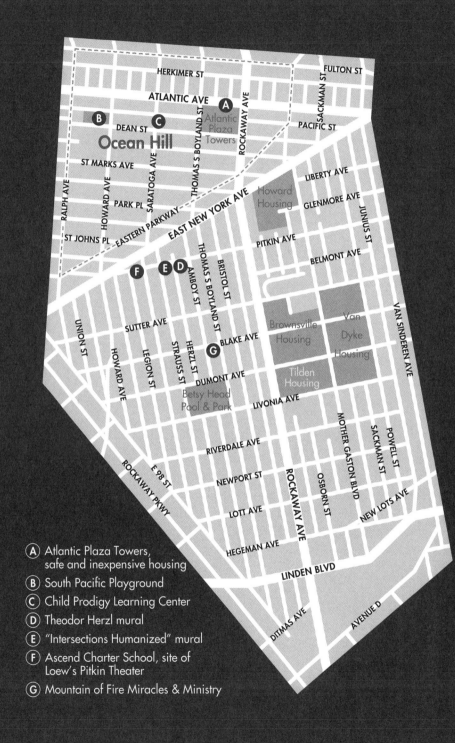

HERKIMER ST

FULTON ST

ATLANTIC AVE

Ⓐ

SACKMAN ST

PACIFIC ST

Ⓑ

DEAN ST

Ⓒ

ROCKAWAY AVE

THOMAS S BOYLAND ST

Atlantic
Plaza
Towers

Ocean Hill

ST MARKS AVE

SARATOGA AVE

LIBERTY AVE

RALPH AVE

HOWARD AVE

PARK PL

Howard
Housing

GLENMORE AVE

JUNIUS ST

ST JOHNS PL

EASTERN PARKWAY

EAST NEW YORK AVE

PITKIN AVE

BELMONT AVE

Ⓕ Ⓔ Ⓓ

BRISTOL ST

THOMAS S BOYLAND ST

AMBOY ST

VAN SINDEREN AVE

UNION ST

SUTTER AVE

LEGION ST

STRAUSS ST

HERZL ST

BLAKE AVE

Ⓖ

Brownsville
Housing

Van
Dyke
Housing

HOWARD AVE

DUMONT AVE

Betsy Head
Pool & Park

Tilden
Housing

LIVONIA AVE

RIVERDALE AVE

ROCKAWAY PKWY

E 98 ST

NEWPORT ST

LOTT AVE

ROCKAWAY AVE

OSBORN ST

MOTHER GASTON BLVD

SACKMAN ST

POWELL ST

NEW LOTS AVE

HEGEMAN AVE

LINDEN BLVD

DITMAS AVE

AVENUE D

Ⓐ Atlantic Plaza Towers,
safe and inexpensive housing

Ⓑ South Pacific Playground

Ⓒ Child Prodigy Learning Center

Ⓓ Theodor Herzl mural

Ⓔ "Intersections Humanized" mural

Ⓕ Ascend Charter School, site of
Loew's Pitkin Theater

Ⓖ Mountain of Fire Miracles & Ministry

BROWNSVILLE

BROWNSVILLE'S BOUNDARIES ARE FULTON STREET ON THE NORTH, Van Sinderen Avenue on the east, Avenue D on the south, and Ralph Avenue and Rockaway Parkway on the west. A smaller area roughly between Eastern Parkway on the south and Fulton street on the north is called Ocean Hill. Until the 1950s, Brownsville was a largely Jewish neighborhood, settled originally by people wishing to escape the slums of the Lower East Side. In the early 1950s, the New York metropolitan area experienced a surge of immigration from Puerto Rico and a wave of African Americans who migrated north to New York. In the name of urban renewal, many of these people were relocated to Brownsville's tenements and public housing projects. This caused a major shift in the community's fortunes—it became a neglected area populated mostly by poor blacks and Hispanics. In those days, the city lacked the resources that it has today to deal with these social and economic problems. It had far less money to spend on improving public housing, expanding public assistance, and in general supporting an economic and social network of programs that would have greatly aided the adjustment of the newcomers. Virtually the same happened to East New York, which was an ethnically mixed white area until the mid-twentieth century.

As is the case with adjacent East New York, Brownsville has experienced very little improvement over the years. In a *New York Times* article from 2012, titled "Where Optimism Feels Out of Reach," Ginia Bellafante writes about how the murder rate there has not fallen since 1998. And the infant mortality rate is the highest in the city, about the same as that of Malaysia.[2] Decades of neglect, lack of private investment, distance from the city center, and large numbers of low-income people have all contributed to this unfortunate state of affairs. There are, and always will be, adventurous souls willing to take a chance on an area and build there, but when it happens in Brownsville, it is likely to be a long and difficult road.

The neighborhood is largely black—African Americans as well as Caribbean and African immigrants. It has good transportation via the A, C, L, and 3 lines. Pitkin Avenue is the main shopping street. It also has the largest concentration of public housing in the city. Like East New York, it is fairly safe during the day, but not at night.

There are, in fact, some decent rental options in Brownsville for those with a low enough income. Two people can rent a one-bedroom apartment with a terrace in a modern hi-rise, with twenty-four-hour security, at 249 Thomas S. Boyland Street (formerly known as Hopkinson Avenue), if their combined annual income is less than $86,000. Rentals vary according to circumstances but can be no more than $1,000 a month (as of 2014). It's a short walk from the subway and the trip to Manhattan is under a half hour on the C/A lines. Many would argue that the presence of such housing is important for Brownsville's future. Students and others with less income will be able to move into such buildings in greater numbers, and new stores and restaurants will open to meet their needs. In fact, it's already beginning to happen. The building has a nice laundry room, but not a gym.

Will Brownsville and, for that matter, East New York, gentrify? You bet. And that day is not so far off, as I learn, speaking with a black developer on Pleasant Place off Atlantic Avenue: "We're doing a gut job on this house for $150,000 and I guess we can get $450,000 to $500,000 for it. I live in Suffolk," he says, "and I come in every day to supervise it. Gentrification? It's already here. We have many offers and so do others. Just look at this block. It's got great brownstones."[3]

He's right. There are many other blocks in the area with housing that can be rehabbed—Gunther Place, Pacific, Dean, and Bergen Streets. Brownsville has more potential than East New York in this respect and is also one neighborhood closer to Manhattan.

South Pacific Playground sounds like a small place, but it's actually the name of a fairly sizeable, beautiful park on Howard Avenue, between Pacific and Dean Streets, that looks spectacular when the red, orange, and yellow leaves of autumn are on display.

A block away, I pass by, at 311 Saratoga Avenue, a storefront operation called the "Child Prodigy Learning Center." Hope is definitely in shorter supply in Brownsville than on the Upper East Side, but it's there. Even the sign can make believers out of parents convinced that their kids have what it takes. Places like this tell us that people in these communities are willing to spend money so their kids can make it. Although not as prevalent, they are in principle no different from identical small operations that dot the streets of the city's Asian neighborhoods.

It's dusk as I continue my walk down Saratoga and approach St. John's Place. A young white man steps out from a car and walks toward me. He is tall, with blue eyes and yellow dyed hair, wearing jeans and a sweater. "Hey," he says, "Do you know where 461 Saratoga is?"

"Up the block," I respond and continue on my way to nowhere in particular, just exploring. As I pass the car from which he emerged, I notice a middle-aged man with large, brown-framed owlish glasses, and I wave hello to him. He smiles, gets out of his older-model BMW, shakes my hand, almost like: "You're my type, so we're friends," and asks: "What's this neighborhood like? That was my son who spoke to you."

Noticing the Maryland plates, I say: "What are you guys doing here?"

"We're looking for an apartment for my son. It was advertised for $900 on Craig's List."

"You're in a not too safe part of Brownsville. Is this what you had in mind?"

It turns out he has no idea where he is. He asks whether Brooklyn Heights or Flatbush would be safer, and he thanks me when I tell him that those sections are not at all dangerous. He is not alone.

I often meet individuals who wander into areas they know nothing about, mostly tourists or people just passing through for any number of reasons. Sometimes they get into trouble. That's just the way it is in any large city. Generally, nothing happens to them, but its best to have an idea of where you are, especially at night.

Notwithstanding the stereotypes about the Mafia, Brownsville was famous as the home of Murder Incorporated, a half Jewish, half Italian "shooting gang," as one organized-crime specialist called it. It was headquartered in Brownsville inside a twenty-four-hour-a-day candy store on the corner of Livonia and Saratoga Avenues, run by a nice old Jewish lady, Rosie Gold. The group's vicious Jewish criminals included Abe "Kid Twist" Reles, Lepke Buchalter, "Tic Toc" Tannenbaum, and Dutch Schultz. The candy store today is a bodega.

One block past St. John's Place, on Pitkin Avenue, I discover two amazing murals. The first, dedicated in September 2014, just off Pitkin on Herzl Street, actually relates to the street that is named after the founder of Zionism, Theodor Herzl. At the top, it proclaims: "Welcome to Brownsville!!!," and on the bottom is Herzl's famous exhortation: "It's not a dream if you will it." These words are particularly relevant to the residents of Brownsville and, in particular, Brownsville's youth. The mural includes a large painting of Herzl, with his long black beard, a look reminiscent of the drawing adorning the Smith Brothers Cough Drops box, a brand started in 1852 and still around today. The mural is a melding of the Jewish life of the neighborhood's past and the African American population of today. In fact, it was black teenage residents of Brownsville who thought of the idea for the mural, not some Jewish organization. Studying the community's history, the teenagers learned that Brownsville was almost 100 percent Jewish in the 1920s. The mural was sponsored by many organizations, including the Pitkin Avenue BID, the New York City Department of Probation, and the National Endowment for the Arts.

Pitkin Avenue and Herzl Street—cross-cultural collaboration

"We dug through the history of Brownsville, aiming to figure out a path for our community in the future," said Sean Turner, one of five Brownsville teenagers who participated in the project. "What is the best way to achieve that other than getting to know our neighborhood first?"

This mural has historical implications too. Between 1950 and 1964, Jewish liberals and African Americans worked together to advance the cause of black people. When the black movement of the 1960s despaired of real progress being made, blacks, led by the militant Black Panthers and others, threw the Jews and other whites out, telling them to, in effect, leave their organizations. Thus began a downward spiral, which culminated in the vicious public school struggle and teachers' strike in Ocean Hill–Brownsville.[4]

Blacks and Jews have had other conflicts too since the 1960s—fights over blacks moving into Jewish and Italian Canarsie; the Yankel Rosenbaum/Lemrick Nelson conflict, when blacks rioted in Crown Heights; and other disagreements. The mural, in my view, doesn't mean that there's a powerful relationship today between the two groups. Rather, it's simply an opportunity to motivate teenagers by using whatever group is available to serve as inspiration.

The second mural, one block away, on Strauss Street, and also just off Pitkin, is equally inspiring. The main part features a tree, with skyscrapers that seem to emerge from it. In the center, green and blue boxes interlock to form a mélange of faces. The mural also features six neighborhood street intersections. The tree's roots are clearly visible, each with words painted on it—spirit, respect, bravery, fortitude, compassion. The 2013 mural is titled "Intersections Humanized." Both of these murals are part of a group of five throughout Brownsville. Together they demonstrate the transformative power of art, literature, and history, to encourage disadvantaged youths to struggle, achieve, and succeed in life.

For nostalgia seekers, the site of the old Loew's Pitkin Theater is but a half block away. In its heyday, the 1930s and 1940s, it was a magnificent theater, serving as a setting for the stage and for films. Among those who performed there were Humphrey Bogart, Al Jolson, and Jackie Gleason. A *New York Times* article described the Pitkin as follows: "The elaborate interior defied classification. It had a Moorish foyer decorated with majolica. The auditorium itself looked like a vast garden under blue sky, enclosed by high sculptured walls, surmounted by carved towers and balconies."[5] In 2010, the theater, which closed decades ago, became a school and retail center. However, the exterior art deco features were restored. This is one of the great benefits of a city that has a sense of history and people who fight to preserve it. You can go home again, physically.

After entering an African/Caribbean church in Brownsville on a Sunday morning, I realize that religion fills the spiritual and emotional needs of many immigrants. The church is called Mountain of Fire and Miracles Ministry and is located at 180 Blake Avenue near Amboy Street. The women wear traditional dress—brightly colored turbans and long, flowing skirts. Hundreds of worshipers are singing ecstatically, swaying in unison, hands pointing upward in celebration. The music and chanting is beautiful, and I am moved by the emotional involvement of the participants. Here again is testimony to the great power of religion in this city—power to bring together its residents, old and new, rich and poor, and many in between. It's what goes on in hundreds of churches throughout the city every Sunday. When a white person walks into a black church, he or she is noticed and, in my case, warmly welcomed. Members of the congregation want you to share in their happiness and feel their joy; they believe so much in what they do that they encourage you to join them, thereby validating their own faith. This church brings together people from Africa, Haiti, Jamaica, and elsewhere. It's an example, too, of pan-Africanism, which is normally a political movement but can also manifest itself in the religious sphere.

ATLANTIC AVE

DOSCHER ST
CRYSTAL ST
PITK'
LOGAN ST
MONTAUK AVE
BERRIMAN ST
ESSEX ST
ELTON ST
ASHFORD ST
JEROME ST
SCHENCK AVE
LIBERTY AVE
VAN SICLEN AVE
BRADFORD ST
VERMONT ST
ALABAMA AVE
PENNSYLVANIA AVE
SHEFFIELD AVE
NEW JERSEY AVE
WYONA ST
MILLER AVE
HENDRIX ST
HINSDALE ST
DUMONT ST

LINWOOD ST

Cypress
Hills
Housing

SUTTER AVE

BLAKE AVE

MILFORD ST

L

DUMONT AVE

LIVONIA AVE

RIVERDALE AVE

NEW LOTS AVE

BARBEY ST
WARWICK ST
ELTON ST
HEGEMAN AVE

New Lots

LINDEN BLVD
CLEVELAND ST
LINWOOD ST
SHEPHERD AVE
ATKINS AVE

Boulevard
Houses

STANLEY AVE
WORTMAN AVE
COZINE AVE

SHEFFIELD AVE

Linden
Houses

FLATLANDS AVE

VANDALIA AVE
SCHROE

WILLIAMS AVE
SNEDIKER AVE
MALTA ST
GEORGIA AVE

Breukelen
Ballfields

Spring Creek
Towers

VAN SICLEN AVE
HENDRIX ST

G

PENNSYLVANIA AVE

LOUISIANA AVE

SEAVIEW AVE

(A) Firefighters memorial
(B) Mrs. Maxwell's Bakery
(C) Elaborate entertainment center
(D) John's Funeral Home
(E) St. Michael's Church
(F) Mafia burial grounds
(G) Spring Creek Towers

EAST NEW YORK

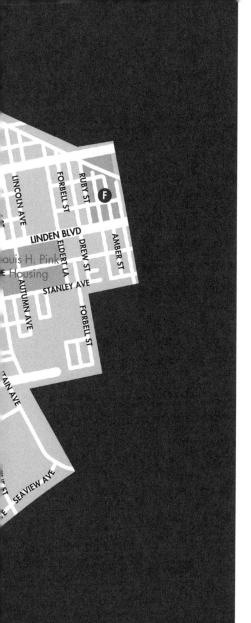

EAST NEW YORK CAN BE SAFELY WALKED during the day if you take the usual precautions, but this neighborhood has the highest crime rate in the city and should not be toured after dark. While gang activity has diminished citywide in the last twenty-five years, it's still a problem in the more troubled neighborhoods. A local version of poetry reflects the continued existence of a gang culture. I use a bathroom in a Laundromat in East New York. Scrawled on the wall are the words, "Let it rain, let it flood; let a Crip killah Blood." There are lots of storefront churches, signposts of poverty, and no fancy brownstones like in Bedford-Stuyvesant. It's a rough area. As recently as the early 1990s, East New York was still popularly referred to as the "murder capital of New York."

The boundaries of the neighborhood are Atlantic Avenue on the north, Conduit Avenue and Queens on the east, Seaview Avenue on the south, and Louisiana and Van Sinderen Avenues on the west. Public transportation is pretty good, with several fast, convenient subway lines—namely, the A and L trains. The population was formerly German, Lithuanian, Polish, Irish,

Italian, and Jewish. Today it's mostly black with substantial numbers of Hispanics, and some South Asians, generally Bangladeshis and Guyanese.[6]

East New York has many community gardens tended by a mix of locals and volunteers from outside the neighborhood, like high school students from Stuyvesant High. The rural roots of many of the area's Hispanic and black residents contribute in no small measure to the popularity of the gardens. There are few parks here; the areas with the fewest public parks tend to have the most gardens.

I'm walking along the outer part of the southern side of Atlantic Avenue toward Queens. It's a normally busy thoroughfare, but in this section, the inner lanes of the street become elevated, passing over Eastern Parkway and continuing for several blocks before descending. It's very quiet here, almost deserted, as I see on my right, behind a tall wire fence, an unusual memorial for two firemen, Captain Scott LaPiedra and Lieutenant James Blackmore, who died in 1998 battling a five-alarm fire alongside 223 other firefighters. Tragically, they had entered a burning building after being told that an elderly woman was trapped there. In fact, she had already been evacuated.

There are many such memorials in the city, but this one is different in several respects. It is located, almost hidden, on a street where few people pass by. It is not in a small park or in front of a firehouse. It is in a place more spacious than usual. The grassy lot has two small white-painted wooden crosses. The names of the victims are inscribed on a large monument on top of which I spot two fire hats with numbers. Presumably, they belonged to the two men who perished. Many flowers have been planted, and there's a large Maltese cross, the fireman's symbol, with flowers next to the plaque. There's even a realistic-looking fire hydrant placed in the grass. A large American flag flies above the scene. Very nicely laid out, it's a powerful, touching memorial; it can be found between Hinsdale and Williams Avenues.

East New York Memorial: A dignified tribute on a forlorn byway

Should it have been placed in a more prominent location? Not really, since this was the place where the five buildings that were destroyed once stood. By not rebuilding here, replacing it instead with a memorial, it becomes hallowed ground, a fitting tribute. This is an opportunity to reflect upon what it means to give one's life to save the lives of strangers. Most important perhaps, it sends a message to local residents, so many of them poor, that the firefighters who work in their neighborhoods are willing to protect them and even die for them. There's no trash in the lot, nor any graffiti. It's clear that this means a lot to the residents.

At 2700 Atlantic Avenue, between Vermont and Wyona Avenues, I come across Mrs. Maxwell's Bakery, with a sign, "Serving the People Since 1928." And indeed, they do quite a job of it. Inside, on this Friday morning, there's a long line of people waiting to pick up their orders. The bakery is both spacious and spotless and the displays are exquisitely arranged. I count at least six people dressed in white clothing, wearing large baker's hats, and preparing delicious-looking pies, cakes, and cookies. The treats come in all

New York's largest party cake store—delicious, efficient, and spotless

colors, shapes, sizes, and flavors, including a seven-inch chocolate cake for diabetics. It's October 31 and the Halloween season is in its climactic final stages, as pumpkin pies and gaily decorated cakes, mostly in white and orange colors, are dispensed. The shop also displays party goods—favors, cards, balloons, flowers. Mrs. Maxwell's bills itself as New York City's largest party cake store.

Eighty-seven years is a long time for a bakery to stay in business, much longer than the life span of most businesses. I wonder why it has been so successful. "Because we take good care of the customers," is one worker's terse response. Most likely, its longevity is due to the business acumen of those who founded it and that of the various owners since then. Its presence at this location for so long means it has catered (literally!) to the needs of the many ethnic groups who have lived in East New York: Jews, Irish, Italians, blacks, and Hispanics. Usually, when one ethnic group moves out, the places that served the group also leave, unable or unwilling to make the transition to the different tastes of the newcomers.

Interestingly, there never was a "Mrs. Maxwell." It was named after Maxwell House coffee and the nearby W. H. Maxwell Career and Technical Education High School. As for "Mrs.," the idea was to give the impression that some little old lady was slaving away baking all these cakes. Apparently it worked. One worker tells me the apocryphal tale: that a former employee at the bakery who defected to Junior's gave them the recipe for their famous cheesecake but that theirs is actually better. Not surprisingly, the people at Junior's say the whole story is nonsense. Regardless, Maxwell's cheesecake is pretty good. And the store's original name was, in fact, "Essential Cheesecake."

At 144 Wyona Street, just off Atlantic Avenue, I spot a remarkable deck on the second floor of an aluminum-sided home with protective wrought-iron bars on every window. The deck extends from the back of the house over the owner's backyard. It's an entertainment center, about sixty feet long and fifteen feet wide, has a fence on either side of it, a metal roof overhead, and contains a refrigerator, freezer, oven, barbecue grill, a full-size pool table, sports trophies, and a number of chairs and tables. Clearly it's a piece of heaven on earth in this very gritty urban setting. Scattered throughout the space are dozens of children's toys, including a small model Escalade and a number of little cars and plastic toy animals, especially dinosaurs. Perhaps the owner is a hunter, for protruding from the rear wall of the house is the stuffed head of a buck deer with antlers. It can best be viewed from Mrs. Maxwell's parking lot.

An elaborate setup like this is more likely to be found in a suburban community, and it raises an interesting question. I have rarely seen something like this in poor neighborhoods. People in these hardscrabble communities are often preoccupied with eking out a living and worry that any conspicuous display could invite burglaries. Why did the owner decide to do it? Since a knock on the door went unanswered I can only speculate. Perhaps he or she wanted to make the most of what they had, wanted to not feel that his modest circumstances prevented him from giving his family a taste of the good life. It's no different actually from the beautifully maintained homes that I occasionally spot in these neighborhoods.

I chat with John Nieman, the director of John's Funeral Home, or, in a nod to the current population, "Funeraria Juan," at the intersection of Van Siclen and Liberty Avenues. He's a gregarious man, as one could expect from someone in his sensitive profession. When I ask him about the occasional white individual I see here—an elderly person, or a young woman wheeling a baby carriage, he says: "Some of the older people never left and the young ones are probably married to a black or Hispanic resident."

John's pretty sanguine about the area's dangerous reputation: "You can certainly walk here in the daytime," he observes. You might think that he's thrilled about the prospect of gentrifiers moving in, as they have in nearby Bushwick, but he isn't: "I hope they're not coming here. I believe they *think* they wanna live here, but when they see it, they change their minds. We're a family business. We depend on generations of people who live here and who die here. The gentrifiers are transients. They don't usually put down roots in the community. They're not gonna help my business." Left unsaid is the fact that they're also young.

Just off Liberty Avenue, on Jerome Street, stands St. Michael's Church, a beautiful ornate Catholic church with an absolutely stunning exterior and interior. It's a priceless standout in a borough with hundreds of churches. There's polished ceramic tile, circular geometric designs; a dark wood, coffered ceiling lined with gilt, turquoise, and gold designs; religious figurines carved into a dome, marble Corinthian pillars with gilt on top, a gorgeous organ, and roman arches containing stained glass windows. The lighting is exquisite too, soft and bold in appropriate locations. And it's spotless, with everything shined to a high gloss. Established in 1845 by German Catholics, it currently serves a Hispanic constituency—mostly Dominicans, but also Puerto Ricans and Mexicans. Many of the churches (and mosques) in East New York are small and simple. This church has been maintained through the years. St. Michael's is an example of what can happen, even here, if people are determined enough.

My walk takes a different turn as I head over to Linden Boulevard and walk up and down Drew, Ruby, Emerald, and Amber Streets, straddling the Brooklyn-Queens border, between Linden and Sutter Avenues, an area known for its connections with the more lurid aspects of Mafia mayhem. As I gaze at this decrepit area and its mostly rundown dwellings, with overgrown lots filled with weeds and debris, and discarded automobiles and unused dumpsters, I am aware that this has reportedly been a burial ground for over half a century. The Gambino, Bonanno, and Gotti families used the area to dispose of hundreds of victims. Occasionally, remains are discovered, including at least one unfortunate soul whose tongue had been cut out. The FBI and other law enforcement agencies have swept the area numerous times over the years, using backhoes, hoping to find evidence for indictments, with mixed success. Residents may talk to you, but understandably, they probably know more than they're willing to reveal.

The Spring Creek section of East New York has low-rise, five-story apartment buildings. Combined with small streets and town squares, the area has a small village feel. It's bounded by Elton Street on the west, Erskine Street on the east, Seaview Avenue on the south, and Flatlands Avenue on the north. There's also the huge residential development, formerly Starrett City, built in 1974, and now called Spring Creek Towers, along with shopping malls and recreational facilities, which include a fitness club, swimming pools, basketball courts, and a boxing studio. With 5,881 apartments it's the largest federally supported development in the country. With other similar projects going forward, this section of East New York has revived, and some homes can even sell for several hundred thousand dollars.[7] This is what the rundown parts of East New York will probably look like ten years from now, especially given the fact that the De Blasio administration has made affordable housing a priority.

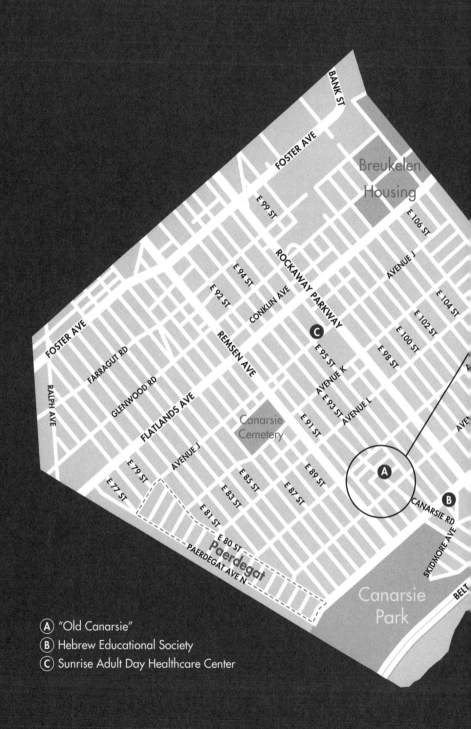

Ⓐ "Old Canarsie"
Ⓑ Hebrew Educational Society
Ⓒ Sunrise Adult Day Healthcare Center

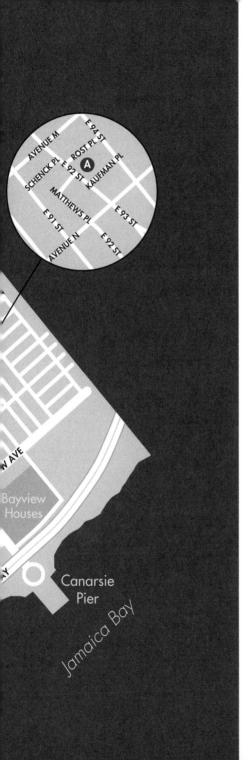

CANARSIE

THIS AREA RANGES FROM SOLIDLY MIDDLE class to poor, with many people in between. There's public housing and very nice single-family detached homes, semidetached, attached, and small apartment buildings. It is, in fact, mostly residential. Flatlands Avenue, Rockaway Parkway, and Avenue L, serve as predominantly commercial areas. Canarsie is bounded on the north by E. 108th Street, on the east by the Belt Parkway, on the south by Paerdegat and Ralph Avenues, and on the west, generally, by Ralph and Foster Avenues. There's also a subsection of Canarsie along the area's southern edge, called Paerdegat. Public transportation is largely by bus and the L subway line, which runs through the area from west to east.

In the nineteenth century, Canarsie was a fishing village, but that industry collapsed when the oysters died out in the polluted waters. In the early twentieth century it had a famous carousel and an amusement center known as Golden City Park. It competed successfully with Coney Island and lasted from 1907 to 1939. In the 1920s Jews and Italians settled in areas of Canarsie that were originally swampland.

The neighborhood shifted gradually in the 1980s and 1990s to a mostly African American population seeking to escape from unsafe neighborhoods like East New York and Brownsville. This did not go unchallenged as Italians in particular, but Jews too, fought the newcomers, resorting at times to violence. Today, the neighborhood is primarily black, with the rest of the population consisting mostly of Hispanics, some Asians, and a sprinkling of Italians, Jews, and Irish who stayed behind.

Recreationally, you have Canarsie Pier, jutting out into Jamaica Bay, which is a very good place for fishing. There's also the 100-acre Canarsie Beach Park, which has skate parks, basketball courts, and baseball fields. There are many nice paths to wander along, and the park is reasonably safe in the daytime. Nevertheless, visitors should exercise caution when walking through infrequently used areas.

Starting my walk on Avenue N, I begin to get a feeling of what Canarsie looked like half a century ago or before. I hang a left and make my way down very quiet Matthews Place (missing from many maps). No traffic, one block long, it has numerous quaint-looking, clapboard homes. Strolling up and down the tiny streets I also discover Rost Place, Schenck Place, and Kaufman Place. At 1524 Canarsie Road, there's a neat-looking old house with a long wraparound porch. It's just one of many charming old houses in this section.[8]

Walking through Canarsie, a cursory glance at religious institutions gives the impression that many white folks still reside here. In truth, however, Canarsie today is no more than 3 percent white. I pass a synagogue on E. 108th Street with the sign still there, but it doesn't appear to be functioning as such, especially since the listed phone number has been disconnected. A few blocks later, I turn left onto Seaview Avenue where the Hebrew Educational Society at 9502 still runs a facility, and most of the seniors who go there

Matthews Place—Old Canarsie lives!

for lunch and socializing are Jewish. They are, however, not local residents, but mostly people who have moved elsewhere, mostly in Brooklyn, and who return because they miss it, forming small affinity groups that enjoy a lunch for just $1.50 and chatting with friends, reminiscing about the old days.

One elderly Jewish lady with a heavy Yiddish accent, wearing a bright yellow scarf with black polka dots, tells me she lived here for forty-four years and likes to return to see her friends. "Sometimes, they lookin' on me, the blacks," she says, "'What you doing here?' But I don't care. Dey don't bodder me. I have a good fruit, a juice. I'm playing bingo, like in the Catskills where I went to the Flagler

Matthews Place—home is what you want it to be

Hotel." Other Jewish institutions, like synagogues, remain and continue to serve a small number of Jews who have stayed on.

Many of the homes in Canarsie are well tended, including a number of detached homes. Most, however, are attached and semi-attached homes made of red brick. There is crime, but it's not a serious problem. As one middle-aged black city worker tells me: "I moved here from East New York in 1991. Canarsie had more crime then and while it's still pretty high, what with crime going down all over the city, it's a lot better than where I came from. I can go out at night, but I know what streets and buildings to avoid. It's worth it because I got a nice home, where I can grill in my backyard and have my friends and relatives over."

An older man is weeding the small patch of grass in front of his modest bungalow home, and I greet him with: "Hi there, I didn't realize white people still live here."

"Yeah, well mostly they don't, but I do. I was born and raised here, and I ain't goin' nowhere." Jim is tall and fit-looking despite some health problems, which he briefs me on. He worked as a custodian for the city and retired on his pension. His children are grown up and live elsewhere, but they visit him regularly. He describes the area in blunt terms: "They dug up all these skeletons from the old days, when the mob dumped the bodies in Fresh Creek Basin a couple of blocks up." Of course, this has nothing to do with crime today. But, in an odd way, notoriety has its own cachet, recalling the glorified way in which the Mafia is portrayed in so many films.

"What's it like living here?" I ask.

"Oh, it's no problem." Jim says. "They all know me and I know them." What does that mean? Basically, that they're all in the same proverbial boat. Most of the homeowners share a common desire to identify and report troublemakers, to keep the area safe, at least in the daytime, as I discover.

"Can you walk around here at night?"

"Oh, forget about it. I don't go out after 5:30. There's drugs and all sortsa stuff going on."

"Then why do you stay here?"

"What else am I gonna do? Move into a nursing home? I can't go anywhere with the money I would get for this place except for a small apartment. If I was thirty I'd be gone, but I'm sixty-seven. Here I have a whole house for me and my wife. In a house, you can walk around naked without any of the neighbors sayin': 'Oh, they're havin' an orgy up there.' Anyway, my orgy days are over. We're two old people."

"Are there any good restaurants around here?" I ask, peering up the block at a small shopping area barely visible on Seaview Avenue.

"Nope."

"So where do you go when you wanna eat out?"

"Nowhere. I don't go. I don't have a car. What for?"

"What about, say, if you wanna go to Manhattan for a trip?"

"I haven't been to Manhattan in ten years. I wouldn't even know what train to take to get there."

"How about when friends come over?"

"I have no friends. Don't want any. The only friends you have are your wife and your bank book. I was in the military. I shoulda stayed in the military. At least I had friends there." He turns pensive for a moment, looking out across the street, and then adds, as though it were an afterthought: "On the other hand, my grandchildren come over. They love to visit grandma and grandpa because we play with them and they love the antiques we got here. The truth is, there's no place that's really safe anywhere in the city. Nobody really bothers me. And if they do then I'll have to do what I did in the old days, when I was younger."

"What's that?"

"Go out and kill people. You think I'm kiddin'? What are you suppose ta do when they come after your family? They mugged my wife a couple a years ago and I swore I was going to get the guy. And I did. Today, everybody's goin' for their gun. And the cops? They stink altogether."

Jim's assertion may well be just so much bravado, but regardless, it suggests a bunker mentality. His whole life, geographically speaking, seems to revolve around his house and, to some extent, his block. He prides himself on toughing it out, though it may be because his options are financially limited. To him, it's "me against them."

Not all whites living in communities like this have the same attitude. Later, I get a different view of things when I meet Brenda, an elderly, simply dressed woman wearing large black-framed owlish glasses, with yellowish-white hair tied in a ponytail. She lives in a New York City project nearby, the Bay View Houses, which has an excellent view of the bay. She has no private home and lives with her older daughter in an apartment. Commenting on nearby Canarsie Beach Park, I say to her: "This park is really nice looking. And it looks as safe as any park in the city."

"It is," she responds. "This all depends on your perspective. I turn on the TV and see there's crime everywhere, even in some of the best neighborhoods." This is the same attitude that Jim has, only in Brenda's case it points to the fact that her community is just as *good* as elsewhere in New York. She continues: "I've lived in Bay View Houses for fifty years and it's quite safe."

"So why did so many people run away from here?"

Brenda chuckles loudly. "You don't know why? Because people have problems. They get afraid. Realtors called them and said: 'If you don't sell, whatever, your house is gonna be worth nothing.' My girlfriend meanwhile sold her house for one price and had she stayed, she'da done much better because her house is now worth $200,000 more than what she sold it for." A typical story, but one that justifies not panicking and leaving. It only applies indirectly to her since she lives in a rental unit, but it is used to justify staying put. Not only that, but, as she sees it, the area is actually better today.

"The houses were bought by middle-class blacks, the ones people are afraid of because they were black. And they're taken care of beautifully, better than the whites before them did."

This is no surprise because, as many studies have shown, whites have far more options in buying homes than minorities, for both racial and economic reasons. For many middle-class blacks, the move is permanent, and they will stay and invest in their home and neighborhood. For many of the white folks, although this was a step up when they first moved into the area, better places were within reach and many decided to leave when they thought the neighborhood would deteriorate.[9] But there's something else going on here that merits mention. Brenda also has ideological or cultural reasons for moving here:

"I grew up in Bensonhurst and my husband was from Flatbush. And all the people living in these places were of one ilk, and I wanted my kid to meet people who were different from her. I didn't want to live across the street from my parents. So I came here so that my kids would grow up with everyone, not just Flatbush and Bensonhurst, where the people really were 'all us.' But I wasn't brought up with an attitude about other people. Of course, there's no diversity now. It's almost all black."

Brenda was an early advocate of integration. She tells me she would have lived in Manhattan to achieve her social goals but was unable to afford it. I bid her good day and continue walking down Seaview, passing a deli with the anonymous, but not really anonymous, name of "Uncle and Cousins," owned, not surprisingly, by Yemenis.

Sometimes institutions remain or are created in the community where whites predominate and blacks attend to their needs. A good example is a large senior citizens complex. I walk into the Sunrise Adult Day Healthcare Center, which has exercise facilities, dental screenings, Alzheimer and dementia programs, nutritional counseling, games, movies, meals, a beauty salon, and much more. It's located between East 96th and 95th Streets on Avenue J and is subsidized by the government and the Federation of Jewish Philanthropies. Hundreds of elderly, mostly Russian, Jews are bussed into Canarsie from Brighton Beach, Sheepshead Bay, and elsewhere to spend their entire day in a beautiful facility. The staff is mostly minority and relationships develop between the caregivers and their mostly Jewish patients. They even blossom into friendships.

Canarsie is sometimes thought of as a place at the end of the world, a stereotype that has survived from the early twentieth century until today. Vaudeville comedians would come on stage and would begin their routine about Brooklyn with "Canarrrrrseee," and everyone would laugh. Brenda tells me: "Canarsie was seen as so far away. My mother used to say when the kids made noise on the bus: 'They're gonna hear you all the way in Canarsie.'" When I was growing up in Manhattan, my teacher told us: "You better behave or I'll send you to Canarsie." And I remember my dad taking me to Canarsie as a kid. When I looked at the marshes and swampland that surrounded many of the houses, I believed that my teacher's threats were real.

E NEW YORK AVE
EMPIRE BLVD
LEFFERTS AVE
RUTLAND RD
E NEW YORK AVE
MAPLE ST
MIDWOOD ST
RUTLAND RD
REMSEN AVE
WINTHROP ST
CLARKSON AVE
LENOX RD
E 49 ST
E 51 ST
E 53 ST
E 55 ST
LINDEN BLVD
MARTENSE ST
CHURCH AVE
E 35 ST
E 37 ST
E 39 ST
E 43 ST
E 45 ST
E
SNYDER AVE
BEDFORD AVE
ERASMUS ST
Erasmus
Rugby
TILDEN AVE
D
ALBEMARLE RD
NOSTRAND AVE
C
Holy Cross Cemetery
TILDEN AVE
ROGERS AVE
BEVERLEY RD
BEVERLEY RD
F
CORTELYOU RD
CLARENDON RD
SCHENECTADY AVE
UTICA AVE
E 52 ST
BEDFORD AVE
E 26 ST
E 28 ST
E 31 ST
ALBANY AVE
TROY AVE
AVENUE D
NEW YORK AVE
BROOKLYN AVE
NEWKIRK AVE
FOSTER AVE
E 46 ST
E 48 ST
FARRAGUT RD
FLATBUSH AVE
E 31 ST
E 34 ST
E 38 ST
E 40 ST
E 42 ST
G
GLENWOOD RD
KINGS HWAY
E 52 ST
Farragut
AVENUE H

EAST FLATBUSH

(A) National Grid plant
(B) Brooklyn Terminal Market
(C) Holy Cross Cemetery
(D) Former home of
Jackie Robinson

(E) Church of the
Restoration Temple
(F) Old Sears Roebuck
Building
(G) "Violence Destroys the
Light of Today" mural
(H) Pieter Claesen
Wyckoff House
(I) Footprints Café

EAST FLATBUSH IS A LARGE, mostly residential area filled with thousands of private homes, especially in the Remsen Village, Rugby, and Farragut sections. The borders have a variety of angles and are a bit difficult to clearly establish. Roughly speaking, it's bounded by East New York Avenue and Empire Boulevard on the north; on the east, at various points, by Rockaway Parkway and Avenue D; on the south also by Avenue D, Foster Avenue, and Avenue H; and, on the west, by Bedford, Flatbush, and Nostrand Avenues. Many, if not most, of the homes are of the red-brick variety you see throughout Brooklyn, small to moderate in size. On the whole, the houses are very well maintained and include beautiful gardens and flowers.

The older sections of Wingate and Erasmus have lots of brick, bow-fronted, two- or three-family row houses, and older apartment buildings, especially near Nostrand and Rogers Avenues. Wingate, incidentally, was called Pig Town until 1954, after the animal farms that originally dotted the area. Utica, Ralph, Remsen, Church (a portion of which has been renamed Bob Marley Boulevard), and Ditmas Avenues are main commercial arteries—auto shops, medical clinics and the like, unappealing to the eye, but highly functional. The subway lines, namely, the 2, 5, B, and Q trains, are just over the border, in Flatbush, walking distance for some, but with most taking a bus or cab for a short distance.

Once upon a time the neighborhood was largely Jewish and Italian. Today, ethnically, East Flatbush is overwhelmingly Caribbean, with residents coming from the West Indies and from Haiti, augmented by considerable numbers of African immigrants. The area is fairly safe, but not completely so. Crime has gone down in recent years, as elsewhere in the city. The people range from working class to middle class. Religion is very big here, and on a Sunday the streets are filled with the music from churches, where people, often dressed in their Sunday best, lift up their voices in song to praise the lord.

The National Grid plant in East Flatbush is a sprawling complex of buildings along Ditmas Avenue. One of them, between Dorset Street and 86th Street, is particularly interesting architecturally. It's a large brick structure, a unique building, the equivalent of seven stories in height, with white stone on the red brick that's decorated with chevrons and keystones, sort of in an art deco style. It also has Romanesque elements, especially near the top, just beneath a large water tower on the roof. It's the most impressive building in the area, literally looming over the East Flatbush landscape. Designed by Benjamin Forrester and completed in 1915, it housed a dye and chemical company, which later became Allied Chemical.

A few blocks away, near Chase Court and 83rd Street, about two blocks east of Ralph Avenue, I enter the Brooklyn Terminal Market. It used to have mostly fish stores, but today it's anchored by two large supermarkets. One, Better Food for Less, has both retail and wholesale divisions. I discover a wide array of Caribbean and African foods, prepared or produced in ways that appeal to these communities—rice, spices, fish, meats, fruits, vegetables.

Beverley Road Sears Roebuck store—an American classic, still alive

People come from the entire metropolitan area to do their ethnic shopping here—all the boroughs, New Jersey, Connecticut, Long Island. There are Haitian and Jamaican sections and African sections featuring products from Liberia, Ghana, Nigeria, and many other countries. Items are also sold in large and giant sizes, just like at Costco. The aisles are wide and neatly arranged and the staff very friendly and knowledgeable; most hail from Africa or the Caribbean.

Across the street I find a very similar place, Gitto Farmer's Market. Browsing through the produce department, I see a large section devoted to yams of every name and description. Also to be found are yucca roots, dozens of varieties of rice, and water coconuts with long roots sticking out. I meet Chudi, a seventy-year-old Nigerian man, in the spice department. He's wearing an Ivy League cap and he's smiling as I approach: "Come here, look at this powder. It's called white melon and can prevent prostate cancer. You put it in food. I came here from Nigeria ten years ago with my wife because of the economic opportunities. Nigeria had political and economic problems. Here you have crime, but mostly it's safe." Chudi's biography reminds me that people can come here even later in life. His children are scattered around the world: in Germany and elsewhere in Europe as well as in Nigeria. That did not deter him from literally starting over again in a new country.

These places are much more than supermarkets. They are a world within a world. The opportunity for people to buy virtually every product they had back home eases the transition from the homeland to the new land. When they sit and eat these foods, they feel almost as though they have recaptured a piece of their past and can derive satisfaction in the fact that they didn't have to give up everything when they came here. When they have a nice dinner they're reminded of feasts and parties in their native villages or cities. In a way, recreating pieces of our past is something that we all do—eating a candy bar we ate as kids, watching a TV show we saw when we were small that we can now view on the Internet. Only here it's even more meaningful because people are connecting with a land that's now far away. Some shoppers I spoke with had traveled many miles in the tristate area to shop here.

I leave the market, walk west on Clarendon Road, eventually make a right onto Schenectady Avenue, and soon arrive at Holy Cross Cemetery, which, like Green-Wood Cemetery, has some pretty famous folks buried in it. One example is Willie Sutton, who, when asked why he robbed banks, allegedly quipped: "Because that's where the money is." Other notables include Gil Hodges, "Diamond Jim" Brady, and famed jockey Edward Garrison. From Brooklyn Avenue at night I can see the towering gravestones of what appears to be a very spooky place. I walk by 5224 Tilden Avenue and notice a small plaque. It identifies the house as home, briefly, to baseball great Jackie Robinson. It's a national landmark, but sadly, today it is neglected and boarded up.

I head north to Church Avenue and make a left. Crossing E. 46th Street I see a crowd outside the Church of the Restoration Temple. Curious, I enter and sit in a wooden pew and listen to the pastor's sermon. As I learn later, most of the members are from Guyana, but some hail from other Caribbean lands and from Africa. I couldn't help but be impressed by the members' love for others and the pastor's avoidance of strident statements about how nonbelievers are going to burn in hell. After the service, the members go into a plainly furnished, long room where food is being prepared. Hundreds of paper bags containing home-cooked turkey or ham dinners are on the table ready for distribution to the needy. Although I was the only white person in the room, it made no difference whatsoever in how I was treated. To them I was just a guy who wandered in. When I returned two hours later, almost all of the dinners had been given out. These events are an essential part of church activities everywhere in the city, and they make a huge difference to those on the receiving end. But what was most striking to me that day was that almost all of the volunteers were teenagers or people in their twenties.

I continue my journey up Church and go left on Bedford Avenue, the border between East Flatbush and Flatbush, to Beverley

Road. I gaze at a classic example of a structure that can evoke strong emotions for some. It's the still-standing Sears, Roebuck Building in Brooklyn, the first one in the city. Located on the corner of Bedford and Beverley, a mile west of the Terminal Market, it is an art deco structure built in 1932 that, like the National Grid center, towers over the two-story homes and small apartment buildings nearby. Eleanor Roosevelt was in attendance when it first opened. Interestingly, the place is still in business; I access it on Bedford. There are three floors above ground and one on the lower level, all with retail establishments.

Those in the know who walk by realize that they're looking at a monument to a forgotten era. As I ponder this building's meaning to those who see it, I realize that New York City is like a time machine. Looking at the Sears Building, I'm in the 1930s, perhaps taking a trip down memory lane; when I visit the new steel apartment buildings along the East River by North Williamsburg, I am catapulted into the twenty-first century.

On Glenwood Road, near E. 46th Street, I see an interesting mural made of several beautifully painted panels. It's the work of numerous teenage artists. Sponsored by the city and supported by Councilman Jumaane Williams and a group identified as "Ground-Swelling Collaboration," it's underneath a train trestle and I probably wouldn't have noticed it driving by. It's titled "Violence Destroys the Light of Today." The panels are each about five feet long and three feet high. The first depicts a skeletal hand inside handcuffs, implying that violence destroys. Its message may also be against police use of violence. The last panel features a bucolic countryside scene of a river flowing through mountains and forests. This mural is in the midst of an industrial area that is mostly deserted, it being a Sunday.

On Clarendon Road, just west of Ralph Avenue, I visit the Pieter Claesen Wyckoff House. An H-frame, this farmhouse, built in 1652 and now restored, is the oldest surviving structure in New York City and, quite possibly, the state. There were once many such buildings in the city. There are gardens outside, where vegetables are thriving, and there's even a small section for flax, from which linen is made. Gazing upon it gives me the feeling of being part of history. The city has so many buildings, but this is *the* oldest one, and that makes it special.

I consider dining at Footprints, 5814 Clarendon Road. While they're big on crabmeat, shrimp, beef, and chicken, Caribbean style, they also offer a spicy vegetarian dish, rasta pasta, prepared by Chef Basil. There's great rap music and hip-hop and everyone's real friendly, whether you're West Indian or Chinese, black or white. People come from all over to eat here. It would be a great way to end my trip if only I didn't have to leave for an evening event.

FLATBUSH

PROSPECT PARK SOUTH

MIDWOOD

FLATLANDS

MARINE PARK

BERGEN BEACH

MILL BASIN

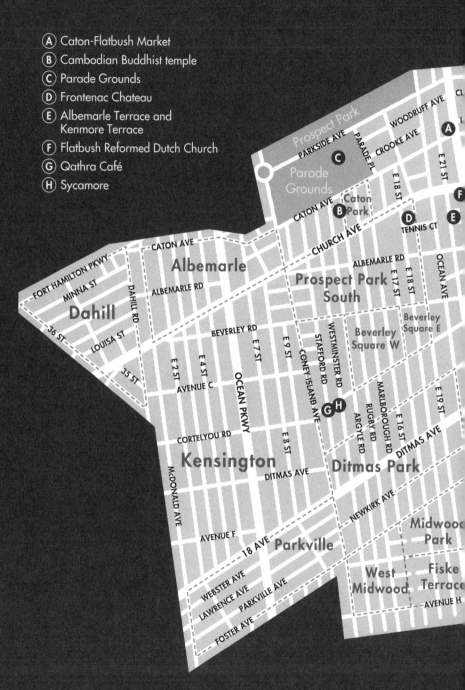

Ⓐ Caton-Flatbush Market
Ⓑ Cambodian Buddhist temple
Ⓒ Parade Grounds
Ⓓ Frontenac Chateau
Ⓔ Albemarle Terrace and
   Kenmore Terrace
Ⓕ Flatbush Reformed Dutch Church
Ⓖ Qathra Café
Ⓗ Sycamore

Prospect Park

PARKSIDE AVE
WOODRUFF AVE
CROOKE AVE
PARADE PL
Ⓒ
Ⓐ
E 21 ST
Ⓕ
Parade
Grounds
CATON AVE
Ⓑ Caton Park
E 18 ST
Ⓓ
Ⓔ
CHURCH AVE
TENNIS CT
CATON AVE
Albemarle
ALBEMARLE RD
Prospect Park
South
ALBEMARLE RD
E 17 ST
E 18 ST
OCEAN AVE
FORT HAMILTON PKWY
MINNA ST
DAHILL RD
ALBEMARLE RD
Dahill
36 ST
LOUISA ST
BEVERLEY RD
E 7 ST
Beverley
Square W
Beverley
Square E
35 ST
E 2 ST
E 4 ST
E 9 ST
WESTMINSTER RD
STAFFORD RD
CONEY ISLAND AVE
AVENUE C
OCEAN PKWY
MARLBOROUGH RD
RUGBY RD
ARGYLE RD
E 16 ST
E 19 ST
Ⓖ Ⓗ
CORTELYOU RD
E 8 ST
Kensington
McDONALD AVE
DITMAS AVE
Ditmas Park
DITMAS AVE
NEWKIRK AVE
AVENUE F
Midwood
Park
18 AVE
Parkville
West
Midwood
Fiske
Terrace
WEBSTER AVE
LAWRENCE AVE
PARKVILLE AVE
AVENUE H
FOSTER AVE

FLATBUSH

THE BOUNDARIES OF FLATBUSH are a bit complex, and not all will agree on their precise locations. They include Parkside Avenue, plus Fort Hamilton Parkway, on the north; Bedford, Flatbush, and Nostrand Avenues on the east; Avenue H on the south; and McDonald Avenue and 36th Street on the west. Although some people view adjacent Midwood as part of Flatbush, its size and demographics combine to justify treating it as a separate community. More than any other neighborhood, Flatbush consists of many subdivisions whose members strongly identify with them—Beverley Square, Ditmas Park, Kensington, and Albemarle and Kenmore Terraces. Many of the streets in these areas have beautiful Victorians, Queen Annes, and colonials that make for rewarding walks. This happened largely because the residents of Flatbush developed strong neighborhood associations that fought hard to preserve and enhance their communities.

Space does not allow for each one to be treated fully. Moreover, this is not a street-by-street guide but rather a selection of relatively unknown or unusual aspects of Brooklyn's communities, along with general observations about

223

them. Thus the areas will be identified or discussed where relevant to this book's main theme. One exception to this approach is Prospect Park South, also located within Flatbush. It is discussed separately as an example of how a beautiful community with many exceptional private homes can peacefully coexist within a commercial and residential area that is quite different from it.

Since these areas vary physically, it's important for the walker to know what each area looks like. The general area from Parkside Avenue on the north to Bedford Avenue on the east, Avenue H on the south, and Ocean Avenue on the west is heavily West Indian, with Haitians making up the largest immigrant group, along with some smaller populations of Hispanics and Africans from a variety of countries. Demographically and residentially, the areas west of Ocean Avenue to Coney Island Avenue and from Church Avenue south to Avenue H tend to be more upscale and diverse.

Flatbush Avenue is a street of stores—dollar outfits, small pharmacies, hair salons, liquor shops, cheap clothing stores, costume jewelry boutiques, tattoo places, fast food joints, factory outlets selling shirts for five dollars, and the like. Church Avenue is similar. These establishments cater primarily to the lower income people who live around here. Farther into Flatbush are the diverse and semigentrified neighborhoods such as West and East Beverley Square and Ditmas Park. As I walk down Stratford, Westminster, Argyle, Rugby, or Marlborough Roads I see many gracious Victorian homes, more than a few with wraparound porches.

Here, as elsewhere, I recognize a contrast in streets that is repeated over and over. A main street, in this case Church, will look somewhat seedy, a place where poor, often unemployed youths and the old-timers congregate, while a parallel street, in this case Martense Street, or Linden Boulevard, is quiet, with pretty row houses or apartment buildings and very few people hanging out. That doesn't mean it's totally safe, and this area does have some crime. There are shootings occasionally, late at night, but nothing like the old days. The cameras, as usual, are everywhere.

At the intersection of Caton and Flatbush Avenues, I take a quick walk through the Flatbush Caton Market. It's a small indoor mall, basically a large, high-ceilinged shed occupied mostly by specialty stores selling clothing, pocketbooks, jewelry, and what New Yorkers call "tchotchkes" of every kind. Many of the stores emphasize ethnic themes, especially from Haiti, which is not surprising since there's a large Haitian presence here.[1] It's not as crowded as the streets and it costs less for a vendor to operate indoors. A barber tells me that his rent is $500 a month compared to $5,000 a month on a well-traveled street.

I decide to try out Orlando's place for a haircut. He's from Colombia and has been practicing his craft for thirty years, ten in Colombia and twenty in New York. He's a friendly chap, and he tells me about the neighborhood, which he considers safe during the daytime hours. Orlando shows me a multicolored, green, red, and black flag whose borders encompass all the lands of Central America and the Caribbean nations, proclaiming them to be both united and part of a "diaspora." There's a feeling by many newcomers to this city that, coming as they do from small countries, they must stick together, and this flag embodies that idea. On the other hand, given the different interests of each group, maintaining a united front is quite challenging.

At 26 Rugby Road, just off Caton Avenue, I discover a genuinely unusual place. It's a Cambodian Buddhist temple in a large private home, one of only two Cambodian temples in the city, the other located in the Bronx. Religious and national flags flutter in the pleasant breeze on a bright, sunny Sunday morning as I approach a man seated in a lounge chair on the porch. Bunnwath greets me with a broad welcoming smile and invites me inside to see a service. About fifty barefoot, mostly Asian people of Cambodian origin are seated on rugs, chanting and listening to soft, somewhat-mournful strains of music, with three bare-chested monks seated on the side, leading the service. In front is a shrine with statues, pottery, and flowers. Red, blue, and yellow flashing lights give the room both a modern and exotic look.

"Why did you establish the temple here?" I ask.

"When we began in 1987 we had more people here, but over time many moved to New Jersey. Still, people come from all over. You see, the communists tried to destroy our Khmer culture and Buddhism, but we want to preserve it and the temple is how we remember and honor our ancient way of life. Those who have visited Angkor Wat can appreciate what was lost. It's still a communist country even if they don't call it that anymore."

Bunnwath's comments express the sense of loss that many political refugees feel, one that can last for generations. It's no different than, say, how Armenians feel about what happened to them. People adjust to new realities but never get over what happened because those who died cannot come back. Services are often held on Sunday mornings, but also at other times. Those wishing to attend will be warmly welcomed. More information is available at their website: www.wattsamakki.org.

Along Caton is an area called the Parade Grounds, a part of Prospect Park. It was once a special area set aside for military drills by Civil War veterans and by the Coast Guard. Today, it has soccer, basketball fields, playgrounds, and among the finest clay tennis courts in the city. I bump into my colleague at CUNY, Juan Battle, a prominent sociologist. He is playing tennis, something he does very well with both passion and finesse. As I walk along Parkside Avenue, I can't help but notice a young attractive woman, listening to music, lying on the ground with the detached metal top of a convertible auto supporting her back. Her two incredibly friendly dachshunds are gamboling nearby. It turns out that Pepsi is doing a commercial across the street and "rented" her convertible, and she's relaxing while waiting for them to finish. Is it an unusual sight, given the fact that there are park benches around? You bet it is, but, as they say, in New York anything goes.

Walking south on Ocean to Tennis Court, I turn right, stop short, and behold, a stunning building on the right called the Chateau Frontenac. Built in 1929, its exterior is one of the prettiest in Brooklyn. It's a red brick building trimmed with white stone, with

Chateau Frontenac—a Canadian chateau transplanted from Quebec

emblems of the French royal court, like the heraldic salamander, carved into it. Note the beautiful pilasters that frame the arched entranceway and the graceful wrought-iron entrance to the inner courtyard. Typical of such buildings, there's a brick, stand-alone guardhouse that is no longer in use.

The building has attracted notables, including some Dodgers players of yore who reportedly made it their home. A John Lennon documentary was filmed there, and in the spring of 2015, it was a setting for the Spanish-language version of *Boardwalk Empire*. I remark to an elderly, elegant-looking black woman with a lilting West Indian accent, entering the locked building, that it looks "really special." She invites me in to see the interior lobby. Standing on a terrazzo floor with an intricate design, my eyes are drawn to the ceiling, which has thick wooden beams set over what appears to be faded cloth fabric.

Back outside, I head up Ocean a short distance and come to two historic streets on the right, Albemarle Terrace and then Kenmore Terrace, both dead-end streets. Standing on these streets, the noisiness of the surrounding area vanishes. It's quiet, and as I look at the row houses dating back to shortly after the beginning of the twentieth century, I feel like I'm back in those times. This is reinforced as I walk by, on E. 21st Street, one of the oldest cemeteries in the city, established by the Flatbush Reformed Dutch Church, circa 1798. The church's front entrance on Flatbush Avenue and Church is around the corner, and on a Sunday morning I sit in a pew, close my eyes, and listen to a service with hymns that takes me back to another imagined era.

Today, Coney Island Avenue is unfortunately an uninteresting place to walk, as it's littered with auto repair and maintenance shops and an assortment of groceries and the like, but the streets immediately east of it are another story. These streets are part of the communities of Prospect Park South (discussed elsewhere in detail), Beverley Square, Ditmas Park, "the Midwoods," and Fiske Terrace, all filled with hundreds of private, free-standing homes, most of them Victorian. Some of them have been used in movies, like *Sophie's Choice*. It would also be fair to say that these areas are in an advanced state of gentrification. There's a real sense of community here in these neighborhoods. As one resident, Michael McKinley, author of the acclaimed book *Finding Jesus*, also a CNN series, explained: "I've never lived in a place that takes such pride in its community. There are parades and other events here all the time. And beautiful decorations go up here on all the holidays, not in a competitive way, but friendly and helping each other. Coney Island Avenue may look dumpy now, but in ten years it's going to be totally different. All you have to do is look at the cafés and shops opening now on Church Avenue. What did that look like five years ago? The future is also very visible on Cortelyou Road."

"You have a daughter. What do you do about schools? Do you send her to the public schools?"

"Yes I do. She goes to a magnet school, which we got into through a lottery. We had her here in a Montessori school but it wasn't very good." So much for the stereotype that all of the gentrifiers' kids go to private schools. There's apparently a whole system where people's children go to magnet public schools that are good, and those are not necessarily the ones down the block from where they live.

Strolling along Cortelyou, with its many cafés, I stop at a typical one, Qathra, at number 1112. It's filled with people, some working on laptops, others enjoying eggs or brownies in a very comfortable outdoor area with wooden tables and chairs and a weird-looking, square-shaped, dark gray fountain made of plastic and rubber with small change in the water. A sign on a wall near the entrance tells me that it's definitely a new age community: "People feeling anxiety? Freeing the subconscious through the arts. All suggestions are welcome with no commitments needed. Group discussions will be completely open to all visitors sharing our anxieties at the Cortelyou Library starting May 30th." Farther up, at 1118, is Sycamore, a flower shop by day and a bar at night. They have, as they call it, "Ditmas Park's only queer party" on the first Thursday of every month.[2]

Between Coney Island and McDonald Avenues, stretching south from Church Avenue to Foster Avenue, are the Kensington and Parkville sections of Flatbush. The homes are a hodgepodge of styles and not especially impressive architecturally, but they are very functional, spacious, and cheap enough for large families who can't afford fancy digs, like the ones in Beverley Square or Fiske Terrace. This part of Flatbush contains an exceptionally large number of immigrants from all over the world—Uzbekistan, Israel, China, Vietnam, Pakistan, Turkey, Bosnia, Korea, Senegal, Nigeria, Egypt, and other lands. There probably aren't many cross-cultural friendships being made here, but an attitude of tolerance prevails.

The northwest section of Flatbush is home to the quaint, small community of Dahill. It's an Irish name, possibly stemming from some Dahills who immigrated here from Ireland in the nineteenth century. It's so quiet that I can almost hear myself think as I walk around.

The homes, simple yet sturdy two-story, red-brick, attached houses, are off Fort Hamilton Parkway where it runs along Green-Wood Cemetery. The streets are named after William Micieli, who bought the farms around 1900 and built the development, and his children, Minna, Clara, and Louisa.

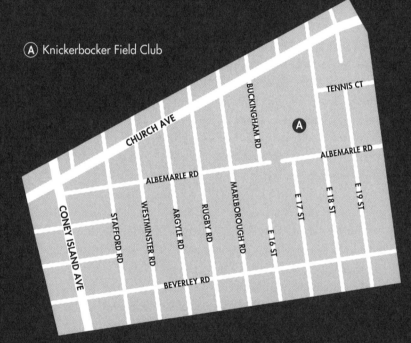

Ⓐ Knickerbocker Field Club

PROSPECT PARK SOUTH

THIS TINY NEIGHBORHOOD, bounded by Church Avenue to the north, Buckingham Road and 16th Street to the east, Beverley Road to the south, and Coney Island Avenue to the west, is a jewel of the borough because of the beautiful homes within its historic district. In the early part of the twentieth century, this was a redoubt of the wealthy, like the directors of the Sperry Corporation (later Sperry Rand) and Gillette. The homes are incredibly varied, consisting mostly of Queen Annes, Colonials, French Revivals, and Italianate styles. Some specific gems include 1440, 1501, and 1510 Albemarle Road, and 104, 125, 131, and 143 Buckingham Road. The homes are expensive, but a diligent search will turn up some apartment rentals in the area that are reasonable. There's not much nightlife here, but Ditmas Park, a short walk away, can accommodate those who desire it.

As I emerge from the Church Avenue stop, a cacophony of noise greets me, from traffic, music blaring from stores and cars, and from African street vendors declaiming the merits of their wares. This and Coney Island Avenue are the main shopping streets within the geographical boundaries of Prospect Park South. It is a predominantly Caribbean neighborhood yet has a mélange of fast food joints—Mexican, West Indian, Chinese, generic, Dunkin' Donuts, and the like. One, Super John's Liquor Store, catches my attention because it's huge but also because it still looks exactly like the 99¢ store it replaced. The design is no frills: glaring, long fluorescent lights with no covers, plain walls. Generally, liquor stores try to appear attractive, especially when they're this big, but this one is all about the product, which, locals tell me, is pretty cheap.

I begin my walk through the rest of the area on 18th Street, which is technically in Flatbush, heading toward another border of the neighborhood, Beverley Road. In a two-block stretch I'm asked for change twice. The street, in the early afternoon, is filled with people, walking, hanging out, with none of the feel of a gentrifying area, and it isn't one. Large brick apartment buildings, whose architecture can best be described as eclectic, loom over the street, their shadows stretching out over the sidewalk, giving the passerby the feeling of traveling through a canyon. People are friendly, speaking in the loud tones that signify comfort in one's environment.

On a whim, I sneak by a building superintendent when his face is turned away and walk along an apartment building's side. Why? Because I want to see if there are any nice gardens in the back, as is sometimes the case. This is a fateful decision, because while there are no gardens, I do come face to face with a high chain link fence with five first-rate tennis courts on the other side. Determined to find out what tennis courts are doing here, I eventually find the entrance, which requires walking through a parking lot, presumably for tenants on the block, that has only a very small neatly lettered white sign with black letters, tucked away, that reads: Knickerbocker Field Club. The street stretching out beyond 18th and dead-ending two blocks away at Ocean Avenue is far more informative, since it's called Tennis Court.

Walking through the lot I turn left and arrive at the entrance. Several elderly and middle-aged men are playing on Har-Tru, well-maintained courts, with each court having cold water and cups available for the players, who are properly attired in the manner befitting a private club. This is the only such club in Brooklyn. Its founding dates back to 1889, when the club also had a golf course, which was sold off later for financial reasons. At its height, there was also a ballroom and dining facilities. While it's technically in Flatbush, just over the border, the club has many members who reside in Prospect Park South, and it's included as part of this neighborhood.

The courts are surrounded by apartment buildings and also straddle the B and Q subway lines, which rumble by every few minutes

Knickerbocker Field Club—move over, US Open!

on outdoor tracks below street level. It's quite scenic, even authentic, and, in any case, truly urban. The only point of comparison for me are the courts where I sometimes play, situated on Lincoln Terrace in Crown Heights. Those courts also have a train running nearby on an elevated track, but these are public courts, of far poorer quality, and usually free, since people check for your park card only intermittently. Want water? Bring your own bottle.

I speak with Raymond Habib, president of the club, who tells me that membership is $900 for the season. It's a bargain, and that's why they have a three-year waiting list of sixty-five people. A member, Charlie, tells me that because of its location as well as its durability through the years it is considered one of the most unusual tennis clubs in the country. I take photos of the place, including one featuring a realistic facsimile subway line sign hanging a few yards away from where the tracks are. Francis Salina, who maintains the club, tells me more: "I'm from Trinidad and Tobago and I've been running the club, taking care of it and things, since 1985, when I came here and stayed to take care of my mother who lived here." He's a seventy-four-year-old man with a West Indian lilt in his voice and a sunny personality that could melt an ice cream cone even in the winter. We're sitting on a wooden deck, which anchors an area that has walls on which ancient-looking wooden rackets from the old days are displayed alongside pictures of how the club looked in the early period and pictures of events held in decades past. All in all, it's a very pleasant place. Todd Snyder, the resident tennis pro since 1994, who's also an amateur musician on the side, informs me that the famous pros who played here—it was a Brooklyn tournament—"include Pancho Segura and Don Budge."

"If you wanted to sell this place you could make a killing," I say.

"That's true," the pro responds. "But you see this plaque? It commemorates the people who, after the clubhouse burned down, provided the financial means so that we didn't have to sell it. Now it has cinderblocks around it so this couldn't happen. We have parties sometimes and it's a very friendly place."

The heart and soul of Prospect Park South can be found on Buckingham, Marlborough, and Albemarle Roads, and their adjacent blocks. The houses are an eclectic collection in a historic district, and are mostly one of a kind. The bucolic scene contrasts sharply with the noised-filled atmosphere on Church and Coney Island Avenues. The streets, with flowerbeds and stately overhanging trees, make me feel as though I'm in a small village, interrupted sometimes by a fire truck or ambulance, sirens blaring, racing through this oasis. I approach a man sitting on a lawn chair trying to get a tan. A native of Poughkeepsie who was drawn to New York City's vibrant lifestyle, he's chatting with a woman. Both of them live in a lone red brick apartment building across the street where the rents are quite reasonable. "The homeowners fought it unsuccessfully, and so here we are and, of course, we love it. It's safe and quiet."

Quiet, suburban living at bargain-basement rates!

Ⓐ Di Fara Pizza
Ⓑ Center for Kosher Culinary Arts
Ⓒ Essen New York Deli
Ⓓ Masbia soup kitchen
Ⓔ Jews for Jesus Center
Ⓕ The Painted Shul
Ⓖ Vasha Kniga
Ⓗ Makki Masjid

MIDWOOD

MIDWOOD IS OFTEN GROUPED TOGETHER with its neighbor, Flatbush, and residents often see themselves as part of Flatbush proper. In many ways it's similar to southwestern Flatbush, but it is nevertheless a distinct area with its own boundaries. These are Avenue H on the north, Nostrand Avenue on the east, Avenue P on the south, and McDonald Avenue on the west. It has a rich and storied history. Vitagraph Studios, which produced many important films, was located in Midwood from 1907 to 1925.[3] It also has two prominent colleges, CUNY's Brooklyn College and Touro College, a school with many locations throughout the city, but with a heavy presence in this area and a predominantly Orthodox Jewish student body.

Overall, Midwood is predominantly middle class, with many spacious, beautiful one-family homes along Avenues K, L, M, N, and O and along Bedford Avenue. You'll find concentrations of apartment buildings along Ocean Avenue and on Ocean Parkway, which was completed in 1880 and is still a grand boulevard. It boasts seven lanes for vehicular traffic and two broad pedestrian walkways, all designed by the architects Frederick Law

Olmsted and Calvert Vaux, who created Central and Prospect Parks and Eastern Parkway. There was actually horse racing here until 1908, and it is where the first bicycle path in the United States was built in 1894. Today, people stroll along its leafy walkways, sit and chat on its benches, and play chess. The street also has one- and two-family dwellings, a number of them quite beautiful.

Midwood became a multiethnic neighborhood in the 1970s and 1980s, when people settled there from many lands, most notably the former Soviet Union, Pakistan, India, Haiti, and Syria. Today, it is primarily an Orthodox Jewish community. Pomegranate, perhaps America's largest kosher supermarket, on Coney Island Avenue near Avenue L, is a worthy rival in design and presentation to Whole Foods. Between Avenue O and Quentin Road, also on "Coney," there's a concentration of Turkish eateries. The main commercial streets are Avenues J, M, P, Coney Island, and Nostrand Avenues.

Midwood has a number of beautiful homes, many of them recently built. One of the most attractive areas is the Nottingham section, between Avenues L and N, from north to south, and running from E. 21st to E. 28th Streets. Meandering along two very quiet diagonal streets near Nottingham—Bay Avenue and Olean Street—is also pleasant. Each street is about two blocks long and each contains a number of very old brick and stucco houses.

Midwood is home to New York's, and quite possibly the world's, most famous pizza shop, Di Fara Pizza. It's located at 1424 Avenue J in an Orthodox Jewish neighborhood. Those who are observant are not allowed to eat in this nonkosher establishment. However, looking isn't the same as eating, and as I watch Orthodox Jews walk by, I see some of them casting a curious glance into the place, possibly wondering why it's always so crowded and maybe thinking that the pizza must be really good. If they want confirmation of its high quality they can get it from Zagat, which has rated it the best in the city, and from Chef Anthony Bourdain, who calls it "the best of the best." They'd probably be surprised to know that two of the many ingredients that go into the pies, oregano and basil, are imported from Israel. The eighty-year-old owner, Domenico DeMarco, who opened the shop over half a century ago, is still at it in 2015, making every pie and using what he regards as the best ingredients—three types of mozzarella cheese, San Marzano tomatoes, and hard cow's milk cheese, called grana padano.

The Orthodox *do* have something to brag about, though it's certainly unknown to most people, including the Orthodox themselves. Midwood is home to the Center for Kosher Culinary Arts, a school that has graduated more than five hundred students since opening eight years ago. It's directed by Jesse Blonder and is the only kosher-oriented culinary school in America. One of the people who works with him, Philippe Kaemmerle, was formerly a pastry chef at Windows on the World (located at the top of the World Trade Center) and at Twenty One. It's open to anyone over the age of sixteen.

I climbed the stairs at 1407 Coney Island Avenue, a building the school shares with Eichler's, a well-known Jewish bookstore located on the ground floor. As it happens, a class on food safety was going on, with several yarmulke-wearing young men listening raptly. The instructor, who is not an Orthodox Jew, peppers his remarks with salty comments that relate the lecture to the community he's in: "When you go over to Essen New York Deli, they'll have a bunch of dried salamis hanging from the ceiling marked 'For Display Only.' Do you know why? If the Board of Health walks in and says: 'That's a meat. What are you doing with this, letting it hang at room temperature? It should be refrigerated.' 'Well, our people are Jews,' they say. 'They've been eating salami for thousands of years, ever since Noah in the Bible, who had salamis hanging from the ark.' Does Essen get away with this? Hopefully, they never sell them to anyone. Why do I teach this course? I've been in the food business for thirty years. One day, long ago, I read an article about a woman who died from sugar toxin forty-eight hours after taking her kids to a fast-food restaurant somewhere in the Midwest. When I read this story I thought: 'Mom took the kids out to dinner and now

A meal to die for if you keep kosher—and even if you don't

these two kids have to grow up without a mother.' I realized that if I could teach classes on food safety I could save lives. That's why I'm here today. I don't want restaurants to kill their customers. This is *nicht git* (Yiddish for 'not good'), like they say in French." Besides teaching about safety and sanitation, there are courses about how to make tasty food, menu design, how to make quality breads and pastries, even career counseling.

A few doors away at 1359 Coney Island, there's Essen New York Deli, for those who want delicious homemade Jewish food that's not exactly low-cholesterol fare. This means—you guessed it— overstuffed and honey-glazed corned beef and hot pastrami sandwiches, golden chicken soup with kreplach and matzoh balls, and a full menu of kosher Chinese food. The last item speaks to the long and venerable lineage of this place, hearkening back to fifty years ago when a place called Schmulka Bernstein's flourished on Essex Street in the center of the Lower East Side. That storied restaurant specialized in making kosher Chinese food taste as good as the real thing while still adhering to Jewish law; the current owners of Essen carry on this strategy. The results taste pretty good. But the real draw that packs them in are the traditional Jewish dishes known to insiders in today's more rigidly observant Orthodox community—chulent (a stew of meat, potatoes, beans, and perhaps a piece of well-done kosher sausage); potato kugel, or pudding; and kishke, a beef intestine stuffed with a seasoned filling. I go there on a Thursday, late at night, and find the place packed with young people enjoying the fare their mother might still make.

Across the street, at 1472 Coney Island, is Masbia, a nonprofit soup kitchen for the poor. It has several locations in Brooklyn and Queens and has served millions of meals since its inception in 2005, receiving funding from UJA Federation and other Jewish organizations. As I walk in, a number of people, most of them alone, are eating what looks like pretty nourishing chow at cafeteria-style tables. But Masbia serves others in need as well. After Hurricane Sandy, it provided 20,000 meals, including hundreds of meals served to stranded seniors temporarily placed in a Park Slope armory. Without these types of support, which come also from a vast network of Jewish, Catholic, Protestant, and nonsectarian groups, the city's efforts to feed, house, and clothe the needy would be immeasurably more difficult.

At 1410, a low-key looking storefront turns out to be a Jews for Jesus operation. To convert Jews, go where the Jews are. But in this neighborhood, the majority of the Jews aren't assimilated or open to changing their religion. They're strongly and proudly identified and certainly don't appreciate what's being sold here. Sensitive to such feelings, the place has no sign atop its door, and the display window is partially concealed by a metal grating. But as I peer through it, I spot a small six-inch sign in black Hebrew letters against a white background in the Yiddish language that asks: "What will be a penance for your soul if not Messiah the son of David (a name for Jesus)?" I doubt they can make much progress here, but the challenge is probably attractive. When I ask a passing Orthodox Jew what he thinks about the group, he laughs and looks at me like I'm crazy, which, in a way, says it all.

The Orthodox Jews in Midwood may appear uniform, but they belong to several communities, each with its own distinct identity. Here's a brief primer on how to recognize them. The ultra-Orthodox, or Hasidim, dress distinctively in black hats (with fur ones worn on the Sabbath, other Jewish holidays, and on special occasions) and are discussed in the sections on Borough Park and Williamsburg. The strictly Orthodox also wear black hats, but of a different type, more angular and, pardon the comparison, somewhat similar to hats mobsters from the 1920s and 1930s wore—black fedoras, with a broad brim and a distinctive front pinch. They are worn at an angle when the wearer wants to look "sharp" and with brim upturned when he feels relaxed, among his friends. Both groups believe the wearing of these hats and black jackets and pants, along with white shirts, to be appropriate according to Jewish tradition and law. Then there are the Modern Orthodox. This group wears modern clothing and is more engaged with the outside world; they have declined significantly in this area over the last thirty years. They attend universities, believing in the value of both a Jewish and secular education, and will go to movies, Broadway plays, and social activities where men and women mix. They also believe in the importance of Israel as an independent state, not simply as a country of residence.

Another very large group of Jews came here, not from Europe, but from Muslim lands. Known as Sephardic Jews, they are largely traditional and their levels of observance vary from Strictly Orthodox, to Modern, to a looser traditional version of observance, which is known as Masorati. Most of those living here hail from Syria and first came to Brooklyn around the turn of the twentieth century. There are also smaller numbers of Conservative, Reform, and unaffiliated Jews who similarly make their homes in Midwood. Once upon a time, in the 1940s and 1950s, they were the dominant group. Today, they are dwarfed in numbers by the Orthodox.

I visit the Sephardic B'nai Yosef Synagogue, or "The Painted Shul," at 1616 Ocean Parkway. It looks totally nondescript from the outside, but it's the opposite inside. The walls of the temple are covered with murals painted by Archie Rand, an art professor at Brooklyn College. Most are drawn from biblical stories, like the flood in Noah's times, the giving of the Torah on Mount Sinai, and one of them, of the Western Wall in Jerusalem, even has fake tufts of grass sticking out from it. While not beautiful in its architecture, this synagogue is worth seeing because it's unique. To the members, however, that's not what's important. What matters to them is that hundreds of people come to services there every day of the week.

Each ethnic group in Midwood has its own niche—houses of worship, restaurants, specialty stores, and so on. For instance, at 451 Avenue P, I walk into Vasha-Kniga, a Russian-language bookshop. It is filled with both softcover and beautifully bound hardcover books, from Shakespeare to Tolstoy. There's also a selection of children's books, including many illustrated Russian fairy tales. Altogether there are 18,000 different titles.

"Who comes here?" I ask Yulia. "Mostly Russians, of course. We're one of the biggest, especially on the Internet and the only major one in Brooklyn. When we opened in 1998, there were many more Russians here. We have the same problems with a decline in book readers as other bookstores. But Russians like to read real books. We sell to hundreds of libraries all over the country—Seattle, Chicago, Los Angeles—wherever there are Russian communities."

Enterprises such as this preserve Russian culture for the newcomers who miss it. They also help immigrants bridge the gap between the homeland and the new land. How long will stores like this last? As long as there's a need for them.

Want Turkish or Pakistani food? One can find it in Midwood on Coney Island Avenue as well as in many grocery stores owned by and catering to the Muslim population. Of course, there's no strictly controlled border between Flatbush and Midwood, so the Muslims straddle both communities and attend one of Brooklyn's largest mosques, Makki Masjid, located in Flatbush, just over the Midwood border, at 1089 Coney Island Avenue, near Glenwood Avenue. The Jews and Muslims here get along quite well, with incidents of any sort a rarity. When members of the Pakistani community first began moving here and no halal meat was available, they happily bought kosher food. Both groups believe strongly in the importance of religion, and their women dress modestly. But they avoid flashpoint topics like politics, and they have very limited social contact with each other.

(A) Flatlands Church of God: former
    site of the Gemini Lounge
(B) Amersfort Park
(C) Anna's Café
(D) Yellow brownstone
(E) Tony's Barber Shop

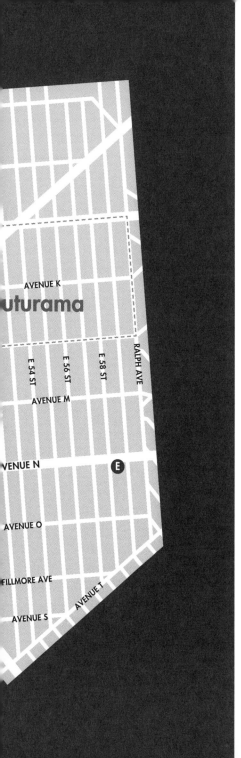

AVENUE K

uturama

E 54 ST E 56 ST E 58 ST RALPH AVE

AVENUE M

VENUE N **E**

AVENUE O

FILLMORE AVE

AVENUE S AVENUE T

FLATLANDS

FLATLANDS IS A STABLE, MIDDLE-CLASS community in southeastern Brooklyn. Its boundaries are Avenue H on the north, Ralph Avenue on the east, Avenue T and Flatlands Avenue on the south, and Flatbush and Nostrand Avenues on the west. It is fairly safe and very quiet, with a mostly black population—predominantly Caribbean people with a strong Haitian representation. Development of the area came relatively late; it was the last town to be annexed to Brooklyn (in 1896). A rural community, it was not developed until the late 1920s.

At one time Flatlands was a white area, with a mostly Italian, Jewish, Irish mix, many of whom eventually departed for the suburbs. As is true of neighboring Marine Park, young Orthodox Jewish families, priced out of nearby Flatbush, have moved here, and their numbers are increasing. Getting to the city via public transportation requires a short bus ride to the subway, and driving in means a trip on the Belt Parkway, which can easily get you to Queens and Long Island, too. There are shopping malls, but not much night life. In short, it's a bedroom community, designed for raising a family and getting ready to move to Florida, Arizona, or elsewhere once the kids have grown up and left.

There's a place in Flatlands near Troy Avenue that is today a church, Flatlands Church of God, at 4021 Flatlands Avenue. The neat two-story brick building (the church occupies the first floor) shows no signs of its notorious past. But a long time ago it was a rowdy bar called the Gemini Lounge, run by Roy DeMeo, a Gambino family operative, who died in 1983. Rumor had it that from the late 1970s to about 1980 victims were killed here and dispatched to the former Fountain Avenue dump in East New York. An estimated one to two hundred murders took place there. Called the "Gemini Method," victims were shot, the blood drained from their heads and hearts, and then dismembered in a basement room. Back in the day there was a live band in the back that may have drowned out the noise of the murders. Today, it's used by the church as a computer room.

This is further graphic evidence of how cities are constantly changing, in this instance, from the Godfather to just God. If you merely walked by the building, you would never know. The bishop has denied knowing about the building's infamous history when he bought it in 1997, but he has no regrets, adding: "I think God sent us here for a reason. After we opened, many of our neighbors said our coming was a sigh of relief. They said if a church is here, God is here, and they could finally sleep at night." He believes the church's presence has saved the souls of those who died here.

Walking up E. 40th Street to Avenue J, I pivot left and arrive in one block at Amersfort Park. New Amersfort, established by the Dutch, was the original name for Flatlands, and the park was founded in 1923. Running from E. 39th to E. 38th Streets and from Avenue I to Avenue J, it's fairly large for a neighborhood park, about 3.5 acres.

There's a beautiful gazebo near the Avenue I entrance, well worth a photo. It features exquisite wrought-iron filigreed musical notes

Amersfort Park—a gazebo pays homage to jazz, rhythm and blues, and boogie-woogie

running around the top of it. On the ground are a series of slates in a circle. In the center of the circle are the engraved words: Celebrating a Century of Jazz—1900 to 2000. Each slate has etched into it different ten-year periods and what type of jazz or related music was popular during that time, accompanied by depictions of the types of instruments used and, in some cases, people dancing to the music. Some examples are: 1910–20—ragtime and Dixieland; 1920–30—hot jazz and boogie-woogie; 1930–40—swing and classic blues; 1940–50—bebop and rhythm and blues—all the way to 1990–2000—mainstream pop jazz.

While the park lacks recreational activities, it is beautifully landscaped and tailor-made for those who want to relax on benches or in the grass beneath shady trees in a peaceful urban oasis. During the summer there are free concerts on the weekends. It is perfectly safe during the daytime. Evening visitors, however, are advised to exercise caution. In fact, the park achieved a certain degree of notoriety, when on August 25, 2011, fifty-six gang members were arrested. They had spread the word via Twitter and other social media about a planned "Crips Holiday," and when they showed up at 7:30 p.m. wearing their blue colors, the police were ready and moved in. This is definitely the kind of cachet neighborhoods seek to avoid.

At Avenue I and Nostrand Avenue I enter an old-style luncheonette called Anna's Cafe and walk into the past. The metal-reinforced, red, plastic-covered revolving stools are there, looking as they did back when I was a kid. The menu is hand-lettered on a signboard, painstakingly printed with a black magic marker—veal cutlet $7.00, manicotti $6.50. There are signs for egg creams, shakes, and frappés, but no prices. Why? No one there knows how to make them, but the owner doesn't want them removed from the list of offerings. One day, this will become an upscale café, but for the moment it hangs on, suspended in time.

My next stop is in front of a well-kept, yellow-brick brownstone just east of Flatbush Avenue on Avenue I. It was built in 1912.

The owner, Serge Numa, an eighty-year-old man from Haiti who fled the brutal Duvalier regime, has lived in it since 1970, when he purchased it from the original owners, a Jewish family. He's a "community character." Everyone seems to know him. In a half-hour period, at least ten people greeted him as he relaxed in a folding chair on the sidewalk.

A tall, thin man, wearing a colorful green-yellow shirt and slacks, sandals, and sunglasses, Serge notes: "I was the first black to move into this street and I got along with everybody. Today, this house is worth a lot more. I was the physical therapist for this family and they sold it to me. The police stopped me and asked: 'What are you doing here?' I told them I was the previous owner's therapist and I'm a Vietnam veteran. I showed them my military ID and they said, 'Okay. No problem.'" Numa is, in an indirect fashion, making a point here, letting me know that his status as a war veteran removed any suspicions the cops might have had about him as a black man.

This is, in fact, the story of the black movement into these middle-class areas: Suspicion, allaying fears, and slow acceptance by most whites, as the years pass. Numa's children are all professionals—a doctor, a lawyer, a successful businessman—the American dream.

I meet a skullcap-wearing Bukharian barber at 5902 Avenue N who appears to be in his late thirties. His name isn't Tony, but above the store window a sign reads, "Tony's Barber Shop." There may be some value in using Tony's name for older Italian men who knew the real Tony. But this barber, who travels here every day from Kew Gardens Hills, Queens, has his own come-on sign next to the first one: "Shomer Shabbos" (Sabbath observer). It's a not-too-subtle appeal to ethnic loyalties, sort of like the old signs that encouraged African Americans to "Buy Black." It seems to be an unwritten rule in the city that you can openly appeal to your own group. Unlike a kosher food establishment, where the man's level of observance matters to customers, it makes no material difference whether the barber keeps the Sabbath or not. But actually, it does matter in a different area—the conversations in the chair. It means a patron has more in common with the barber if he is a similarly observant Jew.

Quite a few working- and middle-class blacks with whom I speak worry that the Orthodox will "kick them out" and take over the neighborhood. These groups don't have much in common, and outreach is limited. The Orthodox want to preserve their culture, and eating together with those from another culture isn't an option because the Orthodox can only eat kosher food.

Whenever I walk into a black church in an area like Flatlands or Canarsie, I can really appreciate the centrality of faith in these precincts. In addition to large houses of worship, there are storefront churches everywhere, sometimes three or four on one block. They can be found on Avenue H in the 40s, and all along Foster, Farragut, Albany, Schenectady, and Troy Avenues. Many are Haitian, filled with people singing, swaying, gesticulating, often waving their hands in the air and undulating. These are the working- and middle-class folks for whom religion is still a constant source of comfort.

The homes here, small Tudors, colonials, and capes, are modest, but well tended and cared for. Interspersed throughout the area are some large spacious residences that would fit in well in the wealthier parts of Brooklyn, like Dyker Heights and Midwood. And there are also brownstones dating back one hundred or more years. One nicely preserved example is a three-story brick structure, built in 1915, at 3415 Avenue I.

Many of the Catholic statues and crèches that adorned the front yards of previously Italian-owned homes are still there, meaning just as much to the more recent black owners, many hailing from the Caribbean. There are signs in the windows proclaiming to all passersby the primacy of God. As I glance at a large smooth stone in a flower-filled front yard at 5502 Avenue I, I'm able to read the inscription: "When you see only one set of footprints, remember, the Lord said: 'I love you, and will never leave you.'" It's neighborhoods like these that challenge the stereotype of black communities as poor, crime ridden, and rundown. Many of the residents are sitting on their porches, relaxing, chatting with friends and relatives, minding their own business, and perhaps yours if you stick around a bit too long.

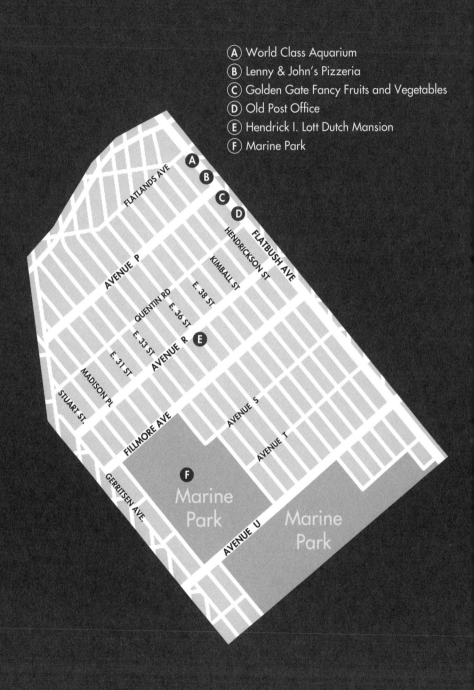

- (A) World Class Aquarium
- (B) Lenny & John's Pizzeria
- (C) Golden Gate Fancy Fruits and Vegetables
- (D) Old Post Office
- (E) Hendrick I. Lott Dutch Mansion
- (F) Marine Park

MARINE PARK

MARINE PARK CAN BE FOUND IN SOUTHEAST BROOKLYN, in a two-fare zone, which means riders of public transportation must take a subway and a bus to get there. The boundaries are Kings Highway on the north, Flatbush Avenue on the east, Avenues V and U on the south, and Gerritsen and Nostrand Avenues on the west. It has a sleepy, old-time look and feel. Like neighboring Flatlands, development only came here in the 1920s. The homes are neat, mostly colonials, ranches, and capes, with a predominantly white population, and the neighborhood is very safe. People know and greet each other on the street, by their homes, and in the local supermarkets and eateries. As one resident put it, comparing it to Park Slope, where she lived before coming here: "Marine Park reminds me of what neighborhoods used to be like before they became advertisements for themselves."[4]

Middle-class communities like this are sometimes resentful of gentrifying neighborhoods. The community folk see them as grabbing all of the attention, which translates into better services and more investment by developers. The president of the Marine Park Civic Association noted that local residents "are constantly reminding elected officials we're here, we're a voting area, we take care of our homes and of each other, and we want to make sure you don't forget us."[5] The problem for gentrifiers is that Marine Park, Manhattan Beach, Mill Basin, and many other nice communities are simply too far away from Manhattan.

As I walk southeast on Flatbush Avenue from Flatlands Avenue, passing fairly nondescript stores—small fruit and vegetable shops, pizzerias, dry-cleaning establishments, a couple of Irish bars, and computer repair places with Russian lettered signs in the windows—I'm a universe or two away from hipster Williamsburg, trendy Cobble Hill, and gentrified Carroll Gardens—no boutiques, no cafés, just ordinary folks. Is there anything here to entice tourists?

And then a sign catches my attention: "World Class Aquarium." Is there really such a place out here? As it turns out the store has a marvelous collection of beautiful fish, some of them rare, like a white red devil cichlid. I meet owner Robert Sackowitz, a man with sky-blue penetrating eyes beneath a full head of white curly hair. He seems a bit bored as I greet him with, "So, is this really as great a place as the sign says?"

"Yeah, look around."

This isn't a big place, like a Petland, but there's a lot in it, notably a large selection of parrots, macaws, and cockatiels, most of them brightly feathered and very talkative, especially when they see my dog. There's also a large selection of custom-built aquariums, something never found in the three-sizes-fits-all chain stores.

Robert and his partner, Allan Roth, are discouraged about the future. A slim, wiry man in his late fifties with thinning straight dark hair, wearing jeans, a plain T-shirt, and work boots, Allan tells me: "I was very idealistic when I was in college. When I was hired to work for a large aquarium, hoping to become a curator, it was my dream job. I loved fish. But I soon discovered that the business was just that, a business. It wasn't about the fish at all. So I got out and went into my own business so I could do what I wanted."

Sounds like another case of burnout. But when Allan began describing the fish in the store he became visibly animated—his voice rose an octave as he spoke: "We have a huge collection of fish. Why? Because that was always my thing. My enthusiasm, and frankly, my willingness to break my ass over the last thirty years to keep these fish alive, whether they sell or not, and giving people advice, honest advice, when they came to me. Most of the people at Petland don't even try to advise you. That's not what they're about. They're about a clerk." I looked into Allan's eyes and saw his passion. He exuded enthusiasm as he grabbed my arm and propelled me toward the

If you love fish, this is the place

fish tanks: "I'm here at the crack of dawn several mornings a week waiting for my delivery. Look at this fish here. It's a black vampire sheatfish. This fish gets as big as you. You can see, he's got really neat teeth."

"You're pretty passionate about these fish," I say.

"Yes, but nobody's interested in this stuff anymore," he said, a look of sadness in his face. But then, when I ask him why he bothers, the sadness washes away, almost immediately. Punctuating the air with his hands, he continues: "I have years and years of what you could call a wet thumb. I know what fish want, what they need. I can't intellectualize it. *I look at the fish and I just know.*"

"What do you know?"

"Whether they're happy, whether they're sick. When their water needs to be changed, when they need medication. I look into their eyes and I can see when they're happy, when they wanna bite me. When they're sad, their eyes get cloudy, they're scratching, they're up near the top. They're doin' something. It has to do with the way they move, a million things, the position of their fins." As I leave the store, I stop by Lenny & John's Pizzeria, a fixture here, with a pretty good reputation.

It's easy to miss a plain-looking fruit and vegetable store on Flatbush called "Golden Gate Fancy Fruits & Vegetables," just beyond Avenue P. My attention was drawn to how old and rickety the place looked, the hand-lettered sign featuring a phone exchange of yesteryear—ESPLANADE 7-2581. Curious, I walked in and literally stepped into the past. John Cortese, a gravelly voiced, ninety-year-old Italian American wearing a faded gray cap came out from a back room and greeted me effusively as though I were an old friend.

John's been in this business since 1939, when he began his career as a helper in his dad's place, same location—a seventy-five-year span. Old crates are scattered about the store, which features an ancient-looking, chipped wooden floor with long thin brownish boards. Above me is a pressed-tin, off-white ceiling divided into little squares. The walls are a shade of green that you don't see today. The only thing that's new are the fruits and vegetables, which seem to be quite fresh. The walls are lined with photos of politicians, entertainers, and professional ballplayers—Tony Bennett, Rudolph Giuliani, Billy Eckstine—as well as former customers.

"You've got one of these old black rotary phones," I remark. "How come you don't get a new one?"

"I like this because when I drop it, it doesn't break. Nuthin' happens. Pick it up, you'll see. I've had this phone more than fifty years."

Everything in this place seems to be trapped in a time warp—the old checkered shirt, the scales, the photos of his family. I think to myself that John is happier than Allan because he enjoys living in the past instead of mourning its passing. No one has forced him to change, and he's still doing what he wants to do—selling and socializing.

On the Marine Park–Flatlands border on E. 45th Street, I stand in front of an old post office, since relocated a few blocks away, on Flatbush Avenue. Painted on the brick, one-story, simple building is an amazing mural consisting almost entirely of postage stamps, mostly imagined, from various eras, with the stamps' cost on date of issue—5¢, 17¢, 36¢, and so on. As far as I can tell, it is the only such painting on a post office in the city, perhaps in the country. They bear the likenesses of many icons of American culture—Elvis Presley, Barbra Streisand, Dwight Eisenhower, JFK, FDR, Martin Luther King. There are also stamps depicting postal workers at various jobs; MIA stamps; a humane treatment for animals stamp, featuring a spaniel; and likenesses of Brooklyn Dodger greats, always a Brooklyn staple for nostalgia buffs, and one for Lou Gehrig, and yet another for Roberto Clemente.

This kaleidoscopic tribute to America was created in 1997 by mural artist Bonnie Siracusa. This exhibit speaks volumes about what slices of Americana matter to the locals. If you spent some time here in a local tavern, chatting with the regulars, as I did, these would be up there as topics of conversation: going to games at

Ebbets Field as a kid; Kennedy, Eisenhower, Elvis, Vietnam, and, more recently, the war stories of combat veterans who served in Iraq. One group that isn't really into this is the Orthodox Jewish community, which is beginning to make some inroads along the western edges of Marine Park. Most of these folks are simply too young to remember the cultural benchmarks and symbols of the older generation. In addition, their interests center more on Jewish music and Jewish education, with some of their stricter members desiring only limited contact with the outside world. They don't clash with the current majority; they just move in different circles.

On 36th Street, near Avenue R, I pass a well-preserved historic Dutch mansion, the Hendrick I. Lott house, dating back to 1800. I'm on my way up to Marine Park, Brooklyn's largest park. It's 798 acres, just 50 acres smaller than Central Park, and it extends from Fillmore Avenue all the way to Jamaica Bay. There's a Salt Marsh Nature Trail near the entrance at Avenue U that extends for miles, has spectacular vistas, and is home to an amazing array of birds— red-winged blackbirds, egrets, herons, ducks, and marsh hawks, to name but a few. There's also a golf course, bocce courts, boating, cricket fields, and bicycle trails. In general, the marshes, with their eight-foot-high reeds and other bushes and trees have a natural beauty that cannot be duplicated in manicured botanical gardens and parks with carefully laid-out paths and large fountains and statues.

Even sports can have religious undertones, I discover. One of the more interesting, perhaps unique, connections between sports and religion I witnessed occurred at a bocce game I was watching. A participant watched another player make a beautiful shot, the ball nestled tightly between the wall and the other ball. "Wow," he exclaimed. "He nailed it to the cross!" And then he repeated it for emphasis. The speaker knew that those in the game were almost surely Catholic, predominantly of Italian heritage, and would appreciate his metaphor, though some Catholics with whom I spoke later found it a bit off-putting. In this way, he expressed the group's solidarity and identity, linking them religiously and declaring it to be a comfort zone for all, a place where they can say what they want without offending anyone. As such, his comment was more than "just a way of talking." I found myself thinking, "Here's a guy who's really comfortable in his own skin. He knows that I, an outsider, am watching the game and I'm standing two feet from him. It makes no difference to him, perhaps also because he's with his friends."

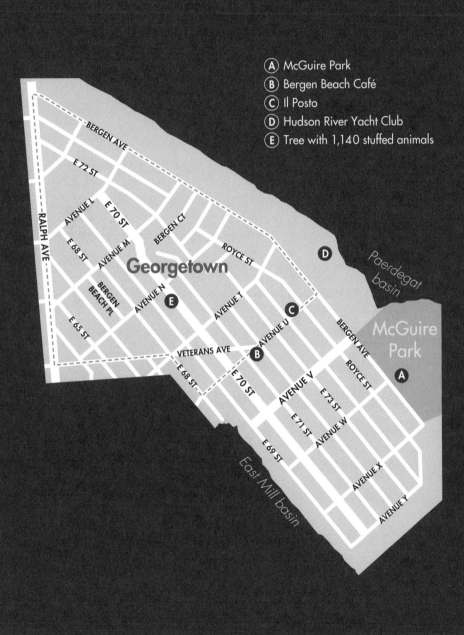

A McGuire Park
B Bergen Beach Café
C Il Posto
D Hudson River Yacht Club
E Tree with 1,140 stuffed animals

BERGEN BEACH

BERGEN BEACH, ALONG WITH ITS NEWER SECTION, GEORGETOWN, is one of, if not the, quietest neighborhoods in Brooklyn. Situated on the southeastern edge of the borough, its boundaries, roughly speaking, are Bergen Avenue on the north, Avenue Y on the east; Veterans Avenue and E. 68th and 69th Streets on the south; and Ralph Avenue on the west. Originally an island, it was settled in the 1600s by Hans Hansen Bergen, a Norwegian. It was connected to the mainland in 1918 as a result of a landfill project. At first, it was a resort area with rides and other amusements. But it couldn't compete with nearby Coney Island and became instead a small residential community of private homes. It remained relatively isolated until the 1960s when construction began on a development known as Georgetown. These were, for the most part, multifamily semiattached and attached houses.

Bergen Beach proper has mostly private homes, some of them quite large, and walking the tree-lined streets is a pleasant experience, especially as you take a stroll up shaded Royce Street. The population is mostly Jewish Russians and Israelis, as well as Italians. It is also home to the privately owned Jamaica Bay Riding Academy, just off the Belt Parkway. Shopping is minimal and there are only a few eateries, mostly on Veterans Avenue and Avenue U, and a shopping center in the Georgetown district on Ralph Avenue, between Avenues K and L. The Mill Basin area, which has lots of dining options, is also nearby.

Will this area be discovered by the restless masses of New Yorkers looking for the next hot place in which to live? Doubtful, since it's so far away from everything. The title of a 2011 article in the *Wall Street Journal*, "Bergen Beach: Connected but Still Remote," says it all.[6] Still, for those willing to rely on the automobile or bus service, the tranquility of Bergen Beach will continue to be a draw for a certain segment of New Yorkers. In fact, hundreds of new homes have been built in the area since 2000. As for public recreation facilities, there's the 77-acre McGuire Park, located at the intersection of Avenue Y and Bergen Avenue. Here you can play roller hockey, tennis, volleyball, football on artificial turf, and can choose from five baseball fields. The beaches and trails off the Belt Parkway, in the Gateway National Recreation Area, are operated by the US National Park Service. This is the nation's largest urban refuge located within a city. It is a paradise for bird lovers; many varieties are on display in their natural habitats. Boats are also available for rental for those who wish to kayak or sail on the grassy marsh inlets.

As I walk through the Georgetown section of Bergen Beach along 70th, 71st, and 72nd Streets, I see newly constructed, semi-attached homes. They look attractive. I pass a seven-story apartment building, one of very few, which was built against the wishes of the neighbors who disliked the idea of an apartment building next to them. A popular local joint along Avenue U is the Bergen Beach Café. A more upscale establishment that has won uniformly rave reviews is Il Posto, at 7409 Avenue U. What caught my attention while perusing Yelp were the comments by one woman who dined there: "So why [only] 4 stars if the food was so delicious? The service is good. The decor is plain, but clean. But there is just a certain something I cannot put my finger on. The vibe seems dull. It is by far, a neighborhood place with a mixed crowd, but most of the patrons are 'mature.' If you are looking to eat traditional Italian fare, you will definitely NOT be disappointed, but the remoteness, lack of people-watching, and hip vibe dominate for me."

Her comments speak volumes about the unattractiveness of living here for younger people and gentrifiers. The area could draw a younger crowd, but it seems that most such residents would be families with children to raise.

Avenue U becomes very residential on the last few streets before it dead-ends into Bergen Avenue. There, across the street, at 2101 Bergen Avenue, is a long dirt road leading to the Hudson River Yacht Club. It's been around since 1873 and has an active membership and an event space. What I like about it is the splendid physical isolation. Even though there are homes two blocks away, I can't see them. It feels like I'm in the Pine Barrens of New Jersey as I gaze at the tall grass, marshes, and the waters of Jamaica Bay.

At 1430 E. 70th Street I stop short. In front of a semiattached brick home is a most amazing tree, amazing because it's filled with stuffed toys of every type of creature in a wild variety of colors. The entire trunk and virtually every branch is covered with the toys, which are tied on with twine. They range in size from as small as five inches to a huge, larger than life Husky dog, a giant bright yellow banana, TV characters like Sponge Bob and Elmo, Mickey Mouse, Woody the Cowboy from Toy Story, Oscar the Grouch, and so on. On top of the tree is an improbably blue-colored large gorilla.

Eugene Fellner created this spectacle. He's a wiry, gray-haired man, with a small handlebar mustache and long sideburns. He's wearing a black and white bandanna and a white T-shirt. Eugene's a recently retired hospital administrative employee who graduated from Brooklyn College in the early 1970s. He majored in sociology, but adds: "I majored in stayin' out of the Vietnam War. These were the days of Kent State. I remember us takin' over the school president's office, drinkin' his whiskey and makin' calls to Australia. That was probably the only time I ever drank such good stuff."

But his greatest love is his tree, which was once just a plain old cherry tree. Not everyone shares his enthusiasm. His neighbor so dislikes it that he built a solid white fence—Eugene derisively refers to it as "the Berlin Wall"—so he wouldn't have to look at it. There's no accounting for taste! As luck would have it the neighbor is just emerging from his car, and Eugene is getting ready to say something to him. Sensing an altercation in the making, I distract him by asking him about his collection. Eugene informs me that at last count

1430 E. 70th Street—1,140 stuffed animals hanging from a cherry tree

there were 1,140 of these toys. A hand-lettered cardboard sign on the tree reads: "Welcome to the World's Most Famous Tree."

Eugene happens to have a terrific memory, and it is a part of his persona. He rattles off facts and figures at the slightest prompt. He can tell me the exact dates when US presidents served their terms, license plate numbers of his neighbors and friends, telephone numbers, and don't get him started on the professional baseball stats going all the way back to the 1950s of any team, not just the Yankees, who happen to be his favorites. I begin by querying him: "How did this collection start?"

"The first was the tiger with sunglasses. I began in 2007. And he looked so realistic. He was just lying around waiting to be thrown out. So I rescued him and put the glasses on him. This is much better than the cherry tree because in July the cherries start getting rotten and fall off. So who needs that? After a while word got around and people just began bringin' me stuff, puttin' it on the lawn even when I wasn't there. What's really incredible is that no one's ever vandalized it in all these years."

"Some of these are really high. How did you do that?"

"Some guy I knew, a lumberjack, used to climb up there, but I think his wife told him not to do it no more, so he don't go up there no more. I use a ladder from a truck to get to the higher spots when I've run out of room further down. Look at this doll of a girl. I press a button and she's singin'." Yes, she is, a version of Olivia Newton John's song, *Let's Get Physical*. Eugene uses this as a segue to list a bunch of songs along with the years in which they were first performed.

With his penchant for knowing everything that's happening in his neighborhood, Eugene qualifies as a community character, of which there are many in this city. But there's a price for his help, as he makes clear: "I watch what goes on and I call the police if I see something. But not necessarily. If I don't like you, then I may not take the trouble to call." He laughs, leaving me to wonder if he's serious about that.

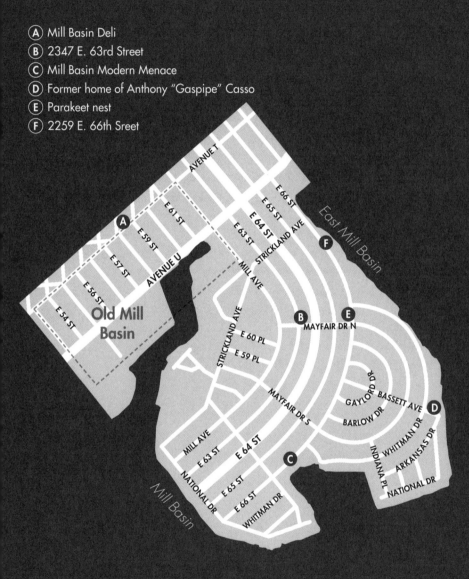

Ⓐ Mill Basin Deli
Ⓑ 2347 E. 63rd Street
Ⓒ Mill Basin Modern Menace
Ⓓ Former home of Anthony "Gaspipe" Casso
Ⓔ Parakeet nest
Ⓕ 2259 E. 66th Sreet

MILL BASIN

COMPARED TO ITS NEIGHBOR, BERGEN BEACH, Mill Basin feels like Times Square, but it's still a quiet, mostly residential neighborhood, deep in southeast Brooklyn. In the early part of the twentieth century, it mostly served industry, with refineries and manufacturing plants like National Lead. There were also some small farms in the area left over from the nineteenth century when Mill Basin was mostly rural. Clammers also found this a lucrative place for shellfish. Eventually, the industrial part died out and residential development began in the 1920s in a small section, called Old Mill Basin, between Avenues T and U, from E. 53rd to E. 68th Streets. After World War II, the southern side of Avenue U, with the help of large amounts of landfill, became the much larger neighborhood, which is today called Mill Basin. The boundaries of Mill Basin/Old Mill Basin are Avenue T to the north and the Mill Basin Inlet to the east and south, and, on the west, the Inlet and National Drive.

Mill Basin is home to Brooklyn's largest indoor mall, Kings Plaza Shopping Center, along Avenue U, built in 1970. The mall is pretty straightforward, nothing especially exciting, unless you want to count the drawing for a Mercedes that was parked on its ground floor when I visited. The mall is anchored by Sears, Macy's, and Best Buy, with other large stores nearby. It can boast of being the first Sbarro location in the nation. As you ascend the ramp to the parking area, you can enjoy a nice view of nearby marinas. There are also small shopping areas farther up Avenue U, on Avenue T, and along Veterans and Mill Avenues. Most of the residents are white, with some Asians, and a good number are immigrants. Economically, it's a mix, ranging from working-class folks residing in simple-frame and fully, or semiattached brick houses, all the way to people living in large opulent homes, some boasting indoor pools and elevators.

In Mill Basin, these homes are called McMansions. For recreation there's Marine Park, entering on Avenue U, one of the city's finest, or the much smaller, but still attractive Alex Lindower Park, along Mill Avenue.

It sits there, sort of in the middle of nowhere, amid a one-block-long row of small retail shops on Avenue T—a Chinese take-out joint, an Italian ices shop with a huge selection of flavors including cantaloupe and honeydew, and a nail salon. But it's far from unknown to a subset of Jewish deli aficionados. The Mill Basin Deli is in the top tier of kosher delis nationwide and is one of the last of its kind. Once there were hundreds in New York City alone, their neon Hebrew National or Isaac Gellis hot dog signs beaming out a welcome to all who passed by. Today there are only two left in Brooklyn, the former heartland of this type of establishment. The offerings include kishka, knishes, sweet and sour tongue, brisket, chopped liver, and pastrami, which a *New York Post* article hailed as even better than the renowned Katz's Deli version. I speak with Jordan Schachner, the manager, a thirty-something man whose father, Mark, is the owner, and whose family has owned delis for three generations: "You don't find many delis like this," he tells me. "We got pastrami for the belly and art for the eyes. You can buy paintings by Erté, Chagall, James Rizzi, and other famous artists. But the deli is a dying business, sadly. If we didn't own the building, we probably wouldn't be here."

"Do you like doing this?"

Jordan ponders the question for a minute, looking out across the street. "Like?" he asks, as though it's a strange question. "It's a very interesting business. It's a very interesting choice of career. But rather than choosing it, it chose me. I guess it's in the blood. But I'm into the artwork as well, which we sell. Anyway, I do several things, the deli, the artwork, and I do real estate." Jordan seems ambivalent. He feels loyalty to his family but he wants to do his own thing too. And this is how he resolves it, by doing both.

For some communities, boating is a central unifying theme and the main reason why members live there. Gerritsen Beach, Bergen Beach, Sheepshead Bay, and other similar areas are distinguished by the number of boats in the nearby water and in the driveways of many homes. Mill Basin, with lots of waterfront property, is typical, boasting more than two hundred private docks.[7]

What is interesting is that this activity automatically expands the horizons (no pun intended) of its residents. It's different from having a subway or bus, because the boats aren't just modes of transportation. They're part of a lifestyle, one that's mobile, one that gives its users the opportunity to get away from it all by going out to sea, where they can relax on their decks and commune with nature. Yet, at the same time, they can easily return to where they live. This shared sense of freedom binds those who avail themselves of it in a way that transcends ordinary activities, for it means they have a pleasurable secret that can be shared and appreciated only with those who have experienced it.

In the 1970s and '80s, most of Mill Basin's homes were modest, and many still are. In recent years, however, the area has become popular with successful immigrants hailing from a variety of lands— Russia, Israel, China, Egypt—who are looking for grander houses and a place with a strong sense of ethnic identity. Location probably plays a role in a decision about where to live, at least for some, since Brighton Beach, an area of first settlement for Russians, both Jewish and non-Jewish, is not far away.

I come across an extraordinary array of large beautiful homes as I walk down E. 66th Street and go up and down Mayfair and Bassett Avenues where they intersect with E. 66th. I also stroll down Barlow and National Drives, and several other streets in this section. On each block, I find several houses worth looking at. At 2347 E. 63rd Street, on the corner of Mayfair Drive, there's a huge, stunning, brick and concrete home with a black mansard roof. There are French doors, pretty keystones, and delicate wrought-iron curlicue designs above them. These mansions seem to project the impression

139 Bassett Avenue—if you've got it, flaunt it!

that people with money to burn decided almost idiosyncratically—"I want a pagoda," "I want a gazebo," "I want a cupola," "I want glass blocks," "*I want it all*." Some look ultramodern, while others have traditional motifs. The only way to fully appreciate them is to see them from up close.

To the neighbors of the newcomers, these successes are often fascinating. They talk about the "new Russian millionaires" in the same way tour guides in Beverly Hills gush about celebrities, providing tidbits of gossip and stories about the people and the parties inside these homes. In its glorification of ostentatiousness, it is but the latest incarnation of the American dream that has captivated and motivated generations of past, and now present, immigrants.

Why some groups have a greater need to flaunt what they have than others would make for an interesting study.

Wanting to get an idea of how the nonmoneyed classes view all this, I ask a young salesman for a pharmaceutical wholesaler, whose arms and legs are covered with tattoos, and who's coming home from work, what he thinks of one of these homes. He and his wife rent an apartment in a very modest two-family house: "My wife and I think it's great and so do our friends. We love looking at it. We rarely see the owner. He seems to be Muslim, but that's all I know about him. If you come here Christmas-time, the displays in these homes are really wild. It's also a safe area and there's a nice park down the street. I think these homes are really cool."

But not everyone agrees. Some find them garish, over the top, even offensive. One home in particular, named the "Mill Basin Modern Menace" by the blog *curbed.com*, is at 2659 E. 66th Street. It's bulky-looking, with a hint of art moderne in the design, and has a brownish large strip that zigzags across the front, in no particular direction. The place last sold for over a million dollars.

Another interesting example of a house that makes its mark is a most unusual private home located at 139 Bassett Avenue, where it intersects with Arkansas Drive. On the left as I face the house are four large American flags flying in the wind. The house, four stories high, is made of light gray cement, with squares and rectangles on the exterior. There are also silver-colored, metallic, abstract sculptures in front of the home. On top of the house is a sculpture consisting of graceful, flying silver birds. The windows feature wavy-looking lines on frosted glass. The grounds are decorated with a bright-red Calder-like stabile, as well as statues of children frolicking in the grass. A large boat sits in the back, next to the water, framed against a brilliant blue sky.

Viewing this extraordinary home is a surreal, memorable experience. Who owns it? An Italian American family that purchased it from the mobster Anthony "Gaspipe" Casso. The family members, the Turanos, are sort of "public community characters," since they also have a very close relationship with former state senator Carl Kruger, who was convicted of corruption. Kruger has reportedly been a frequent guest at their home. I ask several neighbors about the unusual design. If anyone objects to it they're not willing to say so openly. Typical of the reaction is the following comment: "Anyone can do what they want when it comes to designing their homes, even if someone else doesn't like it. They paid for it and it's their own business, not mine."[8]

I hear screeching noises as I approach E. 66th on Mayfair Drive. I look up and see six or seven brightly colored monk parakeets circling around and alighting on top of a large telephone pole. They've built a huge nest. Most people are accustomed to seeing such splendidly colored birds in zoos or as pets in private homes. But this is Brooklyn. The parrots are a fixture in the borough and presumably prefer the telephone poles because the wires provide warmth for their babies when they are in the nest. Nature makes appearances in the most unusual places in cities because cities possess elements of both rural and urban life. Parks sometimes teem with wildlife, coyotes can be nuisances, and so on.

The last and, in a way, most intriguing house I come across is at 2259 E. 66th Street. It's under construction and encased in bright yellow building material. What's intriguing are what looks like two three-story high, very large, yellow, half encircled wheels on each side of the front of the house. The flat, normal-looking center includes an entry, on top of which are two unfinished Juliet balconies. As I continue to stare at it, I notice that the back of the house, facing the marina, slopes very sharply down, making me think of a giant wave. I learn that it's owned by a Chinese couple, but no one seems to know anything about them. I ask people passing by what it looks like and get a variety of responses. One elderly man says it looks like it was made according to the principles of feng shui, a Chinese system of positioning a building to harmonize with the forces of nature. A woman opines that it looks like "a giant beast about to lurch forward." Perhaps it's a take-off on William Butler

Yeats's poem about anarchy, "The Second Coming," which contains the immortal concluding words:

> And what rough beast, its hour come round at last,
> Slouches towards Bethlehem to be born?

Only in this case, it's slouching toward the inlet behind E. 66th Street in what might be called a case of architectural anarchy!

SUNSET PARK

BOROUGH PARK

BAY RIDGE

DYKER HEIGHTS

BENSONHURST

BATH BEACH

SUNSET PARK

THE BOUNDARIES OF SUNSET PARK are 17th Street on the north, Eighth Avenue on the east, 65th Street on the south and First Avenue on the west. Until the early 1960s it had a large Scandinavian population. Sunset Park—an interesting place with lots to see—has all the grit of city life along with some quiet areas, as well as a varied population.

It should be seen in four sections, which sometimes overlap geographically. First, there's Green-Wood Cemetery, a national historic landmark that's worth an entire day's visit if you've never been there. It has nothing to do with the area's population because it came first, in the mid-nineteenth century. Second, there's the industrial area, running from Fourth to First Avenues and from 17th to 65th Streets. Every kind of industry is here, along with lots of old-style factories and warehouses that recall the era the when manufacturing was king. The third section, the Hispanic area, is located between Second and Sixth Avenues, with a commercial street, Fifth Avenue, that runs the length of Sunset Park. The side streets between Fifth and Seventh Avenues actually contain a mixture of Hispanic and Chinese residents. In the fourth section, from Seventh to Eighth, the population becomes predominantly Chinese, extending beyond the current Eighth Avenue informal border into Borough Park about halfway, give or take, toward Ninth Avenue. Simply put, this area is in flux, and Sunset Park's Chinese people are competing with Borough Park's Hasidim, because both populations are growing and need space. In the midst of all this is the outdoor recreational jewel for which the neighborhood is named, Sunset Park, situated between Fifth and Seventh Avenues, running from 41st to 44th Streets.

Green-Wood Cemetery, whose entrance is at 25th Street and Fifth Avenue, isn't exactly unknown, but even many who say they've heard of it think it's just a cemetery with many famous people buried there. They're right about that. Among its "occupants" are Henry Ward Beecher, Leonard Bernstein, Samuel Morse, and William "Boss" Tweed. As early as 1860 it was a tourist attraction with 500,000 visitors annually. I could spend days enjoying the lakes, ponds, and vistas. There are concerts, historical commemorations of Brooklyn's storied history, plays, trolley tours, and lots more. People may find it unnerving that a cemetery, normally a "quiet as a tomb" place for reflection, should be used for such purposes. But it is a National Historic Landmark that both teaches and inspires the multitudes who visit it annually.

Sunset Park's industrial area has the feel, in many places, especially along First and Second Avenues, of being transported in a time machine back to the World War II period and even earlier. The old, huge factories, set in dull colors of gray and off white, loom over the streets, many of the small windowpanes are cracked or missing entirely, and there are few people to be seen in the streets at any time. Some of the streets are still cobbled and have railroad tracks running on them. In those days this was a vibrant place and the side streets, with their small row houses, were home to the thousands of people who worked there in the old Bush industrial park and the

Army Terminal, loading and unloading cargo and shipping army goods. When the war ended, the area declined as heavy industry became less important, and as ports in New Jersey replaced the ones here and more goods were shipped by truck.

Today, First and Second Avenues, plus Third Avenue, where the Gowanus Expressway (a misnomer if there ever was one because traffic almost always crawls on it) runs overhead, are mostly devoted to light industry and supply stores—janitorial services, uniforms at wholesale prices, kitchen cabinet repairs, pipe supplies, trucking companies, tools of all sorts, alarm places, plywood, doors, glass, contact glue, packaging companies, auto repairs. Then there are some unusual enterprises—a spa that teaches relaxation techniques and a Muslim funeral home. At 39th and Second Avenue, there's a "gentleman's lounge," called World Class Cabaret: Peyton's Playpen, next to a hosiery company. Maybe they supply the hosiery for the dancers. The workers need to be entertained and it's common for such clubs to be in industrial areas since they're often not welcome in residential or upscale commercial parts of the city. According to the local buzz, it's a laid back place with "hot girls that aren't especially pushy." Over on First, the railway tracks are still in use.

Fourth Avenue, a heavily trafficked four-lane street, isn't terribly interesting. It's a combination of auto shops, fast food places, and inexpensive retail outlets, but St. Michael's Church, near 42nd Street, is a standout. The Byzantine and Romanesque revival building, with a tall, white dome, is one of Brooklyn's tallest. This church, and Our Lady of Perpetual Help, an imposing granite structure on 59th Street and Fifth Avenue, Brooklyn's largest house of worship, are both worth seeing.

Fifth Avenue is the commercial spine for the area's large Hispanic community, made up largely of Puerto Ricans, Mexicans, Dominicans, El Salvadorians, and people from other Latin American countries, along with a smattering of Gujarati Indians. At 755, there's a place called Baked in Brooklyn. It's spotless, with a big picture window through which I can see bakers hard at work, who smile shyly when I wave hello to them. The breads are fresh and tasty, but is there anything unique about Brooklyn baked bread? Perhaps not, except for one thing. Many people tout Manhattan's drinking water; Brooklyn's water is wonderful too. As one customer explained to me: "It's the water that's so great. A couple a blocks down, a guy who had a pizza shop got tired of the rat race and moved to the Poconos in Pennsylvania. He opened a place there and it failed. It took him a while to figure it out. You know why? He said the water was no good. To make good dough you gotta have good water and we have the best."

Sometimes an entire park, which is officially open to the public, becomes a venue for a particular group. Sunset Park in Brooklyn anchors the Chinese community in which it is situated. It appeals to people of all backgrounds, yet Asians seem to find the park particularly enjoyable. On one visit I saw middle-aged men and women doing yoga and tai chi. One man explained to me, "This is part of my culture and it is also very healthy. You should try it." The park boasts six world-class Ping-Pong tables contributed by a Chinese donor. On a Thursday morning when I visited, all of the players were Chinese, and the same generally is true on other days. Groups of Chinese men use a hilly area near the park's north end to talk and exchange stories. Set high on a hill, the park boasts a terrific view of the Manhattan skyline, the Statue of Liberty, and New York Harbor.

Farther down is an active relic from the past, "Tony's Park Barber Shop, Any Style You Like," at 4409 Fifth Avenue, still offering haircuts and shaves for ten dollars. The sign, which looks original, is faded from both the years and the sun. The name, "Park," is taken from the old Park Theatre that was a half block away from 1915 until 1965. Inside, Tony does his thing, as he has for over half a century. The green chairs look like they did when I was a kid. Vitalis and Wildroot hair tonic are still around, though the bottles are now plastic rather than glass. An old photo hangs on the wall attesting to how unchanged it all is. Next to it is a photo of the more recent Sopranos. There's a pressed tin ceiling, so common in the old days, and the customers on a hot summer day are elderly white men who look like they've stepped out of central casting. Tony says: "I been doing this all my life and the customers are still comin' in so somethin' must be right. But each group likes their hair different. The Scandinavians liked it one way and now we have the Spanish people. I got nuthin against the new immigrants. Hell, I was one too. But they gotta be willin' to work, that's all."

This raises the question: why do some remain in a neighborhood after it changes and how do they decide to do so? For some it's a fondness for the familiar, a dislike of change, or ties to the borough or city as a whole. Others were just so good at their craft that the customers kept coming.

A little farther down I walk into another store from that pressed-tin era—Frank's Shoe Repair at 4515 Fifth. Frank, a genial bespectacled eighty-one-year-old man with a strong Italian accent, and wearing a casual, long-sleeved navy-blue shirt and matching work pants, looks up from his table, where's he's hammering a heel into a shoe. A sign on the wall proclaims: "We Repair Everything But a Broken Heart."

The place is cluttered with pieces of leather, soles, pocketbooks, plus a dust-covered but still functioning wall clock. A sign reminds me of an old brand, Cats Paw, another of one called Neolite. There's also another nonworking wall clock and a grandfather clock, next to which a roll of wire is attached to the store's back wall at a crazy angle. Below it, my glance falls upon a neatly lettered beige sign against a green background that announces: NEW HEELS IN 3 MIN-UTES. Can Frank really do that? He says so, so it must be true. Two sheets hang down from a shelf, for no particular reason, and boxes filled with junk are arrayed next to them, seemingly in danger of tipping over and tumbling to the floor. A real pro who's been there for fifty-one years, he seems to know where everything is. He's friendly, affable, and a real craftsman.

Frank asserts the neighborhood is better than the '80s when, as he put it, "there were a lotta punks around." The place is dimly lit, and as I look at the contents of the store I again feel like I'm in a time warp. An occasional customer drops in. A sixty-one-year-old, heavy-set, Italian American man has come in for a chat, which is mostly one way, as he tells Frank what's going on in his life: "I gotta have a little operation on my stomach, but I'm too busy workin'."

"Why don't you retire?" Frank suggests.

"What I gonna do all day? Stay home? Then I'll get inta trouble with my wife. You know, I can't believe the crazy prices people are payin' for these houses." This is the topic of the day all over Brooklyn, the seemingly astronomical prices of real estate. But the subtext is always: "From where do they get all this money? And why here when these houses were once worth next to nothing." To people who have been living in the same place for decades, it's unbelievable that these unchanged dwellings could fetch such a high price.

I spoke with Dr. Lisa Coico, president of City College of New York, to get a historical perspective. Her comments shed important light on the nature of the community: "To me, growing up in Sunset Park in the 1960s and '70s was interesting because it was always transitional, even when my parents were kids. I grew up in a big Italian family. The 'neighborhood' was comical since it was all of six blocks. If you went to 53rd Street, there was my father's mother; 47th Street was where my mother's mother lived. Then you went to Sixth Avenue, where some of my aunts and uncles lived, down to about Tenth Avenue. This little area was sort of my world. I attended elementary and junior high school in Sunset Park. When I went to my father's mass in September, I walked around there and everything seemed so small. I looked at the stoop we sat on and I thought, 'It looks so little.' But when I was a kid it looked so big."

Time does that and many have spoken of it, as here, in a tone of incredulity. There's a greater meaning too. When you're a child, the whole world seems large and mysterious. In that environment, the neighborhood, which is so familiar, acquires great importance. Coico continues, making it even clearer how this world appeared to her growing up: "In those days you *walked* a neighborhood. No one took a cab, as they do today, for a short distance. And it was such a great place. Fifth Avenue was the spot to go. There were all these little stores where you could get ice cream or candy. My favorite was strawberry ice cream with chocolate sprinkles. We had Melody Lanes, a bowling alley where my cousin Mariellen met her husband." And they both lived in the same neighborhood, just as Coico's parents had. This point is highlighted by Aziz Ansari and Eric Klinenberg in their best-selling book, *Modern Romance*. In the 1950s, they observe, people who married each other were far more likely than today to have grown up within a mile or two of each other.

Yet Sunset Park was different from many other places in the city, even in those earlier times. As opposed to the city's more monoethnic areas then, like Bensonhurst or Gravesend, its ethnic makeup was more varied; Coico recalls it as such: "There were Italians, Irish, and Scandinavians and some Chinese. There were Larsens, Olsens. And then it became Puerto Rican. You could find bodegas where you could get tropical fruits and vegetables that you wouldn't find at the A&P. Of course, my favorite place as a kid, back in the day, was Bella Pizza, near Eighth Avenue and 60th Street. Unfortunately, like so many small businesses, the next generation often had other options and interests, and it's not there today."

The side streets all along Sunset Park, from 18th to 60th Streets have thousands of beautiful two story row houses and brownstones, some in better shape than others. One favorite of mine is a two-story brick home at 530 58th Street between Fifth and Sixth Avenues. Beautiful stone faces are carved on either side of the front doors, one with a man sporting horns atop his head. There is a neat-looking canopy above the door, and five well-tended potted plants on the stairs. The American flag in front of the house is about twenty-five feet high.

At 5722 Sixth Avenue, there is a store with an interesting name—Another Computer Store. "What made you choose this name?" I ask two young techie-type men of Chinese origin.

"Well, when we decided to start this place, people said to us: 'What, you're going to open another computer store? There are so many around here.' And they were right. But a lot of those places have closed since then."

Farther up, along Seventh and Eighth Avenues, are the commercial shopping thoroughfares for the Chinese community. Eighth is more crowded with lots of restaurants, grocery stores, bakeries, and small supermarkets. The best-known restaurant is probably the touristy Pacificana Restaurant on 55th Street, just off Eighth Avenue.[1] But if you're looking for a real insider eatery, the best, in my view, is the Super Lucky Seafood Restaurant at 6022 Eighth Avenue. Despite its name, the seafood and other items are served only at dinnertime; lunch draws a huge crowd for dim sum, a Cantonese dish of small fried or boiled dumplings, which can be an appetizer or main course. When I walked in on a Thursday at 11:30 a.m., the place was packed with maybe 150 people sitting on yellow fabric-covered chairs, all of them Asian, a sure indication of its insider status. Waiters went by the tables in the large dining room with rolling carts of assorted dumplings. The maître d' told me: "We are always full at lunchtime because people love the dim sum."

In the 1980s, those who came here and established Brooklyn's first Chinatown were Cantonese, just like Manhattan's Chinese community. But since then, more and more Fuzhounese have moved here. They are not as well off, and while there have been no open confrontations, the Cantonese are not happy about the overcrowded feel of the community today. Several of them told me there are tensions between the two groups. As I walk the avenues, it is clear

Where "decent" means much more than decent

that this is a very Chinese area, where hardly anyone speaks English well, if at all.

Stores in New York have all sorts of signs, hoping to attract customers. Many of them are grandiose, some would say delusional, for example, "The Best Pizza in the World." So it's refreshing to see one that's modest. At 5801 Fifth Avenue the sign says "Decent Dental Services, Medical & Dental." Not great, not out of this world, or super, just decent. Can this place's modesty attract customers precisely because it's missing the usual outlandish claims? It's owned by a consortium of Indian dentists and doctors, five of them. No one inside knew how the name came about, including one of the dentists.

But not knowing the answer bothered me and it stayed in my mind over the next few days. Researchers like closure. It's a critical goal. So I returned again, this time armed with a copy of my book and a business card, which I hoped would persuade the secretary to grant me a brief audience with someone who knew the answer. Given how crowded the office was with people perfectly happy to see a dentist or physician who was only decent, it wasn't easy. But the approach worked and I was soon ushered into a tiny office, where I met a gray-bearded Gujarati dentist, Dr. J. A. Panchali, who revealed the surprising reason, one I could never have guessed on my own: "When we started this practice thirty years ago, I was looking for a name that would perfectly match the large letters, D.D.S., for dentist. So I came up with Decent Dental Services and that was it."

"But what about, say, 'Dynamic'?" I countered.

"Well, 'Decent' seemed to match up better. We are decent and caring, trying to do a decent job. I'm working very decently, very neat and nicely. And decent is concerned with treating people well. Excellent is a different thing, maybe excellent, maybe not, but decent is a very good thing to be. You know, the prime minister of India, Mr. Modi now, is also a Gujarati. [In Sunset Park] we are, as you may know, a Christian community."

So what can be learned from this experience? First, persistence often pays off. The answer is informative and it's clear that the word *decent* was no accident. Second, one should assume nothing. Dr. Panchali certainly had ample reason to use the name, and he revealed an awareness that calling his place *excellent* might be seen as exaggerated. Finally, English usage among Indians is heavily influenced by the long period of British rule over India. Based on personal encounters with the English and conversations with them, they view the word *decent* as a higher form of praise than Americans do, as in "That was very 'decent' of you."

The last entry for the day in this incredibly varied neighborhood is at 39th Street and First Avenue where, parked in a lot, I notice a stretch limousine, not a new model, painted a bright yellow, to which is attached a large stop sign. The lettering across it proclaims it to be a school bus. And why not? A most unusual type of bus. "Is this luxury transportation or not?" I wonder, as I head home after a long day.

Green-Wood Cemetery
36 ST
37 ST
39 ST
41 ST
43 ST
45 ST
47 ST
48 ST
49 ST
51 ST
53 ST
55 ST
57 ST
59 ST
61 ST
63 ST
64 ST
65 ST
48 ST
8TH AVE
NINTH AVE
10TH AVE
FORT HAMILTON PARKWAY
11TH AVE
12TH AVE
NEW UTRECHT AVE
THIRTEENTH AVE
14TH AVE
15TH AVE
16TH AVE
17TH AVE
18TH AVE
20TH AVE
21ST AVE
Mapleton
A
B
C
D
E
F
G

BOROUGH PARK

IF YOU DRAW A BULL'S-EYE AROUND Brooklyn, Borough Park is at its center. If you're not already in the borough or in mid-Manhattan, it can be a bit difficult to get to, but the trip is well worth it because it's a fascinating place. The boundaries are 36th Street to the north, Dahill Road and McDonald Avenue to the east, 65th Street to the south, and Eighth Avenue to the west.

It contains the largest population of Hasidic Jews in New York City, larger than Williamsburg or Crown Heights. The most prominent groups are the Bobover, followed by the Belzer, Gerer, and Satmar Hasidim. These are all named after the European towns from which most of their followers and descendants came. Boasting the highest birth rate in the city, about twenty-five children per one thousand residents, it has approximately 140,000 residents within a two-square-mile area, and the overwhelming majority are Hasidim. There are also smaller groups of strictly Orthodox, but non-Hasidic, residents. The area also has some Chinese, Russian, Polish, Croatian, and Hispanic residents who work in the area as superintendents, repairmen, or who own small shops that largely service their

McDONALD AVE
DAHILL RD

own groups or who are employed by the larger Hasidic communities in one capacity or another.

Historically, Borough Park was already half Jewish by the 1920s, with the rest of the population consisting mostly of Italians and Irish. In the 1950s many Modern Orthodox Jews lived here, but gradually it became more Hasidic. The Irish population moved to other parts of Brooklyn and beyond; the Italians went south to adjacent Bensonhurst, which had become mostly Italian; and Hispanics settled in neighboring Sunset Park.

The community has many styles of homes. Along Twelfth, Fourteenth, and Fifteenth Avenues are six-story apartment buildings, often of the art deco variety. There are smaller walk-ups, too, and thousands of three-, two-, and single-family homes. A number of these are quite opulent, with columns, archways, pediments, wrought-iron gates, and decorative light fixtures; they can cost $2 million or more. The main shopping street is Thirteenth Avenue, followed by Sixteenth and Eighteenth Avenues. It's a one fare travel zone, with several subway lines running through the area.

As I walk the streets, I am struck by how completely Hasidic it is, the same as I would have observed about black people if I had walked through Harlem in the early 1960s. Most New Yorkers are used to seeing mezuzahs affixed to the entrances of apartments or private homes. These are pieces of parchment with biblical verses inside a metal or wooden case, as prescribed by Jewish law. But in Borough Park they are on the entrances outside large apartment buildings as well, since almost all of the residents are observant Jews and feel it's desirable to have them. They are even on the entrances to elevators on each floor of many public buildings.

My first stop is Breadberry, on the corner of 60th Street and Seventeenth Avenue, a high-end *glatt* kosher supermarket, where I am greeted by a friendly, helpful Hasidic man wearing a black sweater and a white shirt. The store is spotless with wide aisles and attractive light blue, neon-lit signs identifying the deli, bakery, and sushi departments, the last headed by a "Japanese master sushi chef." This and other stores like it are examples of how the Hasidim, lacking the ability to insulate their followers from the outside world, simply incorporate it into their own culture. This way, their adherents don't have to complain about unappealing shopping options, nor do they have to hunt for kosher products in Stop & Shop. Instead, they have their own supermarket where everything's kosher.

The Hasidim do the same cultural incorporation for their children—kosher pizza shops and Chinese restaurants, not to mention the equivalent of McDonalds—Burger Nosh. Ditto for CDs, books, toys, clothing, and so on, all tailor-made for their needs and preferences and compliant with Jewish law. I ask the service manager, Shimshi, what he does to attract customers: "We try to make shopping a nonstressful experience. You can come here and enjoy yourself."

"What do you do that makes them enjoy it?"

"We give them the best service possible. We're friendly and helpful. We have a beautiful place that they like to look at and our prices, while not cheap, are competitive and affordable. And our bread is the best in the world. We make it fresh every morning. Here, try some." I do and it's pretty good.

Breadberry also has non-Orthodox and Gentile clients, as personal observation and a sampling of comments on Yelp revealed. One even complained about the lack of BLT sandwiches (actually, there is a kosher veal bacon BLT). Another noted with pleasure that it's a first-rate shopping emporium that features Danesi coffee at the bar, while a second praised the chocolate babka.

Across the street from Breadberry is the Mapleton (considered a subneighborhood within Borough Park) branch of the Brooklyn Public Library. The first thing I notice as I enter is the computers in use by several young Hasidic Jews, two of whom glanced at me somewhat apprehensively for a moment until they determined, most likely, that I was an outsider to their community. Approaching the librarian, I asked her how often Hasidim used the Internet: "All the time," she said.

"Are you aware," I said, "that use of it for nonbusiness reasons, like reading the newspaper, videos, and the like is strictly forbidden?"

"I am but we're a public library and they can read anything they want. And to tell you the truth, this is clearly more dangerous for their people than watching TV, which they're also not supposed to do, because you can see everything on the Internet." The community continues to discourage such activity. There are even "kosher" cell phones—phones that only allow users to make and receive phone calls and text messages, but prevent access to online programs, except for sites like Talmud classes. It's unknown whether more use these phones or opt for those with Internet access. Many might have both, the bland version to indicate to others their piety and the worldlier one to use when no one's around except for those they trust.

Restricting access to forbidden worlds is nearly impossible in this age.[2] An estimated 5 percent of the population do leave the Hasidic world for a more secular life, and many more imbibe from American culture while remaining within the community, like those I saw in the library at the computer terminals dressed in traditional garb. In recent years there has been a spate of books, mostly by women, who have, as the Hasidim put it, "gone off the *derech* (path)." This branch of the library has some of these books. Looking at her screen, the librarian finds one and continues, "One of them, *Unorthodox: The Scandalous Rejection of My Hasidic Roots*, by Deborah Feldman, was very popular last year." Judging from the numbers, the community is very strong and prosperous today, but it's not possible to predict what will happen to it in the long run. The library also has a collection of books in Hebrew, including volumes of Talmudic and biblical commentaries.

I walk back on 60th Street to New Utrecht Avenue and turn right. At the corner of 55th Street, I enter Gobo's Café. It's small, crowded, but very clean. I sample the caramel-glazed éclair, which is quite tasty. The owner is Chesky Gombo, a young Jewish Borough

Park resident. He has worked elsewhere in the city in food service and his perspective is interesting. I begin by asking him how Borough Park differs from Williamsburg, another Hasidic-dominated community: "This is what I like about Borough Park. It's not closed in. Here, you see people of all types and so by being exposed to others, the people are forced to be more open. You see Modern Orthodox with smaller, knitted yarmulkes. In Williamsburg, they're friendly, nice people and they have a great system of helping people to get to the hospital and take care of them. I lived there and I liked the people. But their *shita* (philosophy) is to keep more to themselves. So things are much more narrow there."

"Is this always going to be the case, these attitudes?"

"I think things are already different among the younger people. The reason is that younger people all grew up with the same things in America—the Internet, music, iPhones, clothing, cars, playing ball. Look, they all like pizza; they all like a *heimische* (traditional, like in the old country) challah, not one with fancy raisins. If I'm doing business with a person my age, we have at least some things in common." This suggests that the outside world does intrude into their consciousness somewhat. It must, for the Hasidim interact with its members.

Brooklyn overall has plenty of all-night spots, Borough Park included. At 55th Street I angle right onto Thirteenth Avenue (New Utrecht is a diagonal thoroughfare) and two blocks later I come to a hangout on 53rd Street and Thirteenth Avenue featuring grocery stores open 24-7 and a SUBWAY-style kosher restaurant. The centerpiece is a synagogue, called Shomer Shabbos, where prayer services are held day and night. But Shomer Shabbos is also known as a place where people can bring food left over from parties or whatever food they have in their homes, drop it off at the synagogue, and it will be gone in an hour, picked up by needy people.

On Fourteenth Avenue and 45th Street, I peer through the window of Artistic Gallery, an art store, and am struck by a painting of gently rolling hills and woods, with a river winding through them.

What's striking is that it empties out into a 3-D waterfall with real water, made up of blue plastic strips that end in a deep pool of water. It's surrounded by rocks and other undefined materials, with a small sailboat in front of it. I ask the owner of the shop about it and he tells me proudly: "It's mostly made of garbage, things people threw away, metal, plastic, wood and it looks beautiful. We can set it up in your house." He estimates that it would go for about $5,000, though his eyes lead me to believe that this is wishful thinking on his part. It strikes me that it's an example of unconscious recycling, though he never uses that word. The Hasidic community isn't into art, at least not the type that hangs in the Metropolitan Museum of Art. However, they do buy paintings for their homes. There are no women in the drawings and the scenery tends toward the bucolic— streets, quaint houses, forests, and the like.

One art genre popular in *haredi*, or very Orthodox homes, is portraits of illustrious rabbis, both paintings and photos. Additionally, there may be depictions of the Orthodox community commemorating a traditional event: a holiday celebration inside a synagogue, dancing with the Torah on the holiday of Simchat Torah. The traditional view of art was that it violated the biblical prohibition against creating graven images. This has given way to the opinion that only a fully three-dimensional sculpture of an entire figure is prohibited.

I go over to 1605 41st Street to see Torah Animal World, run by Rabbi Shaul Shimon Deutsch. In the two-story row house, I discover replicas of animals as well as actual pieces of animals, like the foot of a giraffe, based on all the animals discussed in the Bible, Talmud, and other commentaries. The goal is to explain what the Torah (Bible) meant when it referred to them, often in metaphors and similes that aren't so clear. What animals can be used to make a shofar? Is a camel kosher? No, but a giraffe is. The animals, 350 specimens in all, include an elephant, lion, and a bear. Clearly all aren't kosher, but they are used to teach visitors, many of them youngsters, how to determine if an animal is permissible to eat.

Everyone knows about the muezzin's daily call to prayer in the mosque, a familiar sound in Muslim neighborhoods, but what of the siren? Every Friday in Borough Park, a siren goes off to signal the beginning of the Sabbath. Its wail personifies the feeling one gets that Borough Park is a world onto itself, with its own norms and values. While not empty, the streets have so little vehicular traffic on Saturday that driving schools from all over Brooklyn use them to teach their students how to drive and park. By contrast, Borough Park is heavily trafficked during the week because of the narrow streets and the school buses that service the area's many private schools, or yeshivas. Also, parking rules are not always strictly adhered to, earning it the sobriquet of "Double Park."

I walk by an advertisement pasted to a telephone pole announcing a cantorial concert on a Friday night featuring Cantors Moty and Hillel Boyer at the Crown of Israel Congregation, with a suggested advance donation of $25. "Ladies are welcome," but I know for sure they won't be sitting with the men. The Hasidim do not go clubbing, to the movies, or theater, but they have parties within their communities, cantorial concerts, lectures on Jewish topics, outings to parks and lakes, summer camps for the children, and other similar activities. When young men and women meet, it can be for a drink at a hotel or dinner in a kosher restaurant, though the dating period is short, for the couple must decide rather quickly whether to become engaged, something that also requires parental approval.

As I'm leaving the neighborhood I pass by a humorous advertisement for *shtreimel*s, the round fur hats, usually made of mink, that Hasidic men wear on the Sabbath and on holidays and other special occasions. The ad features a group of minks in the forest animatedly conversing with each other in Yiddish. One proclaims in a death wish statement: "Krausz [a store at 4911 Twelfth Avenue that sells these hats] shtreimels are the king of shtreimels in our generation." Another proudly opines: "Look what Krausz Shtreimels has made out of us!" The other responds: "Yes I saw the new shipment and

Krausz—although they surely wouldn't agree, in the eyes of some, these minks are fulfilling a heavenly purpose they are terrific." Humorous yes . . . politically correct, no. The point is that, as opposed to wearers of fur elsewhere, there's no one here to attack them. If there are Yiddish readers who object, the graffiti free ads suggest that they are unconcerned, perhaps even unaware of such issues. And that's what insularity means.

- (A) Owl's Head Park
- (B) Bay Ridge Place
- (C) Foam Center
- (D) Vesuvio
- (E) Salty Dog
- (F) Handmade on Third
- (G) Tanoreen
- (H) Bay Ridge Jewish Center
- (I) "Hansel & Gretel" Gingerbread House
- (J) Lyon Court
- (K) Wogan Terrace
- (L) John P. Jones Park

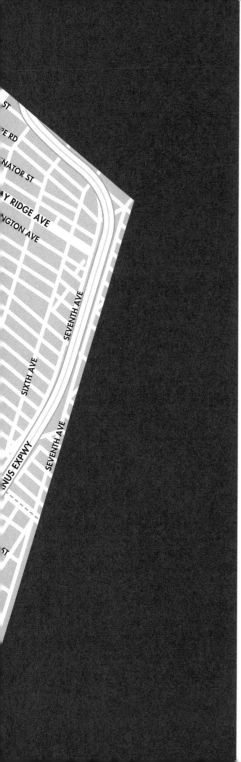

BAY RIDGE

THE ROOTS OF MIDDLE- TO UPPER-MIDDLE-CLASS Bay Ridge are largely Scandinavian, in particular, Norwegian. While most of the original settlers' descendants no longer live in the area, there's still an annual parade up Third Avenue that emphasizes the community's history and culture. It showcases a Miss Norway of Greater New York as it wends its way through the neighborhood, ending in Leif Ericson Park, bounded by 67th and 66th Streets, and Fourth Avenue and Fort Hamilton Parkway. The area has also welcomed significant numbers of Italian and Irish immigrants. Today, it includes a mix of Koreans, Chinese, Greeks, Russians, Jews, and a growing Muslim population, mainly Palestinians, Egyptians, Lebanese, and Syrians.

Bay Ridge's boundaries are 65th Street on the north, the Gowanus Expressway and Seventh Avenue on the east, and Shore Road along the southern and western borders. The main commercial arteries are Third and Fifth Avenues, plus a crowded stretch of businesses along 86th Street. The taverns along Third and Fifth are well known by young people throughout the city as great places to go bar hopping. The Fort

Hamilton section begins south of 86th Street. There's a significant Irish/Scottish presence here, with at least one store, at 9018 Fourth Avenue, offering kilt rentals. Whether or not Fort Hamilton is a separate community from Bay Ridge is debatable since it's inextricably linked to its larger neighbor by geography and the composition of its population.

The area has much that is landmarked, most notably the Senator Street Historic District and thousands of row houses, brownstones, and detached grand-style homes, some of them mansions, along Shore Road. Incidentally, every building in a landmarked district is regulated in the same way as individually landmarked buildings. Walkers and joggers will love Shore Road Park, which runs the length of Bay Ridge, between Shore Road and the Belt Parkway.

Bay Ridge is also well-known in popular culture. It was one of the main settings (along with Bensonhurst and Sunset Park) for the film *Saturday Night Fever*.

Owl's Head Park, located at 68th Street and Colonial Road, is spacious, with wonderful views of New York's harbor and Manhattan's skyscrapers. It's also one of the few parks that has a dog run. But the best feature is the peaceful setting; the landscape has small hills, wooded areas, and well-designed paths. In the Billy Lake Courts playground, there's a nicely done, sculpted cement owl resting atop what looks to be either a Roman column or a representation of a fire hydrant.

On the day I was in the park, I met two groups of visitors that would not normally be together. One was a class of four-year-old Hasidic boys from nearby Borough Park, wearing large black velvet skullcaps that practically covered their small heads. Long earlocks dangling, they sat quietly on a bench as their leader, a Hasidic teacher, explained to me their purpose for coming here—"It's the end of the year, so we just took a bus so they could be outside."

It's important to understand that most New Yorkers feel comfortable going to any park even if it's not in their immediate neighborhood, and the reclusive Hasidim have no hesitancy about traveling to a non-Jewish area to do so, whether it's Owl's Head Park or Brooklyn Bridge Park in DUMBO.

The other group is a class of Muslim middle-school students, the girls dressed mostly in hijabs, playing a game of dodge ball. They're right next to the Hasidic kids and don't give them more than a casual glance. I ask one of them if they would talk to kids from that group. "Sure, if they want to, we'd talk to them." Bay Ridge has a large Muslim community, so this is their home turf. In a way, this is a microcosm of the city as a whole: diversity and tolerance. We tend to think of relations between differing groups as being advanced by programs. Less well known is the impact of chance encounters on peoples' thinking.

Walking east on Bay Ridge Avenue, I come to one of the prettier small blocks in this sprawling neighborhood, Bay Ridge Place, a block east of Ridge Boulevard. The houses here vary in type, and the street is cobbled. The cobblestones were brought over centuries ago when they were used as ballast on ships. The residents like the cobblestones, even though they are badly in need of repair, because they provide character.

At 180 Bay Ridge Avenue, I see an unusual shop called Foam Center. Debra, the middle-aged woman who owns it, cuts foam to size, but she can build anything—cushions, new upholstery, any fabricated materials, whatever. She's an attractive woman with long brownish hair that cascades down her back. She's direct in her clipped responses and sort of makes me feel like she's sharing a secret, no matter what the question. "I've been here for over twenty-seven years. My parents were in this business and now I do it. I do everything, especially one-of-a-kind customized jobs."

"This is a very unusual thing to focus on," I say, looking around at all the stuff that's in here—pillows, backing for wall paintings, quilting, stitching. She also helps people match up items with their walls and rugs. It seems pretty chaotic, but, like Frank's Shoe Repair in Sunset Park, I'm sure she knows where things are or she'd be out

A cobblestone block from the distant past

of business. "I've not seen a retail shop like this in my travels, but you also have other things like wooden masks, drums, antiques, old Pepsi bottles, a strangely shaped walking stick, an ancient-looking mandolin."

"Like I said, we do a lot of things here. And my husband's an antiques collector, so his collection is here as well. But only in a cosmopolitan city like New York could you have a store like this. There wouldn't be enough demand for it in a smaller town."

"I guess you must really love it."

"Not really," she says, to my surprise, a frown beginning to form as she reflects on it. "I mean it's okay but it's so much work. People are always looking for foam. They need it for puppets, for insulation, for art shows. So sometimes you just get tired of it all. I always thought about going into real estate where you can make *real* money, but who's going to hire me at this stage in my life? I have a twenty-four-year-old child, my baby. Today, people want younger employees. My mother got me into this after my kids finished school. She said, 'Why don't you come into this business.' So I did. One thing leads to another. I'm overwhelmed with this, but at the same time I'm comfortable with it."

Debra is a nice person who has probably been doing this a little too long. She sounds tired of the whole thing. While proud of her ability to fix or create things, she feels that somehow she could have done something more lucrative. With her mother's encouragement, she wandered into something that she stayed with because she was good at it and people appreciated her craftsmanship. In short, Debra wants a do-over in life, which, given her stage of life, is not easy to get.

Bay Ridge is, in my view, one of the city's most gorgeous communities. It has miles and miles of brownstones, limestones, row houses, and magnificent large homes, too. The latter are concentrated on Shore Road and on the side streets running from Ridge Boulevard to Shore Road. Along Ridge, Colonial Road, and Narrows Avenue are both private homes and well-preserved and designed apartment buildings. People who live there love it. One woman summed it up as well as anyone: "This place has real history and beauty. You can park here, there's great food, it's very safe. Three blocks away you have Shore Road and you can do an eight mile walk along the water, and the subway is available but runs infrequently enough so it's not caught up in the hubbub of the city. You even have your own Chinatown over in Sunset Park."

Third Avenue is an international thoroughfare, with Mexican, American, Chinese, Japanese, and Arabic food. There's also Vesuvio, near 73rd Street, a well-known pizza parlor that's been around since 1953. Salty Dog is a very popular local sports bar between Bay Ridge Parkway and 76th Street with a large wide open door, at least fourteen TV screens, and a great selection of booze. It's packed on the weekend. A few blocks farther is a lovely gift shop, called Handmade on Third, that specializes in handcrafted gifts from all over the world, some of them exquisite.

Farther down at 7523 Third Avenue, I walk into Tanoreen, a gem of a Middle Eastern dining establishment, perhaps the best one here. It's on the fancy side with a nice decor, linen napkins, and is a real *in* spot for the large Muslim population. It also has a nice selection of vegetarian food. The owner, a Palestinian woman named Rawia Zaatar, who grew up in Nazareth, has copies of her cookbook on display. Rawia greets all of her patrons personally.

The Islamic Society of Bay Ridge is located on Fifth Avenue between Bay Ridge Avenue and 68th Street. On Fridays one mosque on Fifth Avenue is so crowded that worshipers spill out onto the street where they sit on blankets and rugs, blocking the sidewalk. No one seems to complain. It is 1:00 p.m. The men are listening raptly to the loudspeaker that transmits the sermon.

The mannequins in the window of an Arab-run dress shop provide a mirror image of Hasidic Williamsburg. One has no head, another shows the barest outlines of a woman's face, looking as if the features have been filed down. They're wearing traditional, modest Muslim garb, long robes to the ground, with head scarves, some that match and some that don't. But there is adaptation here too. A Muslim woman tells me she lets her child celebrate Halloween because she doesn't want her to be left out of a "fun holiday." The child attends public school.

The Arab population in Bay Ridge is mostly concentrated above Fifth Avenue. A store sign on Fifth tells the story. It's a coffee shop that advertises "Coffee, Tea, Falafel, Carrot Juice, and Hookah," an interesting combination of offerings. Nearby is an insurance company, as well as a dress shop, boutique, and a pharmacy, all with Arabic lettering. Chinese halal restaurants are becoming more popular where there's demand from Muslim residents, and several are located along Fifth Avenue. There are ads for entertainment at a place on the corner of Atlantic and Third Avenue, called Roulette. That area in downtown Brooklyn is a hub of Arab commerce and was an area of first settlement for the community.

There's also a small Jewish presence. The Bay Ridge Jewish Center at 405 81st Street was established in 1919. Over the years its membership dwindled, but recently it has undergone a renaissance, with the arrival of Rabbi Dina Rosenberg, who has been able to attract young families to the congregation. Rabbi Rosenberg also does outreach to the Muslim community. They get along well, in part because it's a mixed community.

Bay Ridge is also home to a one-of-a-kind, though hardly "unknown" home, the "Hansel and Gretel" Gingerbread House, situated on a block-long plot at 8200 Narrows Avenue. Built in 1916–17 in the Arts and Crafts style, which emphasized the use of natural materials, it attracts many visitors from around the world. Currently on sale for $11 million, it has what looks like a thatched, undulating roof, with stained glass windows. Much of the house is made of beautiful solid stone, and the two brick columns at the beginning of the driveway are topped with jagged rocks. They look like crowns and frame the iron gate that leads to the entrance. Interestingly, the former Mafia chieftain Carlo Gambino and his family lived across the street at 8111 Narrows Avenue in a nice, but by no means over the top, home.

The Gingerbread House was bought thirty-five years ago by Jerry and Diane Fishman. Jerry's a tall, fit guy, quick on the draw, with a great sense of humor; he's a man with lots of stories, all of them fascinating. While the house is well known, my interview with Jerry yields much information many people don't know. As we drink iced tea and munch on pistachio nuts in his stunning kitchen, he tells me about himself and the house: "I grew up in Brooklyn, where my father was a builder, as was my grandfather, and so was I. We supplied building materials for the Trumps—Fred and Donald and many other developers. I'm born and raised in Bay Ridge. I'm a member of the Jewish community here and we belong to the temple. There weren't many Jews here. I went to Fort Hamilton High School. There was some anti-Semitism, but nothing like Europe, like what's going on in France today. A kid would call me a dirty Jew, give me a shove, and I would bash him. I can live with that anytime. But there was a lot of antiblack feeling. There were a couple of kids whose fathers were based at the Fort Hamilton army base and they were targets."

"So how did you get the house?"

"We lived in an apartment building not far from here, and my mother tells me that when we went by this house in the carriage I tried to get out to run toward the house. I've loved it since I was a kid; I vowed to buy it and I did, from the Lombardo's. The man was a famous eye doctor. His wife didn't like it. It was too spooky, too scary. I was bidding against the local Greek Orthodox church and I just kept bidding till I got it. I never felt the heat from the local Greek community. Every day I would come home from work and it was $25,000 more. It's a landmarked property and I made sure of that. This has cost me serious money because that means no one can build a twenty-million-dollar apartment complex here, but I feel strongly that it should never be changed because it's of historic importance and the only one of its kind here. It lends real 'character' to Bay Ridge."

Contrary to popular belief, the house doesn't have a bowling alley, nor did bootleggers build a tunnel from the house to the water. But there is an antique 1946 Crosley fire truck in Jerry's basement garage that his father bought for $3,000 on a trip to Kentucky. Interior features of the house include intricate wooden carvings and coffered ceilings, with three-hundred-year-old exquisite stained glass windows, featuring tall English ships with masts and sails, religious icons, and other motifs. Jerry has artworks and collections of all sorts. He's not concerned about possible theft. He has two large rottweilers and other ways to safeguard against that possibility. Incidentally, a tour bus, plus many other visitors, comes by every day. He doesn't mind.

A few blocks away on 95th Street, at number 450, is a six-story co-op apartment building called Lyon Court, constructed in 1937, with a drawing of a lion on the awning. I look up and see about one hundred carved lions above the top floor windows standing on their hind legs, facing each other in pairs and painted a bright blue. This blue color is what caught my attention in the first place. The lion carvings are delicate, and taken together, very impressive and possibly unique. As usual, I wonder what inspired the builder to go to the trouble of creating this. After all, no one driving by, or even walking past it, would notice it unless they happened to look up. I ask the super but he has no idea, despite having worked there for twelve years.

Walking around the corner at Fort Hamilton Parkway, I go up 94th Street and see an exquisite short street called Wogan Terrace with only a few homes. They are all attached English Tudors; this is an excellent example of the many short, dead-end blocks through-out the city that most people, except for residents in the immediate vicinity, are completely unaware of.

I return to Fort Hamilton Parkway and walk south until it dead-ends into John Paul Jones Park at 101st Street, which is situated adjacent to and partially underneath the Verrazano-Narrows Bridge, constructed in 1964. In fact, the eastern tower of the bridge can be seen here at an unusual angle, looking up, one that gives the viewer the feeling it's reaching into the sky. The park is quite attractive and well landscaped, but there is a steady roar of the highway above as autos traverse the bridge. Not so well known is that there was a plan to build a tunnel from Bay Ridge, at Owl's Head Park, to Staten Island. Construction actually began in 1921, during John Hylan's tenure as mayor, but it was never built. Exactly why is not clear.[3] Right now, a water tunnel is in fact being built to Staten Island. Reflecting on this, I'm reminded once again of how the city is always changing. It wouldn't surprise me if one day there were a tunnel for a subway here.

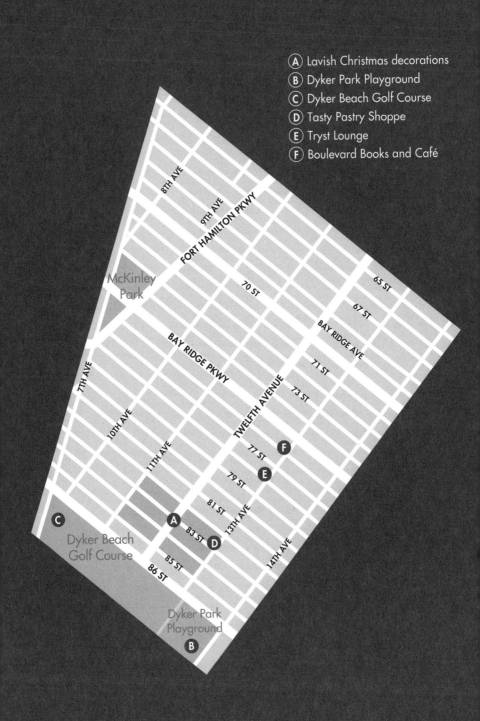

(A) Lavish Christmas decorations
(B) Dyker Park Playground
(C) Dyker Beach Golf Course
(D) Tasty Pastry Shoppe
(E) Tryst Lounge
(F) Boulevard Books and Café

8TH AVE
9TH AVE
FORT HAMILTON PKWY
65 ST
67 ST
McKinley Park
70 ST
BAY RIDGE AVE
BAY RIDGE PKWY
71 ST
7TH AVE
TWELFTH AVENUE
73 ST
10TH AVE
77 ST
(F)
11TH AVE
79 ST
(E)
81 ST
13TH AVE
(A)
(C)
83 ST
(D)
Dyker Beach Golf Course
85 ST
14TH AVE
86 ST
Dyker Park Playground
(B)

DYKER HEIGHTS

SOME WOULD SAY THAT DYKER HEIGHTS is really part of Bay Ridge, but, in truth, it has its own identity. It's an upscale neighborhood with many American and Italian flags side by side, accompanied by Virgin Mary statuettes and nativity scenes. It's bounded by 65th Street on the north, Fourteenth Avenue on the east, 86th Street on the south, and Seventh Avenue on the west. The area was settled by Scandinavians in the nineteenth century. Today, it's primarily Italian American, with Russians and Chinese moving in as well. Except for Thirteenth Avenue, the main shopping drag, it's almost exclusively residential; few buildings are taller than two or three stories.

It takes some effort to get to Dyker Heights, as the nearest subway stop is a mile away. To the outside world it's known for the elaborate Christmas decorations on display during the holiday season. An area of gracious private residences, roughly between 85th and 82nd Streets and from Thirteenth to Eleventh Avenues, is where to see the decorations. People lavishly bedeck their homes with beautiful, expensive decorations—reindeer, wooden soldiers, elaborate wreaths, trees—in a festival of dazzling displays and multicolored lights. Some of them are even motorized, and one wonders if the owners are attempting to one-up each other.

Cars go slowly up and down the streets, their occupants gazing, often gawking, at this million-dollar extravaganza. Many have seen it before but delight in watching the faces of their friends who are experiencing it for the first time. Others willing to brave the cold walk the streets, their feet tripping gaily up and down the stairs in front of these million-dollar homes, a good number of which are palatial, with circular staircases, marble surfaces, and Roman columns and arches.

Boulevard Books—a dying breed puts down roots, and adapts

I have spoken with people from all over the world—Norway, China, Argentina—for whom this neighborhood is part of the itinerary on their visit to New York City during the holidays, an insider's journey that is becoming less so as the word spreads. Is touring the area a religious experience or simply a fun, touristy type of thing to do? Conversations with visitors suggest it's a little of each. A young man from Taiwan, visiting with his wife, said, "We love the lights and the way the houses look. But it's also a way of getting into the holiday spirit, and feeling the joy that Jesus brings into the hearts of those who believe." Less well known is that this place is well worth visiting during the rest of the year. When everything's blooming, the well-manicured, beautifully landscaped gardens are a horticulturalist's delight. Home after home looks magnificent, and it is worth spending time walking up and down the streets, especially those in the 80s between Tenth and Thirteenth Avenues.

In the city's parks and playgrounds, even at 7:30 a.m., there is plenty going on. At Dyker Park Playground, things are happening at this hour. Asian men and women are exercising—tai-chi, deep knee bends, arm circles, jogging. Older men are striding across soccer fields. I also notice a homeless man fast asleep on a park bench, his shopping cart filled with his clothing and a couple of empty Poland Spring water bottles. Homelessness is widespread; the problem is especially sad when contrasted with the city's vast wealth.

The outstanding recreational site in this neighborhood is the well-maintained Dyker Beach Golf Course. For those interested in golfing there, it's a 6,438 yard, par 72 course. It's also a popular site for weddings, communions, corporate events, and parties in general. One woman gushed about it on Yelp: "Everyone kept telling us how beautiful this place was. You would never think you were in the middle of Brooklyn." Not sure what "the middle of Brooklyn" means. That it's urban? That the borough doesn't look like the golf course? Who knows? Whatever, it's a gorgeous-looking course.

I pass by a bakery, Tasty Pastry Shoppe, near 85th Street on Thirteenth Avenue, that claims to have one of the largest selections of sugar-free cakes and cookies in the city. The staff is friendly, and cannolis are their most popular offering. I enter and see every type of mouth-watering pastry. The Italian men kibitzing outside are only too happy to show me around the store; the one who told me to go in insists that he deserves a 10 percent commission for showing me the place. It's all in good fun.

A store at 7912 Thirteenth has an original red-faded sign from the old days reading OPTIMO cigars. Farther along I pass by the Tryst Lounge. What's striking is a small but very well done mural of an American flag along the brick wall of the tavern. What makes it special is that it's so realistic. It looks like it's waving in the air, or in the nonexisting wind, on a brick wall. At 76th Street I glance at the Rising Sun Laundromat, a grandiose and, at the same time, very appropriate name. I also pass Boulevard Books and Café. To find this last of a dying breed at 7518 in a quiet part of Brooklyn is quite unusual. The area is much more likely to have salumerias, bakeries, and storefront medical offices. How does the shop survive? I wonder. The answer is probably service. They have community events—poetry readings, book signings, arts and crafts programs, and book clubs. They also feature an excellent selection of kids books, which is essential in this family-oriented part of the borough. Add to that owners who understand the community and their success is understandable.

As I walk on I pass Italian men sitting on the benches interspersed along Thirteenth, enjoying the early morning sun, chatting, mostly in Italian. Beyond Bay Ridge Avenue, the street has more Chinese-owned establishments. This section could perhaps be called Lower Dyker Heights; it's a lot less ritzy, as a stroll down the residential streets makes clear. Architecturally, the area more closely resembles its neighbor, Bensonhurst. If I had to select a community in Brooklyn that was representative of what Brooklyn was like in the old days—mostly white, family oriented, with working-, middle-, and upper-middle class people, Dyker Heights would be a pretty good choice.

BENSONHURST

BENSONHURST, WHICH BEGAN DEVELOPING around 1915, was originally split 50–50 between Italians and Jews. After World War II, there was a heavy influx of Italians into the area, and the Jewish population began to decline. The area has, in fact, been enshrined as such in popular culture. Among the TV shows that have focused on the Italians, either in terms of street scenes or characters living there, are *General Hospital*; *Mob Wives*; *Welcome Back, Kotter*; and *Saturday Night Live*. And then there are the films, including *Saturday Night Fever*, *The Warriors*, *The French Connection*, and *Jungle Fever*.

The area's boundaries are 65th Street on the north, roughly Avenue P and Bay Parkway on the east, 86th Street on the south, and Fourteenth Avenue on the west. Ethnically, Bensonhurst has undergone great change; the earlier, now aging, population of Italians, Jews, and other white ethnics has left for sunnier climes or has simply died out. Today, it has one of the largest immigrant populations in the city, with significant numbers of Chinese, who have their own version of Chinatown along Eighteenth Avenue and Bay Parkway. In addition, Russians, Albanians, Turks,

(A) Brooklyn Musical Arts
(B) J & V Pizzeria
(C) Acting Out
(D) Golden Bay Chinese Restaurant
(E) Kabbalah Center
(F) Steve's Place

Palestinians, Egyptians, Mexicans, Puerto Ricans, and other groups have also made this area home. This can be seen in the stores along the main thoroughfares, the most commercial being Eighteenth Avenue, and by spending some time in the local parks. Many of Bensonhurst's streets are lined with one- and two-family homes, of which a large portion are stucco, brick, or stone dwellings dating back a century or more. These are augmented by four- and five-story walkup apartment buildings, many of them art deco, art moderne, or a mix of the two. There's also the 5,000-unit Shore Haven complex along Twenty-First Avenue, built by Fred Trump, Donald's father.

At 7306 Eighteenth Avenue (Cristoforo Colombo Boulevard), I come across the Brooklyn Musical Arts center, featuring in its front window a large TV screen showing a young Chinese girl of perhaps seven or eight, dressed in a white blouse and navy jumper. The girl is sitting on a stage, playing a baby grand piano. The repetition of this two-minute scene, looped to play over and over, effectively conveys the school's idea that practice makes perfect and that one must be totally dedicated if one wishes to succeed. I cannot hear the music from the street, but I am certain it is great. In any event it's a wonderful way to sell the school, one of hundreds that, along with test preparation and tutoring centers, have sprouted as storefront operations in Asian neighborhoods throughout the city.

Walking along Eighteenth Avenue, I pass J&V Pizzeria on the corner of 64th Street, a block outside Bensonhurst, but really part of it in the minds of the residents. This place has an excellent reputation for great eats. Vito, a family member who works here, highly recommends the chicken parmesan sandwich, called the Jo-Jo, after his nephew. This naming is a popular form of recognition. It makes everyone happy except, perhaps, those who aren't named. It's no different from the common practice in New York of building owners naming their properties after the first names of children, spouses, or parents. What's the store's secret for success? The usual, from

Vito: "We use the best Italian ingredients, with four different types of mozzarella and great, fresh tomato sauce." Yes, but it's also how the pie is made. And as I've learned over the years, making pizza is more of an art than a science.

Seniors frequently gather in restaurants, parks, and on streets. Physically, Bensonhurst is quintessentially Brooklyn. Some streets are tree lined, others are bare, and most are in between. In this neighborhood, middle-aged and elderly men hang out in front of the buildings, sitting on stoops or folding chairs, or in nearby coffee shops and Burger Kings, where they have their favorite tables. Typically, they are dressed in flannel shirts and plain pants, wearing windbreakers that may read "Korean War Vet" or "Mets," and thick, square work shoes. The words on their caps often reflect where they worked, the beers they favored, and the teams they loved, most often the standard white *B* for Brooklyn Dodgers on their blue, often faded caps. They speak in animated tones, gesturing, laughing, and jabbing each other playfully to emphasize their points. The conversations most often revolve around their families, their work, past and present, and, most important, which team to bet on—the Lions, the Patriots, the Jets, as well as on the ever-changing fortunes of their Yankees and Mets.

And yet the new Brooklyn is in Bensonhurst too, pushing its way into the consciousness of these old-timers. They can't help but notice the passing crowds of Asians and Russians thronging the 86th Street shopping area: the ethnic stores; the multilingual signs; the travel agencies advertising low fares to every corner of the globe; and the restaurants, a veritable United Nations, offering Turkish, Russian, Japanese, Mexican, Peruvian, Chinese, Korean, Vietnamese, and Afghan food. Change has come, and the oldsters know it. Yet for now, they do their best to hold on, clinging to each other for comfort.

While hanging around in candy stores and delis in Bensonhurst, I watched and listened as groups of teenagers from nearby public schools came in, chattering and primping during recess, buying snacks such as Devil Dogs or Wise potato chips and cans of soda. The students were oblivious to my presence, and I noticed that words like "dem" and "dose" rolled easily off their tongues, as did questions like, "Is you'se goin'?" or "Is you'se buyin' this?" These remarks were not made in any kind of mocking or joking tone, and there was no reaction by the listeners, who usually responded in kind. They were a mix of whites, possibly Italian Americans, and Asians. I wondered how these vestiges of what I thought was a vanished past survived. Were they transmitted through families? Clearly second-generation children from Russia and China learned these pronunciations, not from their immigrant parents, but from their American-born classmates.

At 7426 Fifteenth Avenue, I step inside Acting Out, which advertises itself as "Brooklyn's Premier Acting School." The class I watch has about twenty young children enthusiastically participating. Besides acting classes, they offer "Audition Prep," singing, piano, and guitar lessons. I ask the owner why people like his program, and he responds: "All of our people have advanced degrees in acting, directing, etc., just like in Manhattan, but we give you the same for less and closer to home."

The Asians in Bensonhurst (and Bath Beach) hail mostly from Hong Kong. One man, Chakyin, a sixty-eight-year-old recently retired construction worker, has been here for twenty years. He speaks little English because he always worked for Chinese bosses and didn't need to know the language. "How does this affect you?" I ask through a local who has volunteered to interpret for me: "Well, I can't get friendly with my American neighbors except to wave hello, because I cannot communicate with them. I only speak Cantonese."

"Was going to America a good decision for you and your mother?"

"Yes, because the economy here is good and my family is here. My sons have good jobs in the US. Twenty years ago, education was very difficult to get in China. Here they were able to go to university. One is in banking, the other in jewelry."

"Do you ever go to Manhattan?"

"Yes, I go to Chinatown to buy moon cakes because the bakeries there are better. I also go to see my doctor." Moon cakes are a delicacy; they commemorate the Mid-Autumn Festival, one of the most important traditional Chinese holidays.

A ninety-year-old woman, Jia Luo, tells me she spends most of her time playing mah-jongg at a senior citizen's center. She came to the United States because other Hong Kong Chinese were moving here. She's very spry and alert with a ready smile. She attributes her longevity to daily exercise and eating one egg and three spoonfuls of oatmeal every day. She loves the United States because as an old person she cannot work and the government gives the elderly financial assistance. She doesn't miss China because life here is good.

As a group I have found the Chinese I spoke with very happy about their decision to come to these shores. Pragmatically, it's because America has great economic and educational opportunities. They are resigned to not knowing English, but are glad that their children will learn the language.

I'm invited into the modest, spotless home of an immigrant Chinese couple who speak English reasonably well despite having come here only eight years ago in midlife. Two large glossy maps hang on their living room wall. One is of the entire United States with the names of the states and major cities, all of which have been translated into Cantonese. The other is a Cantonese subway transit map. This is a traveling couple. They have vacationed in Maine and intend to see California and the state of Washington, where they have friends. What matters most to them? Ensuring that their children acquire a good education. That's why they left Staten Island. The good colleges, in their view, were in Manhattan, namely, City College of New York. In Bensonhurst, they recommend the Golden Bay restaurant on 86th Street for dim sum. The place is especially popular on Sunday mornings.

I chance upon what could only be described as an amazing shrine to Brooklyn's history and culture, with all its revered icons. Were I

2056 85th Street—iconic Brooklyn at its core, and frozen in time

not walking every block in the area, I would not have discovered it. It's a private house at 2056 85th Street, right down the block, paradoxically, from Brooklyn's only Kabbalah Center. I assume the two do not have more than a passing acquaintanceship. The unique house is a striking example of the borough's richness and diversity.

The bronze sign in front reads, "This property has been placed in the National Register of Historic Places by the U.S. Department of the Interior." It's a white brick colonial with a porch attached to the second story, vinyl siding on the third floor, and many plaster statues arrayed in front of the house and along the driveway. There's a garbage can with a small monster peering out near a red and yellow sign that reads, "Welcome to Steve's Place." On the right is a three-foot-tall brown statue of a man dressed in a trench coat and a black hat. In the middle is a 1950s-era gangster clad in a black leather jacket and a hat pulled down low. He has long sideburns, sunglasses, and a cigarette dangling from his mouth. There's also a biker mannequin with a guitar. Then there's a cigarette girl wearing a scanty outfit and a little hat. She's carrying a small tray of fake tulips. Next to that is a seated Godfather-type figure, leisurely reclining and holding a cigar in his hand. The sign says, "Original Capone Gangster." At the top it reads, "Jury Convicts Capone." By contrast, next to Capone's likeness is a symbol of the US Army. On the window behind it are several gremlins. Nearby is a statue of a marine standing at attention, and alongside him is a statue of a derelict. Above that is the famous photo of the marines planting the American flag on Iwo Jima. An assortment of jungle animals dots the area as well.

Jutting out from the second floor is a statue of Superman appearing to break out of the house. On one side of him is a Batman poster, and on the other is one of Robin. Above a knight in armor is a face attached to the wall. There's also Betty Boop near a barber shop pole and a sign encouraging the viewer or customer to "ask for Wildroot," a hair lotion from the old days. There's Elvis and his guitar, his song, "Don't Be Cruel" etched behind him, along with

You never know from whence your salvation will come!

a scale of red-colored notes. He is next to Marilyn Monroe, who is standing above the famous grating where the wind is blowing up her skirt.

At the front of the driveway is a brightly colored garage door with a dotted stripe down the middle, just like a road. It's done in 3-D trompe l'oeil style so that it looks as if you're driving into it. And where are you driving into? Why, the Brooklyn Battery Tunnel, with signs reading, "EZ Pass," "CASH," and, "Leaving Brooklyn." There's also a statue of Humphrey Bogart. And then Superman makes a second appearance as Clark Kent emerging from a phone booth after a quick change of clothing. I almost feel as if I'm spying on him, especially when I see the famous quote from Perry White, publisher of the *Daily Planet*, exclaiming, "Great Caesar's Ghost!" There's a pirate of a Captain Kidd type, Dracula, Frankenstein, Forrest Gump, and Arthur Herbert Fonzarelli, a.k.a. the Fonz.

There's much more, including iconic photos of Brooklyn, like one of Ebbets Field. Inside the garage—which is larger than the house, having been owned before by a limousine company—are seven vintage cars in great condition, including a bright pink Cadillac, as well as literally thousands of items from the past—gumball machines, games played in mid-twentieth century Brooklyn, old games in general, clothing from that era, rare framed photographs, and more. All in all, the entire scene is a rich tapestry of the borough's history as well as the era in which it played out, depicting characters and real people that residents of Brooklyn liked. It's also an effort to demonstrate that despite all that's happened in the last thirty-five years, Brooklyn has hewed to its cultural trappings and its history, unique in some aspects and tied into the larger society in others. To sum up, this unusually decorated home is a part of America and at the same time apart from it. If there are such complex exhibits elsewhere in the five boroughs—other than Christmas displays—I'm not aware of them. It's an amazing space on private property but there for all who pass by to see.

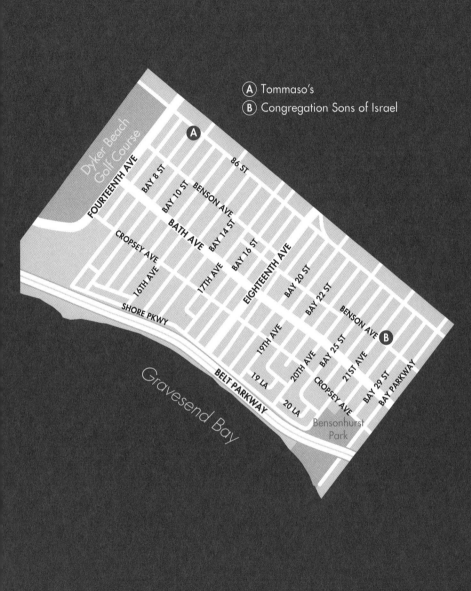

A Tommaso's
B Congregation Sons of Israel

Dyker Beach Golf Course

Gravesend Bay

FOURTEENTH AVE

BAY 8 ST
BAY 10 ST
BENSON AVE
86 ST

CROPSEY AVE
BATH AVE
BAY 14 ST
BAY 16 ST

16TH AVE
17TH AVE
EIGHTEENTH AVE
BAY 20 ST
BAY 22 ST
BENSON AVE

SHORE PKWY

19TH AVE
20TH AVE
BAY 25 ST
21 ST AVE
BAY 29 ST
BAY PARKWAY

BELT PARKWAY
19 LA
20 LA
CROPSEY AVE

Bensonhurst Park

BATH BEACH

BATH BEACH IS A SMALL NEIGHBORHOOD adjacent to Bensonhurst. Its boundaries are 86th Street to the north, Bay Parkway to the east, the Belt Parkway to the south, and Fourteenth Avenue to the west. It's a quiet place, with mostly small homes and some apartment buildings. The major commercial streets are 86th, Bay Parkway, and, to a lesser extent, Bath and Benson Avenues. In the mid-1800s there was a settlement of freed slaves living around Eighteenth and Bath Avenues. The settlement was anchored by the Mount Zion Baptist Church, which is today located on Gates Avenue in Bedford-Stuyvesant. Bath Beach once had a beach, but today it's buried under Shore Parkway, Bensonhurst Park, and a large shopping center. It was also featured in two major films, *The French Connection* and *Saturday Night Fever*. Ethnically, it's a mix, mostly of Chinese and Russians, plus elderly Italians and some Jews.

Several restaurants in the city could be called "iconic Italian." They feature the traditional hearty food of Italy, with generous portions, lots of seasoning, photos of famous Hollywood stars and politicians who have dined there, and an atmosphere of conviviality mixed with a hint of mob connections somewhere in the past. There's Don Peppe's in Ozone Park, Queens; Parkside Restaurant in Corona, Queens; Bamonte's in Williamsburg, Brooklyn; and Tommaso's, in Bath Beach, at 1464 86th Street.

It's my lucky day as I enter Tommaso's on a hot late morning in July. The tables are beautifully set, but there are no customers since they haven't officially opened yet. Seeing no one, I open the kitchen door and I'm face to face with Tommaso Verdillo himself. He's wearing a striped chef's smock and is busy preparing the food for the day. I tell him I'm writing a book about Brooklyn. "You don't need to interview me. My place is all over the Internet."

"Yes, but I want you to tell me about things that aren't there, that people don't know about. Like, where are these beautiful dolls from." I'm referring to colorful, dainty dolls and other figurines scattered throughout the dining room. "They're made of ceramic and I've collected them through the years, many of them from Mexico. Listen, we're doing fine, though sometimes I wonder if I shouldn't have moved to Manhattan." This is a lament I've heard before from other restaurateurs. They look at places there that charge, and get, three times as much for dishes that they feel they can make even better. They may be right, but it takes courage and self-confidence, plus financial acumen, salesmanship, and good luck to make the jump to Manhattan. I have a feeling Tommaso has all that, but perhaps he's not so sure, or he may simply feel he's doing well enough. In addition, he would have to modify his menu to appeal to a younger crowd with different tastes. He is still offering the old favorites, and the latest arrivals, Russians, like the food well enough to come in, not to mention the Italians and Jews who still live in Bath Beach. The Chinese, it turns out, are not so adventurous.

The residential part of the neighborhood is a mix of row houses that look like brownstones but are made of light beige brick, as well as old colonials, updated homes with shake shingles, and new brick homes, generally inhabited by Chinese and Russians. As I walk up and down the small streets, usually preceded by "Bay" as in Bay 8th or Bay 20th, I'm struck by how similar they are to Bensonhurst, Gravesend, and Sheepshead Bay, both visually and in terms of who lives there. I see a changing of the guard, with the older generation of white ethnics moving on and out, to be replaced by Chinese, Russians, Orthodox Jews, blacks, and Hispanics.

I chat with Tommy, a ninety-two-year-old army veteran. He's wearing a navy blue cap, on which is stitched in yellow letters the name of the unit he served in, the 110th. He's hard of hearing, but his mind is all there. "How do you feel about the neighborhood these days?"

"It's all changed. I remember how when I was a kid we'd walk to the beach and have a great time, but that's all gone now. And so are the people." He chuckles. "I guess I outlived them."

"Do you have anything in common with the new people?"

"Well, not the way it used to be when it was Italian. But I'll tell ya this. The Chinese are the greatest." He points to a brick house across the street. "Those people over there, they always say hello and when they heard I was celebrating my sixty-fifth anniversary with my wife, he gave me an envelope and there was a hundred bucks in it. It doesn't get any better than that. I have other Chinese neighbors and they're wonderful too. They stay to themselves, but they don't bother nobody." I've heard this from the white ethnics over and over. The locals see Asians as a model minority—quiet, industrious, law abiding—and that's enough to render their cultural distinctiveness a moot point. They feel similarly about the Russians, complaining only occasionally about their loud parties. Tommy worked for customs inspection at Kennedy Airport. "They used ta call Kennedy Idlewild, ya know," he tells me. Today, he appears to be a happy man. His wife is still alive and his daughter takes care of him whenever necessary, though he's still managing in his own house. When I ask about crime in the neighborhood, he responds: "It's still pretty safe. I hate to say it because I don't approve of them, but in the old days the Mafia kept things quiet around here and there was never a problem." Left unsaid is the fact that Bath Beach had a reputation as a mob dumping ground. There's this ambivalence among Italian Americans about the Mafia. They don't like the stereotype and its basis in reality, but they do see the Mafia as protectors.

Houses of worship are important spaces in a neighborhood but not only to those they currently serve. They matter a great deal to those who no longer live in the area, too. Many people who used to live in the neighborhood travel back to see what's left, and a church or temple is often on the itinerary. This thought enters my head as I stand in front of a magnificent Jewish temple in the

Congregation Sons of Israel—a century of history in one building

round, Congregation Sons of Israel, 2115 Benson Avenue, built in 1919 when there was a significant Jewish population. In fact, Bath Beach was a summer resort area that attracted Jews in the late nineteenth century. These days, the temple caters to a largely Russian population.

As I gaze at it, I start thinking. What happened to all those kids who attended its youth groups, its afternoon school; what about the adult members, the committees on which they served—Ritual, House, Membership, Burial, Social Activities, Young Couples? Lives were lived here, political intrigues were played out, religious events were celebrated. And lifelong friendships began inside its walls. But I am only an observer. For those who come back to the old neighborhood to visit and remember, such a trip is filled with memories, and the building, to the extent that it remains intact, is the vehicle that lends special meaning and even comfort. In that sense the old building, even if it has been transformed into a church or bingo hall, keeps alive the past that its former occupants wish to preserve.

GRAVESEND

SHEEPSHEAD BAY

GERRITSEN BEACH

MANHATTAN BEACH

BRIGHTON BEACH

CONEY ISLAND

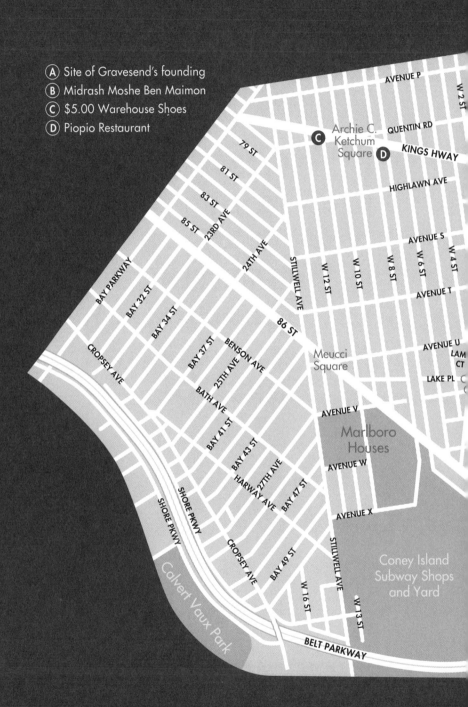

(A) Site of Gravesend's founding
(B) Midrash Moshe Ben Maimon
(C) $5.00 Warehouse Shoes
(D) Piopio Restaurant

AVENUE P

W 2 ST

Archie C.
Ketchum
Square

QUENTIN RD

KINGS HWY

HIGHLAWN AVE

79 ST

81 ST

83 ST

85 ST

23RD AVE

24TH AVE

STILLWELL AVE

W 12 ST

W 10 ST

W 8 ST

W 6 ST

W 4 ST

AVENUE S

AVENUE T

BAY PARKWAY

BAY 32 ST

BAY 34 ST

BAY 37 ST

BENSON AVE

25TH AVE

86 ST

Meucci
Square

AVENUE U

LAM
CT

LAKE PL

CROPSEY AVE

BATH AVE

BAY 41 ST

BAY 43 ST

27TH AVE

HARWAY AVE

BAY 47 ST

AVENUE V

AVENUE W

Marlboro
Houses

SHORE PKWY

SHORE PKWY

CROPSEY AVE

BAY 49 ST

W 16 ST

STILLWELL AVE

W 13 ST

AVENUE X

Coney Island
Subway Shops
and Yard

Calvert Vaux Park

BELT PARKWAY

GRAVESEND

GRAVESEND IS A FAIRLY QUIET neighborhood in south Brooklyn, roughly bounded on the north by Avenue P, Ocean Parkway on the east, and the Belt Parkway on the south and west. It's the only English town of the original six towns in Brooklyn; the other five were Dutch. The Dutch government granted autonomy in 1645 to a group of religious dissidents led by an Englishwoman, Lady Deborah Moody. It soon became a haven for such people, especially Quakers. It was annexed to Brooklyn in 1894 and residentially developed at that time. Until the 1990s the population was mostly Italian and, to a lesser extent, Jewish. Today it's a mix of those groups, plus Chinese and Koreans, Indians, Russians, and Hispanics from various countries.

Among the major commercial thoroughfares are Avenue U, parts of Avenue X, Kings Highway, McDonald Avenue, 86th Street, and Stillwell Avenue. Residentially, the area has a section of expensive homes between McDonald and Ocean Parkway. The rest of the community has more modest two- and one-family homes, attached, semiattached, and detached, as well as apartment buildings of various heights, and some public housing. It's safe, diverse, and well served by the D, N, and F subway lines and, a bit farther away, the B and Q lines.

I walk up and down E. 2nd, E. 3rd, E. 4th, and E. 5th Streets from Kings Highway to Gravesend Neck Road. This little enclave is the epicenter of the Syrian Jewish community; it features large, beautiful homes, mostly brick. Generally, the ones on the corners of the street are the most spacious. But contrary to the popular image of this neighborhood as a redoubt for the wealthy, there are many more homes that are not especially large—semiattached and two-family. Following the trend, these smaller residences may eventually be replaced by larger, elegant homes.

At the intersection of E. 2nd Street, Avenue V, and Gravesend Neck Road lies a small grassy triangle, with several oak trees and some inkberry bushes. This is where Gravesend was founded. It was named either for the seaport of Gravesend, in Kent, England, or after a Dutch town called Gravenzande. The walkways are lined with Belgian paving stones. Farther up the block is the Trinity Tabernacle Church, which sits on a site formerly occupied by the Dutch Reformed Church, established in 1655. This is an area rich in history, as evidenced by the Old Gravesend Cemetery, on Gravesend Neck Road near McDonald Avenue, also dating back to the 1650s. As I peer through the gates of the site, I can see small gravestones, some tilting at crazy angles, with grass growing around them. It looks and feels like something from a long-gone era, and I'm amazed it has survived for so long. The same can be said for various Dutch homes in the immediate vicinity. A good example is the Ryder Van-Cleef House at 38 Village Road North. In my search for the historical places in Gravesend I found forgotten-ny.com to be the best source of information.

At 59 Gravesend Neck Road there's a modern synagogue, Midrash Moshe ben Maimon, which has several beautiful crystal chandeliers. As I watch the mostly Sephardic worshipers leave the temple following morning services, I'm reminded that it was Sephardic

Jews from Recife, Brazil, who settled in New Amsterdam in 1652; this is a strange twist of history, connecting the past with the present. Those here now hail from Syria, the earlier ones lived in Brazil, and before that, Spain and Portugal.

As I leave the immediate area and cross McDonald Avenue, I see furniture outlets, plumbing supply places, and automotive parts and repair shops under the tracks of the elevated F train. Farther up Gravesend Neck, I pass the former Coney Island Christian Church, which serves the Korean community and is now called the First Korean Church of Brooklyn. Between Avenue U and Gravesend Neck, along Van Sicklen Street, there's a one-block road called Lama Place that exudes peace and quiet, with modest nice homes stretching its length. There are so many tiny streets like these dotting the city—oases of solitude often known only to their inhabitants.

On Avenue U, a few blocks west of McDonald Avenue, I stop to chat with a grocery store owner. He tells me that there's very little business now that school's out for the summer. He also says, "The biggest problem is that ten years ago kids walked around in groups, but now you don't see them. They're all on their computers." If so, it's an unintended but significant consequence of technology that applies to group life in general.

I have a conversation with the owner of a local bar, a genial Irishman who talks happily about the weather until I observe that this is such a nice, quiet area. Suddenly his face turns dark and brooding. "Do you know how many undercover cops there are here and all over Coney Island, on the beach? I talk to the boys when they come in and they say 'Always be alert.' Look at all the people killed by these terrorists on the beach in Tunisia. These things don't happen so much here because everybody's watching." New York City is certainly security conscious; his remarks underscore how concern over security is firmly embedded in the public's consciousness.

Making a right off Avenue U, I see an interesting name for a store, "Wild Bagel" on Stillwell Avenue. Expecting to find bagels with exotic flavors, I am disappointed. None of the workers have any idea why it's called that, and to me, it looks like any other routine selection of bagels. But, as we see from the fact that I asked the question, it's a good draw.

At Kings Highway, one of Brooklyn's most important boulevards, I turn right and at W. 11th Street there's a shoe emporium called "$5.00 Warehouse Shoes." There are a few others like it, scattered around the boroughs, but I've never been inside one. At five bucks, what can I lose? If it fits and lasts a few months I'm ahead of the game. So I decide to take a look. Much to my surprise, the shoes, most of them women's shoes, look fairly attractive and certainly colorful, not to mention brand new. I wonder how many people would be able to tell they're so cheap. Many are described as designer shoes. The brand names sound vaguely like designers' names—Qupid, DeRivage, Marco Vitale. I ask a well-dressed, middle-aged Asian woman why they're so cheap. "Because they're man-made and come from China," she says.

A sign above some men's shoes selling for $12, says, "leather made." "Are they really leather?" I ask the saleslady. "No, it's not leather," she responds. I don't have the heart to challenge the sign. I ask a young woman, stylishly dressed, how they can cost so little. "They only cost a dollar to make," she quips, with a laugh. Outside, I talk to a man from Uganda. He's visiting his daughter-in-law, who hails from Ukraine. I ask him if he can get shoes for that price in Uganda. He doesn't think so. He's skeptical about how good the ladies shoes are. But when I tell him there are men's shoes being sold for $12, he excuses himself and immediately goes into the store to look for them. In truth, many think the quality is poor, but more than a few find the idea of a bargain irresistible.

The entire area from Stillwell to McDonald and from Kings Highway to 86th Street is mostly Chinese and Russian, but the groups are very intermingled geographically. There's no all-Chinese or all-Russian neighborhood. A Chinese realtor with whom I chat observes: "The Chinese stick to themselves but it's not that they're unfriendly. It's mostly a language barrier. Also, as a people we tend to be more reserved."

Continuing on Kings Highway I step inside Piopio Restaurant, a Peruvian eatery at number 282. It's clean and pleasantly decorated, and the food is reportedly good. "Do Peruvians live here?" I ask the man inside.

"No," he responds.

"So who eats here?"

"Russians."

"What about Chinese?"

"No," is the response. "They eat in their own restaurants."

"Do Peruvians eat in Russian or Chinese restaurants?" He laughs heartily and treats it as a funny question.

"Ha! They would never do that. They eat Spanish food." Perhaps the Russians are more daring, more willing to try new food, I conclude, thinking the topic of preferences would be worth investigating. I move on to 86th Street. The blocks between Twenty-Third Avenue and Bay Parkway and the surrounding area remind me of Manhattan's Chinatown. There's Thanksgiving Supermarket, Super Feng Discount Store, and LC Discount Store. Crowds of Asian shoppers spill out onto the sidewalk examining the wares, filling up their baskets with vegetables and fruits.

All in all, Gravesend is a community of incredible diversity, ethnically as well as economically, and for those who live here, it's affordable, safe, and a place where newcomers can truly feel at home among their own. Some immigrants will never leave the area, especially if they were older when they arrived. Others will see it as their home for a period of time and then move on to more upscale areas like Bay Ridge or Mill Basin.

KINGS HWY

QUENTIN RD

AVENUE P M L

AVENUE R

HARING ST

Madison

AVENUE S

H **K**

AVENUE T

E 28 ST
E 26 ST
E 23 ST
E 21 ST
E 19 ST
E 17 ST
E 15 ST
E 13 ST
E 12 ST
E 9 ST
E 7 ST

J **I**

Kelly Park

Homecrest

OCEAN PARKWAY

G **F**

AVENUE U

AVENUE V

GRAVESEND NECK RD

OCEAN AVE

CONEY ISLAND AVE

HOMECREST AVE

AVENUE W

AVENUE W
LANCASTER AVE
CRAWFORD AVE

SHEEPSHEAD BAY RD

AVENUE X

She

H

AVENUE Y

BEDFORD AVE

E 27 ST

E 11 ST

AVENUE Z

SHEEPSHEAD BAY RD

JEROME AVE

E 23 ST

VOORHIES A

OCEAN PARKWAY

HUBBARD ST
E 6 ST

MANOR CT

SHORE PKWY

SHORE PKWY

BE

D **C** **E**

B

EMMONS AVE

Sheepshead Bay

SHEEPSHEAD BAY

SHEEPSHEAD BAY IS LUMPED TOGETHER with Homecrest and Madison because of these communities' location next to each other. Sheepshead Bay is actually somewhat different from the other two in terms of its proximity to the bay and its history and attractions, but there are also similarities in terms of ethnicity and socioeconomic makeup. The boundaries of these communities are Avenue P and Kings Highway on the north, Gerritsen Avenue and Knapp Street on the east, Emmons and Voorhies Avenues on the south, and Ocean Parkway on the west.

In the 1880s the area was home to a 112-acre racetrack that ran along Ocean Avenue. One remnant of that is a small African American community along 15th Street near Gravesend Neck Road, consisting of the descendants of those who once worked at the track. Sheepshead Bay was developed as a residential community during the 1920s, which included apartment buildings along Ocean Avenue and elsewhere. Two New York City Housing Authority projects are now located in the area.

Today, it has large numbers of Russian, Chinese, Jewish, and Italian inhabitants. The main commercial thoroughfares are Nostrand Avenue, Coney Island Avenue, and Sheepshead Bay Road. Emmons Avenue, which runs along the bay, is entertainment oriented, with pleasure boats, restaurants, and nightclubs. It feels a bit like some of the summer communities along the Jersey shore.

It's a beautiful, though hot, June day as I explore Sheepshead Bay, beginning with a stroll down Emmons Avenue. To my right are condos and small detached or semiattached homes. This section, one block wide, between Emmons and the Belt Parkway, sits apart from the rest of Sheepshead Bay. This is also where Nostrand Avenue, which runs the length of Brooklyn, passing through Hasidic, black, and white communities, dead-ends into the bay. So what can one do here in this narrow inlet facing the bay besides take an excursion on a pleasure or fishing boat?

Welcome to Bernie's Bait & Tackle Shop, at 3035 Emmons. Here I can get a fishing license, buy every type of fishing rod, have them repaired, and purchase a variety of baits for fish I'd love to catch. Because of the location by the ocean, I thought they might only sell bait for saltwater fish, but they also have delectable food for freshwater fish. I ask the owner how long he's been here. He replies, "About sixty-one years, in various locations."

"Have the people who come in stayed the same?"

"You have more shore fishermen and far fewer fishing boats. The price for the boats became too expensive, like sixty bucks an hour. We have the largest selection of reels, rods, and tackle in Brooklyn." Farther down, at 2702, I find his competitor, Stella Maris Bait & Tackle, which has been around even longer, sixty-eight years. The store has an original looking sign—green capital letters for the name, with red Coca Cola signs flanking it. The word on the street is that Bernie's is better for tackle and rods and Stella Maris has better bait, with both rated highly in general.

Continuing along Emmons, I come across a muscular man in his thirties with wavy black hair and a nice tan who's walking his huge, beige-colored Spanish mastiff. "Cute, but pretty tough-looking. Is he friendly?" I ask.

"Well, not exactly. Look at my arm. You see these marks?" They're more than marks. They're very serious bite-marks. Earl continues: "He's bitten me a couple of times, as well as my son, and my wife."

"Then why do you keep him? That's dangerous."

"Well. He's a kid, only a year old, and I keep hoping he'll grow out of it. The guy I got him from said, if he really wanted to hurt you, he could have easily taken off your arm."

I marvel that this man would keep such an animal, beautiful as he might be. But then an answer presents itself: "How much did he cost?"

"Six thousand dollars."

"Aha," I think. Cognitive dissonance. If he paid six grand, he needs to justify the money he spent. Therefore, if the dog shapes up, he will be vindicated. But there's more to it, I suspect, based on the following remark Earl made: "I see this dog like a child. You wouldn't get rid of a child just because he misbehaves a lot." This dog is his baby and he's not getting rid of him just because he's a troublemaker. Clearly, some people would cut their losses, but not Earl, I guess. I've seen this incredibly strong attachment to dogs over and over again in this city. It's part of the fabric of life in New York. Without their dogs (or cats, for that matter) the lives of many urban dwellers would be greatly impoverished.

I stand in front of a wooden house that must be a hundred years old and ask an elderly man who's walking by with his wife: "How long has this place been here? It looks so old and out of place among the condo buildings."

"It was here when I was growing up in the 1940s. I moved away many years ago, but I like to visit and it still looks the same. But now there are more Russians, and when I grew up everybody was either

Jewish or Italian. A lot of the kids lived in the projects and they all thought it was a great place to grow up in."

It turns out that Malcolm Rothman, who has lived in Chicago for most of his adult life after serving in the armed forces, had an interesting career as a professional actor. He hands me a thick, laminated business card that looks and feels like a baseball card, which has a photo of him on one side, with the exclamation "Holy Cow!!!" beneath it, is a reference to a well-known baseball announcer, Harry Caray, whom he imitates professionally (Yankee announcer Phil Rizzuto also used the expression): "I wasn't famous, but I was pretty good. Chicago had the second tier actors, while LA and New York got the top ones. I've performed for all types of groups—Anheuser-Busch, Chicago Magazine, Fidelity Investments, Washington University in St. Louis, you name it. It's been a great career and I'm still doing it even though I'm in my seventies. I even got a good pension out of it from the actors' union."

Malcolm and his wife look quite good for their age. The twinkle in his eyes projects good humor and alertness and he relishes trips like these. "I'm taking pictures for my friends who used to live here, of where they lived. My Aunt Molly lived on Avenue V and Bedford Avenue. I always loved this place and I still do. When we were kids you could get a special pass that allowed us to go out for free on the fishing boats."

No surprises there, as millions of people routinely visit the communities of their childhood, though to my knowledge the phenomenon has not been given much, if any, attention by sociologists. From my own research, however, I've learned that a critical factor in nostalgia of this sort is that folks don't just recall the places, but remember as well *who* they were in those days—young, vibrant, with their lives ahead of them.

There are many nice dining places along Emmons, including one longtime survivor, Randazzo's. It's unpretentious, with good, down-home Italian fare. The most famous restaurant was, of course, Lundy's at 1901 Emmons, which started when Irving Lundy began selling raw clams in 1900 from a pushcart. In 1934, he opened as a real restaurant; at one time it was the biggest food emporium in the country, with a seating capacity of 2,800. It was landmarked in 1992 and closed for good in 2007, which was a lucky thing since the location was flooded in 2012 during Hurricane Sandy. It was renowned for its clams and the huckleberry pie served a la mode, with Breyers ice cream.

And while walking on Emmons, I visit Yogurt City, which, if it were a real city, would be the cleanest one in the world. Absolutely spotless, with attractive looking chairs—green, yellow, blue, and red, at each table—a patron can "literally eat off the floor."

I turn around and head over to Nostrand Avenue. At 3432, near Avenue U, I discover a different sort of place, definitely not for health food enthusiasts, but one with a very long history. Brennan and Carr, a seventy-eight-year-old place, is famed for its juicy, flavorful roast beef, which the proprietors call "Hot Beef." It's a working-class place that takes cash only. The old-timey feel is enhanced by the stand-alone brick building with a wood paneled interior. Despite the presence of waiters with clean white jackets, one can get a sandwich for about six bucks, followed by some tasty blueberry pie a la mode, and even watch a ball game at the bar. Framed prints of America's history hang on the wall.

A little farther down, at number 2718, there's another, quite different type of place that also serves roast beef, Jay & Lloyd's kosher deli, that's been there for ages. The owners are very welcoming and the pastrami is a worthy, if not nearly as well known, challenger to the legendary Katz's on the Lower East Side, as are the kasha varnishkes and chicken soup with kreplach.

This area was once home to Richard Yee's, a fabled restaurant for those who love Chinese fare, and also a well-known watering hole. It opened in 1952 in an area that had no Chinese population, serving Cantonese food in an upscale environment. After it closed in 2008, the *Village Voice* predicted it would no doubt be replaced by a fast food joint. But that's not what happened. When I walked by it was under construction. Eddie, who runs the highly regarded G&S Pork Store next door at 2611 (which takes particular pride in its guaranteed very fresh prime beef) told me that the property, owned by Richard's son, Robert, would soon be replaced by Cherry Hill, a gourmet glatt kosher supermarket. This demonstrates how unwise it is to predict neighborhood change, even in passing. The movement of the Orthodox into these parts was not widely expected even ten years ago. And, in an ironic twist, a reborn Richard, perhaps "Robert Yee's" would have been in the middle of a fast-growing Chinese community, which is what's happening now.

Homecrest's housing is quite varied—colonials, capes, row houses, clapboard and shingle, one- and two-family homes, and eclectic styles not easily categorized. Walking up Kings Highway, I pass by a catering hall near Coney Island Avenue that has undergone several name changes as different owners have come and gone. For most of its existence, dating back at least to the 1930s, it was known as the Aperion Manor, where thousands of events were held. Today it's in the last stages of survival. There are no events, just an office, and the manager, sitting behind an old wooden desk, tells me the wrecker's ball is coming. The plan is for a hotel to go up.

Walking east on Avenue U the population becomes primarily Chinese, with most of the residents from Hong Kong. Practically every shop has Chinese lettering, and it feels like the Chinatowns of Sunset Park and Bensonhurst. I ask a young Chinese couple why they moved here. Their response, in halting English: "We used to live in crowded apartment in Sunset Park, but now this place becoming more popular for Chinese people. We have nice small house and we can get all our food and be with our own people. This is good for our children too."

I wander around Kelly Park, running from Avenue S halfway up to Avenue R and between E. 14th Street and the B/Q subway lines that run between E. 15th and 16th Streets. There are a number of tennis and basketball courts, and I notice that the participants in a full-court game come from varied backgrounds. A large, concrete, white-painted polar bear stands guard near the entrance. Supposedly, it was done as a nod to the Russian population that uses the park, but people also find it to be an unpretentious sculpture for kids to climb on and have their pictures taken. The only complaint I heard about the park was that home run balls from the baseball field land with too much frequency on some of the nearby tennis courts.

At 2165 Coney Island Avenue I find the Tayba Islamic Center, a mosque, right next door to the Orthodox-run Perla's Day Care Center. They're neighbors and they must have some contact. As it turns out, a Russian man standing outside smoking a cigar, a longtime resident, asserts that everyone gets along but that the cars that double park on Fridays are a real pain. Personally, I find some humor in the sign above the day care center's entrance: "Lincense by New York City." It seems to me that a place with a license ought to spell license correctly!

There's a real gem of a mural along Coney Island on the wall of the Verizon Building near Avenue R. It consists of seven well-drawn panels, painted in color, depicting the history of communication from the beginning of time, starting with a loincloth-clad, bearded man sending out smoke signals. The last panel shows two people talking on the phone. Don't miss this one!

The name of the Madison area, as it's known by many, is derived from James Madison High School, which was and continues to be one of the borough's premier high schools. It's located at 3787 Bedford Avenue. This is also a neighborhood that can be considered to be within Sheepshead Bay, Midwood, or even Flatbush, depending on which maps are consulted and which people are asked. It has many pretty homes throughout.

I come to the Madison Jewish Center, a Conservative Egalitarian temple—meaning women participate fully in the service and administration of the temple—on Nostrand Avenue, just south of Avenue P. It's a large structure, and in a sense a dinosaur, because the area is now overwhelmingly Orthodox. Even so it still serves an

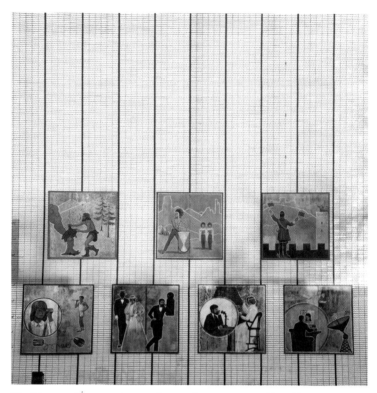

The history of communication from earliest times, as told by Verizon

important purpose, attracting several hundred worshipers on the High Holy Days.

The changing demographics affect the Christian community, too, as new populations of Chinese and Russian immigrants are moving in. Congregations that formerly served Italians and Irish residents are beginning to offer services in other languages to attract new members.

On the corner of Avenue P and E. 24th Street there's a synagogue and "kollel," a place where young married men engage in Talmud study, inside a very large, beautiful private home. Called the Beis Medrash Imrei Zvi, it is a most unusual place. Outside, there's an elevator for the family of its leader, Rabbi Moshe Scheinerman, who live on the upper floors, and for parties held in the basement. But it is the beauty of the interior that makes this synagogue special. The inside is stunning, especially given its small size. Large temples are often ornately designed, but small ones, serving perhaps a hundred or so members, are generally simple affairs—a couple of long tables, for which folding chairs or simple benches are good enough. Here, the floor consists of beige blocks of gleaming marble. It's ornate yet very tasteful. The built-in wooden, carved bookcases, with literally more than a thousand leather-bound volumes, are constructed from what appears to be an oak that's a rich, glossy, honey color. The tabletops look like polished cherrywood, and the thick upholstered, patterned chairs are probably made from mahogany. The ark housing the Torahs is quite magnificent, made again of carved wood with intricate designs of grapes and vines. There are also Ionic/Corinthian pillars made of polished, maple-colored wood. There's a menorah etched into a glass surface, hanging on the wall. The inscription atop the ark reads, "I put God before me always." The five chandeliers in the room are elegant and constructed of dark polished brass. As I gaze upon all this on a quiet weekday afternoon I'm left with a feeling of deep serenity.

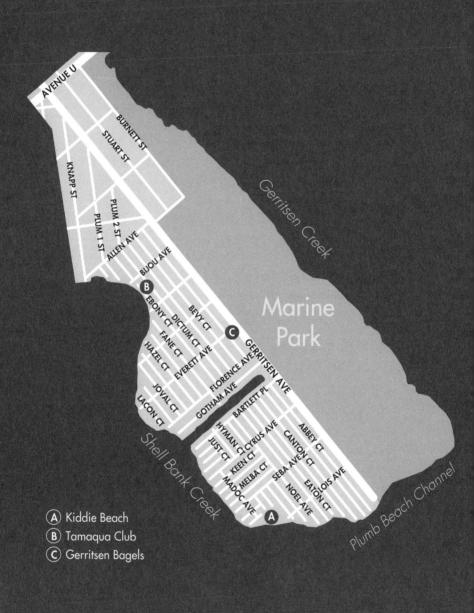

AVENUE U

BURNETT ST

STUART ST

KNAPP ST

PLUM 2 ST

PLUM 1 ST

ALLEN AVE

BIJOU AVE

BEVY CT

EBONY CT

DICTUM CT

FANE CT

EVERETT AVE

HAZEL CT

JOVAL CT

LACON CT

FLORENCE AVE

GOTHAM AVE

BARTLETT PL

GERRITSEN AVE

Gerritsen Creek

Marine Park

Shell Bank Creek

HYMAN CT

JUST CT

KEEN CT

MADOC AVE

CYRUS AVE

MELBA CT

CANTON CT

SEBA AVE

NOEL AVE

ABBEY CT

EATON CT

LOIS AVE

Plumb Beach Channel

B

C

A

(A) Kiddie Beach
(B) Tamaqua Club
(C) Gerritsen Bagels

GERRITSEN BEACH

IT LIES THERE, ALMOST IN REPOSE, A SUPER-QUIET, SMALL COMMUNITY tucked away in the far southern reaches of Brooklyn. You can very easily miss it if you're just driving along one of its borders, Knapp Street, because it's completely hidden from view until you actually enter it; you also need to know where to turn off. Gerritsen Avenue, another boundary marker, is seen mostly as a driving shortcut, except by the locals who shop there. In fact, many people in adjacent Sheepshead Bay and Marine Park, not to mention the rest of Brooklyn, have never even heard of Gerritsen Beach. The borders are Avenue U to the north, Gerritsen Avenue to the east, Plumb Beach Channel to the south, and to the west, Shell Bank Creek and Knapp Street. Within these boundaries, the northern part of Gerritsen Beach is separated from the southern half by the Shell Bank Canal, which runs east to west. The northern half has more brick homes and commercial establishments, while the southern half more closely resembles a quaint New England fishing village. Despite these differences, it is still considered to be one community, with a long strip of stores along Gerritsen Avenue serving both halves of the neighborhood.

Named after Wolfert Gerritsen, who built a house and a mill in the area in the early 1600s, it became a middle-class summer resort in the 1920s—with hundreds of bungalows built along very narrow streets with tiny sidewalks. Eventually, workers and others bought the houses and expanded them, adding small backyards. Today, there are about 1,600 homes. The population is still mostly Italian, German, and Irish, with a little Dutch and Norwegian mixed in. It has remained a blue-collar community, mostly cops, firefighters, sandhogs (workers who build tunnels or lay foundations), bus drivers, and the like, with many homes being passed on to several generations of descendants. One middle-aged woman tells me about the time she was renovating the house: "I'm spending your inheritance," she said to her son. "No you're not. You're fixing up my house," he replied. Most of the residents are water enthusiasts, and many of their boats are moored along the waterways, which are visited sometimes by party boats.

While the area is still very homogeneous, ethnic change is coming, albeit slowly. There are a few Jews, Hispanics, and Asians living in Gerritsen Beach today as well as other "outsiders." As John Douglas, head of Gerritsen Beach Cares, a local community group, stated: "We have more people from outside moving in because it's open housing and people like the peace, quiet, and small-town feel, and so, in that way, we've been discovered."

Volunteerism is a strong tradition here. Gerritsen Beach has the only volunteer fire department in the city. John moved here after becoming familiar with the neighborhood because of his route as a UPS driver: "We'd been living in Midwood nearby, but most of the neighbors were Orthodox Jews. They were okay, saying 'Hello,' but we had nothing in common with them; nor did our kids. So we came here. I'd grown up in Huntington and in Wading River, Long Island, and I liked the similar village feel and the water nearby."

One interesting case of changing attitudes toward outsiders is an Indian couple who reportedly extol the community's virtues, either because they fervently believe them to be true or because they wish to gain favor with their neighbors and win acceptance. Maybe it's a combination of both. It does not hurt that the Indian is a doctor. After all, what if someone in the community needs medical assistance? And there may even be some deflected status. He does not threaten the community's ethos of the value of being a working man, because he's "different" anyway. This is in distinction to those few who are insiders and achieve high status in society at large.

On the other hand, one group that has not been viewed favorably is Russians, mostly from Brighton Beach and Sheepshead Bay, who have begun building large homes here. Russians like living in communities near the water. It doesn't help that they tend to stick to themselves. And there have been some squabbles between locals and Russian developers about expanding the area.

Residents are aware that the community is often caricatured as made up of "rednecks," conservative, not very educated, white working class. Several incidents in which outsiders have been attacked has reinforced this belief. In one case, locals reportedly set upon black teenagers. The community's insularity is heightened by the fact that there's a large, mostly black housing project fifteen minutes' walk away across Knapp Street.[1] One man was reluctant to discuss it in detail, commenting only that, "I've heard several versions. Some say they might have come in to steal bikes, which happens, or that they were just passing through." When I mention that the *New York Times* article describing the event said that the police complained about residents who refused to cooperate with them, he admitted: "Yeah. It's an attitude. Like, when kids are charged with underage drinking, the parents will say, 'Hell, they were only drinking beer.'"

I meet Joe, a retired plumber and boating aficionado whose views represent the old ways of thinking. A friendly but blunt seventy-one-year-old, stocky, with flashing blue eyes, and a shock of gray-white hair, he gives me a friendly hello. When I tell him I'm writing a book about Brooklyn, he jokes: "Well, you haven't written about me, have you?"

"No," I say, laughing. "But it's never too late."

"Okay," he chuckles, "So how about a beer? Come sit here on my deck." I accept and look out at the boats, some of them yachts, swaying gently as the waves lap at their undersides, and think about how so many people living in New York City have no idea that this idyllic setting exists. My reverie is interrupted by Joe, who says, "I must be crazy. Who grows fifty tomato plants when he only eats a couple a day, not even? But I like doing it, I guess. This is a great community. I got generations who lived here. It's got great people and it's a warm friendly place." He goes on: "The only presidents I liked were Eisenhower—hey, he was a general—even Truman, these people had guts. I also liked Bush—the second one. I keep his picture up here." He shows me a faded newspaper photo of Teddy Roosevelt scotch-taped to the inside wall of his garage. "There was a man. 'There shall be only one language in this land. And that language is English.'"

I gaze at the mementos, family photos, and military insignias and realize that Joe has invited me into his inner sanctum. I ask him what bothers him most about this country. He thinks for a long moment and answers: "9/11 was the worst day ever. I went over to help out with boats goin' across the river." His eyes moisten and I can see he's reliving the experience. He's also very angry as he describes what happened: "It was such a sad day. What a mess. I started the boat and took 1,157 people home to New Jersey. We told the younger people to go down to the bottom deck and let the older ones sit upstairs. I say to everybody: 'I'm a Brooklyn boy. Don't anybody look now but when we turn around you're gonna see the World Trade Center burnin' like crazy.' It was a terrible day, a very long day. I got home at three in the morning. How could we let shit like this happen?"

In a very real sense, a large part of Joe lives in the past. He loves past presidents, some of them anyway. He feels his grandparents knew the meaning of work. He doesn't like the new immigrants and he doesn't like De Blasio either. But he does like Gerritsen Beach, perhaps because his way of thinking is shared by many others here. And, as is true of so many New Yorkers, the defining 9/11 moment is front and center. I thank Joe for his time and he wishes me good luck with my book.

John Douglas's son, Dan, is more critical of the area, saying that it is very conservative in its values and describing how his friends thought it was "weird" that he was in graduate school, going for a PhD in sociology, adding that "there's so much politics going on in the community, backbiting and such."

At the same time, he describes a really fun childhood where he had a circle of about seventy acquaintances and a number of close friends with whom he used to "hang," playing ball and going to parties. He knows, however, that he seems like an outsider to them today. Regardless of where they grow up, kids like to have fun by pulling pranks, whether it's throwing water balloons from windows or ringing people's bells in apartment buildings and running away. In Gerritsen Beach a favorite pastime is giving wrong directions to lost drivers who turn up in the community. The driver ends up facing the water on a dead-end street. These pranks have the effect of binding residents together in later life as well, as they reminisce about their youth.

Hurricane Sandy hit people here very hard because of the exposed waterways and small homes. In such circumstances people have to pull together. It helped that Steve Buscemi paid a visit to the neighborhood. But sometimes working together brings out differences. As John Douglas recalls: "We rebuilt this park after convincing local politicians and the parks department that there was one here many years ago and that the community needed it for the kids. Then there have been other people who are always against change. They opposed it, saying: 'It'll bring outsiders in and there will be fights.' Meanwhile, that turned out to be untrue. The kids came in from outside, but all they wanted to do was skateboard and they got along fine with our kids." The local librarian, who was asked if her innovative programming was bringing outsiders in, expressed another version. She retorted, "If by outsiders you mean people who read, well, then, yes, it is."

One attraction here is Kiddie Beach, a private beach and club for residents near Madoc Avenue. It's so-named because once the children reach adolescence, they're eager to leave the friendly but small beach of their early childhood. Adults like to swim there as well, happy to use the saltwater pool. It's only crowded on weekends. Describing its attraction for people, one resident recalled nostalgically: "What was really fun was rolling a wagon down the street to the beach that was filled with bottles and cans of beer and then getting absolutely smashed while the kids ran along the beach." This is, at

A fisherman's village in New York City

least here, the kind of experience that gives people a warm feeling when they think about having been raised in Gerritsen Beach.

Another center of activity is the Tamaqua Bar and Marina on Ebony Court in the northern portion of the neighborhood. There's beer, food, a view of the marina, and a large dancing area with loud music. And Gerritsen Bagels on Gerritsen Avenue has a stellar reputation for bagels. Reportedly, it was the Filipino who rolled the bagels that made them taste so good.

Perhaps the most enticing aspect of this community is walking through its small narrow streets and along its shoreline. I know I'm in another world. The quiet in the air on a lazy summer afternoon is somehow very soothing. But would it be so to an African

American wandering these streets? Almost every neighborhood in this town, or at least parts of it, is its own universe, one created and defined by its history and by the people who inhabit it—Bed-Stuy, Borough Park, Sunset Park, Bushwick. The segmented distribution of populations, each in their own ghettoized geographical areas—Hong Kong Chinese, Bobover Hasidim, Haitians, young gentrifiers, people hell-bent on diversity, remind me that the balance between territoriality and openness to new ideas is very delicate and constantly changing. When it comes to self-perception, Brooklynites have one thing in common. They are acutely aware of the new status that Brooklyn now has, asking me almost rhetorically how it's perceived. When I confirm the change, they say, "Yeah, Brooklyn's really comin' up. It's hot!"[2]

Sheepshead Bay

SHORE BLVD D

C B

CORBIN PL

GIRARD ST

IRVIN ST

S

HAMPTON AVE

WEST END AVE

AMHERST ST

COLERIDGE ST

EXETER ST

FALMOUTH ST

HASTINGS ST

JAFFRAY ST

LANGHAM ST

NORFOLK ST

ORIENTAL BLVD

BEAUMONT ST

DOVER ST

OCEAN AVE

Manhattan Beach Park

E

Coney Island Channel

MANHATTAN BEACH

PEMBROKE ST

DECATUR AVE

SEAWALK AVE

Kingsborough
Community
College

(A)

JOHN BERRY BLVD

Oriental
Beach

THE BOUNDARIES OF MANHATTAN BEACH are Shore Boulevard on the north, the Atlantic Ocean on the east and south, and Corbin Place on the west. It's on the same peninsula as Coney Island but that's about all they have in common. The area is decidedly upscale with mostly middle- and upper-middle-class, overwhelmingly white residents, some of them Russian oligarchs, living in McMansions. It was originally developed in the nineteenth century by Austin Corbin, a past president of the Long Island Railroad, as a resort for the wealthy. Corbin, a leader of the Society for the Suppression of Jews, was an anti-Semite who refused to allow Jews to live in the area. Things have certainly changed, since most of today's residents are Jews of various denominations. In fact, when Corbin's bigotry came to light several years ago, a cry went up to remove the name *Corbin* from the street named Corbin Place. The result was an interesting, almost Solomonic, compromise by the local community board: The street name would be kept, but named after

357

The Brooklyn Riviera!—with a shortcut to dining and shopping in Sheepshead Bay

a different Corbin who was not known to have been anti-Semitic! This person was Margaret Corbin, the first woman to have been injured in an American battle, namely, in the Revolutionary War. She was not a soldier, but in those times, women sometimes accompanied their husbands to tend to them if they were injured during an engagement. There's no real shopping area in Manhattan Beach, just a few stores here and there on Oriental Boulevard and West End Avenue. The nearest subways are a mile away, but there is bus service.

Living the good life in Brooklyn

The main institution of any size here is Kingsborough Community College, with a lovely campus that sits astride the Atlantic Ocean. Not surprisingly, it has a program in marine technology and oceanography and boasts a small aquarium to boot. One student tells me that the school is also referred to as "Kingsborough Country Club." This may be somewhat misleading since it was named one of the top four community colleges in the nation by the Aspen Institute College Excellence Program.

One relatively unknown amenity is the college's Oriental Beach, which is open to the public. An older woman I met gave it high marks: "This is a great place. My husband and I come here from Manhattan. They have a nice cafeteria, shady areas, a nice beach that's not crowded, and it's not expensive. You just have to fill out an application and they'll send you a special pass. You only pay for parking. And you can make a donation if you want."

The beach is technically free, and membership is open to the public. However, there's a daily ten-dollar parking charge, but a one-time fee of $250 is good for the season. It's well maintained, looks beautiful, and feels very private. The woman has a Russian accent and feels comfortable here because "her own people" take full advantage of the club. The cafeteria has several vendors selling burgers, Chinese food, and the like. It also has a beautiful collection of flags from about 140 countries.

Overall, the neighborhood is very safe with lots of nice homes. Walking up and down the side streets is certainly an enjoyable activity. Shore Boulevard, facing Sheepshead Bay, is especially pretty, with many spacious homes that have a waterfront view. One very large home at 906 Shore Boulevard, a little garish and a hodgepodge of different styles, is quite eye-catching. It looks like someone's fantasy house and is made of stone and cement. At 820, there's a beautiful, more traditional stucco home with a tile roof; next door is a handsome brick colonial, with a slate roof. Number 340 features a large home with white stone and marble pathways; the structure is surrounded by tall columns and has statues inside. The metal gate entrance has gold trim, with a gold figure of a lion. There's also a gazebo, covered with filigreed iron.

Manhattan Beach Park offers a beach that's nice, but somewhat crowded, even on a Monday afternoon. Still, it's clean and not nearly as packed as Brighton and Coney Island beaches. The park itself has baseball fields, tennis, volleyball, and other sports. This is a gem of a neighborhood for a day's outing.

What makes this area so different from others is that it has almost none of the characteristics found even in other tranquil neighborhoods. Walking past the homes, many of them exquisitely designed, you feel almost as if you've wandered into a wealthy town in New Jersey or Connecticut. Everything's very quiet, shopping is almost nonexistent, the water surrounds the community on three sides, apartment buildings are largely absent, limited to a four block area. To sum up, it feels as if the rest of Brooklyn, not to mention the entire city, is somewhere far off, on a distant horizon.

A Oceana Condominium and Club
B 711 Brightwater Court
C Tatiana Club
D Old brick houses on Banner 3rd Road
E Eyup Sultan Cultural Center
F St. Petersburg Global Trade House
G National nightclub
H Master Theater

SHORE PKWY
BELT PARKWAY
SHORE PKWY
SHORE PKWY
E 11 ST
BANNER AVE
E 12 ST
HOMECREST AVE
BANNER AVE
GUIDER AVE
BANNER 3RD RD
BRIGHTON 3 ST
CASS PL
NEPTUNE AVE
BRIGHTON 8 ST
CONEY ISLAND AVE
BRIGHTON 10 ST
BRIGHTON 11 ST
CORBIN PL
OCEAN PARKWAY
BRIGHTON 1 ST
OCEAN VIEW AVE
BRIGHTON 3 ST
BRIGHTON 4 ST
BRIGHTON 5 ST
BRIGHTON 6 ST
BRIGHTON 7 ST
BRIGHTON 13 ST
BRIGHTON 2 ST
BRIGHTON BEACH AVE
SEACOAST TERR
Oceana Condominium and Club
CORBIN PL
BRIGHTWATER CT
Boardwalk
Brighton Beach
Atlantic Ocean

BRIGHTON BEACH

THIS COMMUNITY, SOMETIMES CALLED "LITTLE ODESSA BY THE SEA," lies between Manhattan Beach and Coney Island. Wealthier and younger Russians have moved to nearby Mill Basin, Sheepshead Bay, and even to Staten Island; they view Brighton Beach much like Eastern European Jews saw the Lower East Side—a poor, crowded place to escape from. Yet the area still has a majority population of immigrants from the former Soviet Union, most of them elderly. This can easily be seen by taking a walk along the main shopping street, Brighton Beach Avenue. There is the usual array of restaurants, shops, video places, pharmacies, and medical offices, but what distinguishes them is that they all have Russian signage. This, more than anything else, tells you who lives here. In recent years, many Muslims from the Central Russian republics have also come here. At the same time, about 30 percent of the population is a mix of Turks, Chinese, Uzbeks, Kazaks, Pakistanis, and Indians, Hispanics, blacks, and American-born whites of various backgrounds who lived in the area before the Russians started coming in the 1970s.

Brighton Beach's boundaries are the Belt Parkway to the north, Corbin Place to the east, Brighton Beach to the south, and Ocean Parkway to the west. The buildings are a mixture of apartment buildings from the 1920s and 1930s, predominantly art deco in style, and old frame houses, many in varying states of neglect and decay. These are augmented by newer condominiums, some luxury apartment complexes, and a few glass and steel buildings of the type more common in gentrified Williamsburg and Greenpoint.

Transportation is available via the Q and B lines and by bus. It's a congested area and finding parking is sometimes a challenge. The best thing going for this part of Brooklyn is a lovely boardwalk and large beach area. It's also quite safe now, as opposed to in the 1980s and early '90s, when crime and illegal activity of all sorts flourished north of Brighton Beach Avenue. The locals give credit for this to both the police and the Russian Mafia, most of whose leaders, both Jewish and non-Jewish, came from Odessa.[3]

As I walk along the luxury Oceana Condominium and Club development, I can hear the strains of piano music coming from various apartments. It reminds me that classical music is very much a part of Russian culture. I also remember my son's demanding Russian teacher, the concert pianist, Oxana Yablonskaya, who occasionally rewarded my son's momentary inattention with a light rap across his knuckles. She was renowned in her native land and gave concerts at Carnegie Hall. Yet she bemoaned her fate here because occasional performances were not enough to sustain her family. This is what can happen when highly educated immigrants start over again in mid-life. It's a struggle. I also take note of fluttering Israeli flags hanging from a number of windows. For many Russian Jews, Israel is a central part of their lives.

Oceana, which begins at the southeastern intersection of Coney Island and Brighton Beach Avenues, has hundreds of apartments ranging in price from $500,000 to over a million for a three-bedroom unit. It has a complete health club with indoor and outdoor pools and well-manicured lawns and flowerbeds. It rests on the site of the Brighton Beach Baths, a club established in 1907 that had over 13,000 members in its heyday. In addition to the usual leisure-time activities—saunas, handball courts, and such, Brighton Beach Baths had the popular egg cream and knish-eating contests. I guess Nathan's needed some competition!

Security is pretty good at Oceana, but I wanted to see it from the inside. This was easier than I thought it would be. Like many such complexes, finding an open gate is quite simple because the maintenance workers, furniture deliverers, and others invariably prop the gates open so they don't have to bother dealing with them. From there it's simply a question of dressing like the others, in this case shorts, a T-shirt, and, for good measure, sunglasses. As they say: If you look like you belong, then you belong. Suffice it to say, there are many strategies for getting into secure places in New York, cameras, fences, and guards notwithstanding.

My efforts were worthwhile because visually it's a beautiful, peaceful fifteen-acre oasis, well worth exploring. But it seems to have some shortcomings. According to some nonresidents, the walls are paper thin, the air-conditioning stinks, and there are leaky ceilings. But this is a common, perhaps even sour grapes, complaint made by New Yorkers, who love to contrast the thick walls and oak floors in their prewar buildings with their more modern counterparts, cheerfully ignoring the old bathrooms, small windows, ancient lobbies, and musty smells, and elevators that often break down, which they must endure.

Meandering over to Brightwater Court, I stop in front of a really beautiful art deco building, number 711, on the corner of Coney Island Avenue. It has all sorts of terra cotta designs and pyramids, suns, chevrons, elaborate multicolored brick and shiny tiles, and angled bricks in rich hues of blue, bright orange, and black extending all the way to the top of the structure. The tapestry-like motif above the entranceway is especially striking.

I chat with Phil, a balding, middle-aged man wearing a dark blue tank top, green shorts with a couple of light spots on them, and weathered New Balance sneakers. He's cradling a shih tzu in his arms. "What's this neighborhood like?" I inquire.

"It's okay," he says. "Mostly Russian. I grew up here, left for a while and then came back when I inherited the apartment from my grandmother. It's a good area now. In the 1980s there was prostitution across the subway. My wife and I like the convenience of the beach a block away. You do have the problem of the people coming out of the Tatiana club on the weekends—loud, drunk, and fighting, but there's a lot of advantages to living here. It's rent stabilized, by the ocean, and pretty safe." Phil's an insurance salesman who graduated from Berkeley, where he was a communications major. "I wanted to be a broadcaster but that didn't work out so I went into insurance. You could do worse." He has stereotypical attitudes toward the Russians based on scanty evidence, more like impressions. Here's one: "Look I've never been an immigrant, but within a month or two after coming here they're driving a Mercedes and I gotta assume they're getting it from the Russian Mafia. It's a mentality." He may be referring to their flashiness, but when pressed, he can't explain why the mob would give them these fancy cars other than to ask rhetorically: "Well, where else would they get 'em from? You'll notice that on the avenue there'll be three flower shops or three clothing stores all on one block and then if they don't do well and go out of business, there's a new one a week later. In other words, they take it over. How can that be unless the mob controls it?" Again, no proof but to him it's a mystery in search of an explanation. In general, the Mafia, of whatever variety, is always a great gossip topic, and quite a few known Russian mobsters immigrated here after the fall of communism.

And then, on my left, I approach a canopied entrance that's sort of the back way into Tatiana, one of the most famous Russian nightclubs in Brighton Beach. The main way into the place is on the boardwalk, one block south. I stride up a carpeted walkway lined with photos of people who've dined there. Most aren't famous but some, like James Earl Jones, Ed Koch, and Charles Schumer, are. This status by association is a game thoroughly enjoyed by people everywhere but particularly noticeable in the Big Apple, which has so many celebrities. Outside the restrooms are two life-size statues of women, one painted black, the other bright red, atop of which is a lamp. An ad on the wall advertises a Vegas-style floor show with girls clad only in "fur bikinis." A female employee speaking heavily-accented English tells me: "That was last year. Every year is samting different." I emerge into the outdoor sitting area and meet the manager. They're getting ready for lunch; Russian music is blaring.

One of the best ways to get a feel for this place is to spend an hour or two wandering along Brighton Beach Avenue and along some of the mostly residential side streets. The brick houses on Banner off Third Road are a great example of what the area looked like in earlier days. Brighton Beach has a Turkish community, and there's an interesting looking Turkish mosque and community center farther up 3rd Street at number 2814 that flies both the American and Turkish flags. Called the Eyup Sultan Cultural Center, the four-story building has large arched, rectangular windows framed by bricks of different colors with unusual motifs. The interior is dominated by a bright, large, triple-tiered round chandelier. The walls are decorated with blue, white, and gold mosaic tiles that form intricate designs; I'm reminded of the tiles around Hearst Castle's indoor swimming pool.

At 230 Brighton Beach Avenue I enter the St. Petersburg Global Trade House. It's a large place where one can get souvenirs of all kinds from Russia, select from thousands of Russian-language DVDs, and browse Russian books and paintings. There's also a special section for items related to the "occult," a topic many Russians seem to be into. It's a billion-dollar industry in Russia, with almost half a million practicing occultists and psychics.

I venture into the National nightclub at 273 Brighton Beach Avenue; it's famous and is one of the granddaddies of such venues. I talk with the owner, Mark, and his sister. "What's so good about your place? Is it better than Tatiana?"

"They our competition. They outside on the beach, but other than that I better. And we are bigger." He shows me around. They're not really open on this day. The setup here is quite elaborate, with a big stage. Like Tatiana, they also have famous visitors. A basic Russian meal is $75, including the show. They're selling tradition, and the music goes on until 3:00 a.m. I glance at photos of Ed Koch and Alphonse D'Amato, both with frozen smiles on their faces.

There are other night clubs offering similar fare and formats. They all have a touristy feel but are worth seeing for a representation of Russian culture. In many cases the patrons are Jews whose forebears came from Russia to the United States in the early twentieth

Tatiana—where everyone can be Russian for an evening

century. To attend a Russian concert, go to the Master Theater on 1029 Brighton Beach Avenue. For gourmet food emporiums, there are two excellent options: the Russian Gold Label shop at 281–85 Brighton Beach Avenue and the Turkish place next door called Vintage.

Exploring this thoroughfare gives one an idea of how varied the groups living here are. As time passes and the older Russians pass away, there will be "ethnic succession," just as happened elsewhere in places like Little Italy, Brownsville, and Washington Heights. This is the story of New York City—always changing and forever reinventing itself.

Ⓐ Terra cotta reliefs
Ⓑ Seaside Handball Courts
Ⓒ Nathan's
Ⓓ Coney Art Walls
Ⓔ MCU Park
Ⓕ Sea Gate community

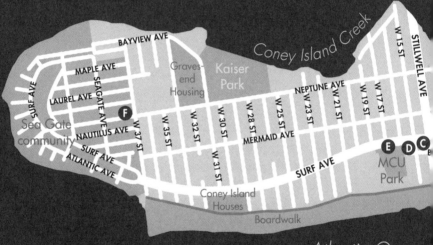

BAYVIEW AVE

Coney Island Creek

MAPLE AVE

Graves-end Housing

Kaiser Park

SURF AVE

LAUREL AVE

SEAGATE AVE

NEPTUNE AVE

W 15 ST

STILLWELL AVE

W 17 ST

W 19 ST

W 21 ST

W 23 ST

W 25 ST

W 28 ST

W 30 ST

W 32 ST

W 35 ST

W 37 ST

Ⓕ

Sea Gate community

NAUTILUS AVE

SURF AVE

ATLANTIC AVE

MERMAID AVE

Ⓔ Ⓓ Ⓒ Ⓑ

W 31 ST

Coney Island Houses

SURF AVE

MCU Park

Boardwalk

Atlantic Ocean

CONEY ISLAND

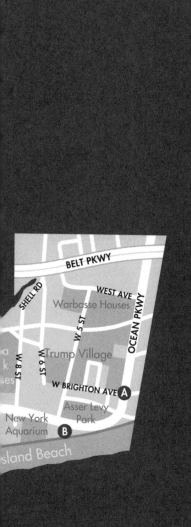

CONEY ISLAND, part of the same peninsula that contains two other distinct communities, Manhattan Beach and Brighton Beach, is literally a mixed bag. Its borders are the Belt Parkway and Coney Island Creek to the north, Ocean Parkway to the east, Coney Island Beach to the south, and Surf Avenue to the west. Of course, there are the well-known amusement rides here, like the Cyclone and the Wonder Wheel, built in the 1920s, and Luna, Dreamland, and Steeplechase Parks. The amusement area extends along the boardwalk and Surf Avenue, from about W. 8th to W. 17th Streets. And there's a world famous aquarium on Surf Avenue.

Over the years, various plans for developing Coney Island have been proposed, including a year-round refurbished amusement park and a variety of commercial business enterprises. Corporate sponsorships create goodwill and even tax write-offs. They have also created concern that the corporations may have too much influence in the community and might use their leverage for personal gain. These plans, centered on turning Coney Island into a world-class amusement center, have also included designs for large-scale housing,

371

both affordable and at market rates. But despite the involvement of major real estate figures and the general support of several city administrations, the efforts have often become mired in controversy between competing interests. As a result, concrete accomplishments have been few.[4]

This neighborhood is already home to a multiethnic community, one with whites, blacks, and Hispanics. These include Italians, Irish, Jews, Chinese, West Indians, Mexicans, and Puerto Ricans. Of late, more and more Russians have been moving in, as they did earlier in neighboring Brighton Beach. It contains Mitchell-Lama co-op housing, private low- and middle-income developments like Trump Village, and large public housing projects that are spread out along Mermaid, Neptune, Surf, and West Brighton Avenues and the many side streets, plus a small number of privately owned houses. The main commercial thoroughfares are Neptune, Mermaid, and Stillwell Avenues. A gated community called Sea Gate can be found at the very end of Coney Island on 37th Street. Because of its location on the ocean, the existence of a very nice boardwalk, and its storied history, Coney Island continues to be viewed as an area with great potential.

As I begin walking the area south along the western side of Ocean Parkway, Coney Island's eastern edge, I come face to face with a large, unglazed, brownish-red, terra-cotta-colored relief made of cast concrete, dubbed "Brooklyn." It's located on the surface of a supporting viaduct immediately beneath the tracks of the Ocean Parkway subway station of the Q line on West Brighton Avenue. It consists of a group of people, some standing, others seated in a roller-coaster. Most are wearing bathing suits. To the left on a separate panel is a bare-breasted mermaid. I cross the street and see a similarly designed relief, depicting people lying on a beach, called "Sideshow." Some of the women are wearing bikinis, others appear to be sunbathing topless. A few are lolling in the shade of an umbrella. Both reliefs were created by the sculptor Deborah Masters and are called

Terra Cotta Reliefs—Coney Island's lure for all to see

the "Coney Island Reliefs." They are surrounded by diamond- and square-shaped colorful ceramic tiles. The purpose is to portray the unusual history and legends of Coney Island. A must see!

I continue to Surf Avenue and go right. As a youngster, handball, the Chinese or American version, was always a big-time game for me and my friends everywhere in the city. As I looked at the games in progress at the Seaside Courts on Surf, near W. 5th Street on a warm July evening, I could see this was an intense, serious place. Players of all nationalities and ages, their bodies glistening with sweat, competed fiercely for every point, enduring critical comments and rare compliments from those sitting on the bench waiting their turn to play.

I speak to Oliver, a regular here. He's a large man with thick, brown, wavy hair with bleached highlights, a ruddy complexion, and a broad smile. He greets me effusively: "You haven't been down here in a while! How ya doin?" I'm sure he knows I've never been here. It's just a way of saying: "You look like a friend."

"Yeah, how's the neighborhood?"

"Well, the police are trying to clean it up, but it's hard, especially around the projects. What's interesting is you could have a whole new ethnic group come in, but Brooklyn has a certain essence that always stays the same. My father lives upstate in Swan Lake. It's in the middle of nowhere. He says Bob Dylan lives a few blocks away, but that's not gonna do it for me. What would I do there all day?"

"Are there times when you have serious matches?" I ask, as I look at the courts. It's 5:00 p.m. on a Tuesday and they're now fully occupied.

"Well, I just beat a guy for ten dollars. I don't know if you call that a serious match." I let him know that I do.

"I was terrible at this game until I looked myself in the mirror and said: 'You gotta use every bit of your brain to coordinate the physical parts of your game and figure out the right strategy.' It's a very cerebral sport. This here is a nice game, between Marty and Fred, two Russian Jews. Look how I inundate you into the game right away. Come, sit down here on the bench and enjoy. It's the Brooklyn way. You sit down and you blend right into the culture. I've even gotten the Orthodox Jews to play. Look at this picture of me seven years ago. Look how great I looked. I'm trying to get back to this."

No doubt his view of me is related to the fact that I'm a fellow New Yorker. There's also a certain pride in being a Brooklynite, as he lets me know several times. The faux gruffness, concealing deliberately while at the same time allowing a certain warmth and camaraderie to emerge, is all part of his "presentation of self," as the sociologist Erving Goffman would have said. People like to have the validity of their self-image reaffirmed by using nonnatives as a sounding board.

At 2896 W. 12th Street I visit the New York Fencing Academy, one of only two in Brooklyn. It's a good location, as fencing is a popular sport among the Russians living in the area. I go up the stairs to have a look. Hanging on the walls outside are fencing awards won by those at the academy, a way of letting the visitor know that this is a serious and successful place. The young Russian at the desk enlightens me: "We have about eighty students, many of them Russian. It's a great sport for kids because you learn agility, coordination, and strengthen your muscles. We have people who trained here who became champions in the sport. It also helps train you to think better in terms of strategy." Fencing is indeed a major sport in Russia, and the world championship games have been held in the country several times, most recently in July 2015.

I first went to Coney Island as a kid, with my dad and my older brother, Mark, who was then fourteen. He had bought tickets for the famed Cyclone roller coaster, for two consecutive rides. But the first one so sickened Mark—I well remember his greenish complexion after he stumbled off the car—that he declined a repeat performance. For me, everything about going there, and we went there numerous times, was memorable. Some of the rides, especially the bumper cars, where you could crash into other cars with gusto but with no consequences except for a dirty look or minor retaliation in kind, are indelibly imprinted on my consciousness. The same for the boardwalk, where we delighted in staring at the waves as they crashed ashore, and consumed all manner of delectable treats—potato knishes, hot dogs, and ice cream in crisp, dark sugar cones.

Some of the old rides are still operating, but they exist in a setting that's a cross between venerating the old and embracing the new. Nathan's, which turned one hundred in 2016, is still there, the signage recognizable as well as the menu, offering many of the old standbys—the crinkle-cut fries and hot dogs, frog legs, ears of buttered corn, and Chow Mein on a bun, but not the real glasses in which orange drinks were once served. Nathan's Wall of Fame lists all of the recent winners of the Annual International Hot

Dog Eating Contest, dominated by two world class *fressers*—Joey Chestnut and Takeru Kobayashi. Another sign fairly shouts out: "They Came, They Ate, They Conquered." This is especially true of Chestnut, holder of the current world record, sixty-nine hot dogs, and Sonya Thomas, a.k.a. Lee Sung Kyong, and top dog among the women, with forty-five franks.

Today there's also Applebee's, Popeye Chicken, and a new site for a national candy chain called IT'SUGAR. The Grimaldis have a pizza outlet here too. There are many new rides, like the Thunderbolt, which will turn riders upside down at high speed in more ways than you can imagine. The scariest one of all, according to riders and from what I could see visually, is the Slingshot, where riders are suspended along wires at crazy angles in a small bowl-like contraption, built for two. The advantage? "You can see the world," as one person put it, from 150 feet in the air. Even the actor Mark Wahlberg and his brothers, Donnie and Paul, have invested in an outlet of their popular chain, called "Wahlburger's." "There's a million people in New York! Somebody's got to feed them," declared Donnie in an interview with the online website *Grub Stop*. And of course there's a new boardwalk, rebuilt after Sandy, along a nice-sized beach, one used regularly by bathers, walkers, and joggers. But make no mistake. This is not yet a Disneyfied place like Times Square. It still has a certain vaguely seedy feel about it. Panhandlers operate pretty freely, and the crowds are raucous and sometimes unruly. There is some crime, and the trains constantly rumbling overhead into the city's biggest subway yards, add both noise and color to the scene.

Some of the old buildings are still there, there's ample seating at Nathan's, and I lose myself in the past as I listen to what's been called the "bubble gum songs" of summer. The crowds are a mix of locals and tourists from all over the country, in fact, the world. A cop tells me it's safe, "but you should probably stay away from the projects further down," he said, referring no doubt to the area in the 20s and 30s. To really understand Brooklyn's perception of self, it's important to visit this historically important neighborhood.

A new addition to the area is an outdoor museum devoted to large mural panels, sort of, in graffiti artist style. Called "Coney Art Walls," it's at 1320 Bowery Street, the heart of the entertainment district, near Stillwell Avenue. Most of the artists represented are really talented—no "scribble scrabble." Unlike the rides, admission is free. While it doesn't yet rival murals in Bushwick/East Williamsburg, it's definitely worth touring.

Farther up, on 17th Street, is MCU Park, home to the Mets-owned farm club, the Brooklyn Cyclones, where I can watch a game and the ocean at the same time while sitting in the most expensive field box for just $19. The park also has other types of entertainment, like boxing matches and concerts, and it can also be rented for private parties.

Be advised that venturing beyond W. 20th Street, just three blocks away, is not advisable for any but the most intrepid adventurers. That's where the public housing projects begin, running, roughly, from W. 20th to W. 37th Streets, east to west, and from Neptune to Surf Avenues, north to south. Many of the NYCHA buildings are in need of serious repairs and renovations, and portions of them are clearly abandoned. There are some exceptions, where the buildings look better, like on W. 23th Street between Neptune and Mermaid Avenues, where there are some nice gardens. Many of the smaller houses around them are also dilapidated, with barred windows and signs of neglect. A wall mural with the slogan "We must stop the Violence," and "RIP," accompanied by the Lord's Prayer and a pair of hands raised in supplication tells an incredibly sad story, with the names of some eighty victims listed—Allen "Jungle" Lewis, Treat Rogers, Butter Troy Harris, and so many others who died young. A walk up Mermaid or Neptune Avenue will easily confirm that this is a grim part of the city with idle young men hanging out on the streets by day and many homeless people. It may not be as dangerous as the Louis Pink Houses in East New York, or some of the projects in Brownsville, but it's not advisable to take a chance here.

Sea Gate—gateway to peace and tranquility in another world

Sea Gate, which begins on W. 37th Street, is part of Coney Island, but, as the name implies, it's a gated community, one of four in the city. The others are Silver Beach Gardens and Edgewater Park, in the Throgs Neck section of the Bronx; and Breezy Point in the Rockaways portion of Queens. Sea Gate is the oldest, established in 1898, and the most integrated of the four. It has the feel, in any case, of not being part of greater Coney Island. It's quiet, has its own beaches and a visitor needs permission from a guard to gain entry. People who live here have an opportunity to feel they live in an exclusive community, but one that's, theoretically at least, within walking distance of the subway. The subway is actually a mile away and would require walking through an unsafe area.

There is a fence or wall surrounding most of the community. It is a mere few blocks away from public housing in Coney Island. The houses are middle to lower-middle class—mostly attached brick row houses, but detached homes as well, especially closer to the ocean. There are a few apartment buildings. Inside, there is no shopping to speak of. It's peaceful and bucolic but quite boring for teenagers, as

I learn from speaking with them. There's a large Orthodox Jewish population here, a good number of them Holocaust survivors or their children and grandchildren. Isaac Bashevis Singer, winner of the Nobel Prize in literature, wrote a great novel about the survivors living here, called *Enemies, A Love Story*.

Immediately outside the gates and across the street are the projects, looming over the area. Their size and poor condition dampens some of the enthusiasm about Coney Island's future. The residents in Sea Gate, however, are not unduly concerned about the projects despite the presence of some criminal elements there because they feel they have an effective private police force. But they generally ride to the subway, shopping, or the city on buses, cabs, and in their own cars. An express bus takes the rider to the city in eighty minutes.

Coney Island, in many ways, typifies much of Brooklyn. It has something special to offer, namely, the amusements and the boardwalk. But it also has its downside: sections that are unsafe. It's also a community that is changing in many ways, with a diverse ethnic and racial population. Moreover, its people are often likely to engage outsiders in ways that are friendly and sometimes charming. Its self-image is in flux because at this point no one knows what its future will be. In short, it's a microcosm of Brooklyn as a whole.

> *Brooklyn's a place I couldn't wait to get out of*
> *And now can't afford to move back to.*

Anonymous

ACKNOWLEDGMENTS

I want to first thank the people at Princeton for their assistance and guidance through this process. Peter Dougherty, director of Princeton University Press, supported this project in every way, as he has other projects in the past. My editor, Meagan Levinson, set high standards, was fully and enthusiastically engaged in the project, and made many improvements to the manuscript, both conceptually and in the countless details necessary to produce this book. It was a genuinely collaborative effort in so many ways, and I truly appreciate it. Thanks also to Harvey Molotch and the other, anonymous reviewer of my manuscript. Others at Princeton who played key roles were Mark Bellis, Kathleen Cioffi, Seth Ditchik, Julia Haav, Maria Lindenfeldar, Ryan Mulligan, and Laurie Schlesinger. Special thanks to my copyeditor, Dawn Hall, my proofreader, Marcia Glass, my talented photographer, Tony Bennett, who has a great eye for what looks good, and the mapmaker, Shane Kelley. Finally, my appreciation to everyone else at the press whom I don't know personally, but who worked hard to bring this book to fruition.

A number of people read all or portions of the book and made insightful comments and helpful suggestions, for which I am deeply indebted. These include Richard Alba, Sheldon and Tobie Czapnik, Norman Fisher, Esther Friedman, Hershey and Linda Friedman, Murray Gewirtz, Steve and Joan Goldberg, Giselle Goldschmidt, Harvey and Helen Ishofsky, Robert Katz, Sydelle and Rob Knepper, Bill Kornblum, Phil and Joyce Levine, Paul and Irene Marcus, Jack Nass, Irene Prager, Brooklyn Borough Historian Ron Schweiger, Rebecca and Fred Terna, Oriel Weinberg, Jeff Wiesenfeld, Edward Wydra, and Zach Dicker. Special thanks to Jessica Schwartz, who thought of the five-borough idea and Eric Schwartz, who pushed it forward, and to Mitchell Duneier, friend and colleague, who greatly sharpened my thinking on how to do it.

Many individuals helped me in a myriad of ways for which I am very grateful. Among them are: Carole Agus, Charlie Ames, Elijah Anderson who always stands by me, Joseph Berger, Alex Bilu, Bernard Bochner, Francesco Bollorini, Vince Boudreau, Mehdi Bozorgmehr, Steve and Eva Campanella, Yin Pak Chen, Lillian Chubak, Kenneth Cohen, Lisa Coico, Mary Curtis, Thomas DiNapoli, Andrew Dolkart, Dan Douglas, Mitchell Duneier, Eugene Fellner, Karin and Gerald Feldhamer, Norman and Sylvia Fisher, Jerry Fishman, Howard Fuchs, Cynthia Fuchs-Epstein, Matt Green, Avi Hadar, Pearl and Nathan Halegua, Allan and Judy Halpern, Josh Halpern, Gabriel Haslip-Viera, Alan Helmreich, Ramona Hernandez, David Hoenig, Riley Hooper, Philip and Margie Jacobs, Phil Kasinitz, Ivan Kaufman, Beth Klein, Jon Kule, L'Heureux Lewis-McCoy, Billy and Nechama Liss-Levenson, Jack Levinson, Esther Lipstein, Sesil Lissberger, Rebecca Litt, Iris Lopez, Mike Makatron, Hollis Martino, Joyce Matkowsky, Richard Mazzara, Michael McKinley, Mitchell Meltzer, Albert Miller, Barry Mitchell, Jessica Pellien, Colin Powell, Constance Rosenblum, Ruben Rumbaut, Allan Rudolf, Parmatma and Rupam Saran, Bill Spier, Baruch and Pamela Toledano, Ashley Velie, Daniel Vitow, Hadassah Wachstock, Roger Waldinger, Russell Warren, Albert Weinstein, Charlotte Wendel, Malcolm Woodier, Helen Zimmerman, and Sharon Zukin.

It's my great fortune to have a talented family of writers. All of my children, Jeff, Joe, and Deb, read the manuscript carefully, making many valuable and incisive observations. I can't thank them enough.

My greatest thanks goes to my brilliant and wonderful wife, Helaine, who is an extremely talented professional novelist and biographer. She accompanied me on many of my walks, read every word of what I wrote, as she has always done, and made hundreds of insightful and critical observations that were invaluable to me in every way. Plus, she happens to be a Brooklyn native! Finally, although she may not know how she contributed, I must thank Heidi, our super-friendly and adaptable dog who served as a great ice-breaker whenever she came along.

APPENDIX

East New York falls into a category of Brooklyn neighborhoods that can be quite dangerous. Others, in varying degrees, include Brownsville, Bushwick, Bedford-Stuyvesant, and Coney Island. Some of these areas are gentrifying but still have unsafe sections. East New York is the largest in area and has the highest crime rate, followed closely by neighboring Brownsville.

So why include them in a book like this? Because one can still walk them in relative safety, by day at least, provided caution is exercised. The statistical risk of being attacked in these neighborhoods is actually quite low in absolute terms, but it's far more likely to happen here than in, say, the Upper East Side, Bay Ridge, Brooklyn Heights, or Riverdale.

Some will be motivated by curiosity about what life looks like in these communities. Also, these areas are actually quite interesting in terms of buildings, stores, and life there in general. The vast majority of residents are honest, hard-working folks who will be friendly if approached the way anyone should be approached. That said, if the reader is the type of person who worries a lot about crime, then my suggestion is to avoid these areas. It's fair to say that in the many talks I gave after *The New York Nobody Knows* appeared, this was by far the question I was most often asked.

I offer the following tips to those readers who wish to tour these neighborhoods:

1. Be alert at all times.
2. Dress innocuously and not very well—no loud colors, especially gang ones—bright blue or red.
3. Never stare at anyone, but if you should make eye contact, and the person isn't looking at you in a hostile manner, smile and say "Hi." It's a counterintuitive, disarming

approach that has served me well, though gauging this can sometimes be tricky.

4. Avoid groups of people congregating on the street, especially teenagers, but do not cross the street if you feel they've already seen you approaching. You don't want to look nervous or fearful. This is obviously not easy to determine with certainty.

5. Walking at night, on weekends, and in the summer is riskier than at other times.

6. Do not walk with more than one person since you don't want to attract attention.

7. Avoid areas where it's difficult to exit, such as neighborhoods without nearby transportation.

8. Avoid deserted areas.

9. Don't carry a lot of cash, but have some. Having nothing on you may increase the likelihood of physical attack from a disappointed assailant. Never fight back unless all else is lost.

10. Be careful about giving money to panhandlers. Generosity can lead to trouble, especially if others take notice.

11. Always be respectful. If someone is walking toward you be ready to give way as you are not on your home turf.

12. Never try to project an image of toughness. It won't work and, in fact, people may judge you as either insecure or challenging them if you try it.

These are not hard and fast rules. Circumstances may dictate a different response or approach. Each situation is, by definition, unique, and one needs to be flexible and adapt. Having and using common sense is an essential quality.

Women, as a rule, should exercise more caution and should not walk in these areas alone. Walking with a man is less likely to attract attention. Walking with a man and a dog is even better. It suggests that you are local, or at least visiting someone local. Older people, provided they are physically fit and can walk at a reasonable pace and without using a cane, are actually at less risk than those who are younger. A younger person who looks like an outsider, meaning of a different race or ethnicity, may be seen as a challenge to a resident of similar age. People who look like they could be a cop or worker in the area, for example, teacher, social worker, delivery person, store employee, are at less risk.

On a personal note, I walked 6,864 miles of city streets in recent years at all times of the day and night and was never attacked. Why? I grew up in a rough area of the city and was familiar with life there. I hung out on the streets and developed the usual sixth sense about danger. Even more important perhaps, I was just plain lucky. One incident brought this home to me. I once walked into a public housing project at midday. As I passed a teenager who glanced at me, I said, "How ya doin?" His face was expressionless as he said something in Spanish into a walkie-talkie. I looked around and saw seven heads go up about fifteen yards away across a small grass oval. Without any hesitation, I said "Have a nice day," and walked out, not quickly or slowly, toward the street, never looking back. I had, I suspected, interrupted a drug deal or other illegal activity. My goal was to indicate that I wasn't a threat to what they were doing. In this case, being seen as a cop might have made things worse.

Nothing happened to me. I was fortunate.

NOTES

INTRODUCTION

1. To determine the neighborhoods' boundaries, I relied on my own walks, Kenneth Jackson's *The Encyclopedia of New York City*, and John Manbeck's *The Neighborhoods of Brooklyn*. The maps are primarily designed to help readers find the locations discussed, and they don't always show either a community's actual borders or all of its streets.

GREENPOINT, WILLIAMSBURG, DUMBO, VINEGAR HILL, BROOKLYN HEIGHTS, COBBLE HILL, DOWNTOWN BROOKLYN

1. Cordes 2009.
2. Kornblum 2002, 164. Newtown Creek has long suffered from pollution. It has recently been declared a "Superfund" site, making it eligible for improvement with government funding.
3. Zukin 2010.
4. Foner (2005) has called 9/11 "a dispersed tragedy" because people from every part of the city and the surrounding suburbs were killed or injured. In Brooklyn, as in the other boroughs, many streets are named after the victims and there are signs on almost every firehouse proclaiming "never forget," often accompanied by the victims' names.
5. East Williamsburg is an informal name for the area, bounded generally by Flushing Avenue on the south, Bushwick Avenue on the west, Maspeth Avenue on the north, and the Queens border on the east.
6. Gonzalez 2010.
7. Anasi 2012.
8. Luken 2015.
9. Poll 1962; Mayer 2010.
10. Foderaro 2015.
11. Sorkin 2009, 7.
12. Brownstoner.com. For more on the Amity Street home, see Rosenblum 2011.

BOERUM HILL, CARROLL GARDENS, RED HOOK, GOWANUS, PARK SLOPE, WINDSOR TERRACE

1. Zukin 2010.
2. Alexiou 2015.
3. For more on the Ansonia Clock Factory, see Morrone 2008.
4. Sohn 2009, 13–14.
5. For a very good book about Prospect Park, see Colley 2013.
6. For an excellent discussion of Farrell's, see Dennis Hamill's introduction in Merlis and Rosenzweig 2010.
7. Hamill 1994.

FORT GREENE, CLINTON HILL, PROSPECT HEIGHTS, BEDFORD-STUYVESANT, CROWN HEIGHTS, PROSPECT LEFFERTS GARDENS

1. For more on BAM, see Morrone 2010.
2. For more on Fort Greene's black middle class, see Morrone 2010.
3. Abramson 2010.
4. It's not clear whether any of the Pfizers actually lived there. See Morrone 2010.
5. Anderson 2011.
6. Bernstein 2011.
7. Williams 2015. The article cited here talks about artists and musicians moving to Los Angeles from New York City because Los Angeles has become more hip. But these are always the first wave and they are often followed by the more economically invested gentrifiers in industry and commerce. Of course, they'll be competing with indigenous Angeleno gentrifiers too.
8. Zukin 2010.
9. Kasinitz 1992.
10. Goldschmidt 2006.

BUSHWICK, CYPRESS HILLS, BROWNSVILLE, EAST NEW YORK, CANARSIE, EAST FLATBUSH

1. Ehrenhalt 2012, 65–88.
2. Bellafante 2012.
3. Rosenberg 2015.
4. Pritchett 2002.
5. Pristin 2010. The *Times* quoted other sources too for this description.

6. Thabit 2003.
7. Stern, Fishman, and Tilove 2006, 1191–201.
8. For more on the old roads and lanes of Canarsie, see Merlis and Rosenzweig 2008.
9. Rieder 1985.

FLATBUSH, PROSPECT PARK SOUTH, MIDWOOD, FLATLANDS, MARINE PARK, BERGEN BEACH, MILL BASIN

1. Roberts 2010.
2. For more on Ditmas Park, see Joseph Berger's excellent book on New York, 2007, 19–31.
3. Merlis, Rosenzweig, and Israelowitz 2011.
4. Beyer 2008; Anasi 2012.
5. Berger 2012. See also Chiusano 2014.
6. Lefkowitz 2011.
7. Kornblum and Hooreweghe, 2010, 74.
8. Gray 2012.

SUNSET PARK, BOROUGH PARK, BAY RIDGE, DYKER HEIGHTS, BENSONHURST, BATH BEACH

1. Hum 2014.
2. This has long been the case, though today the problems, because of modern technology, are even greater. See Poll 1962; Mayer 2010.
3. Merlis and Rosenzweig 2000.

GRAVESEND, SHEEPSHEAD BAY, GERRITSEN BEACH, MANHATTAN BEACH, BRIGHTON BEACH, CONEY ISLAND

1. Buckley 2006.
2. For a good history of Gerritsen Beach, see Merlis, Rosenzweig, and Miller 1997.
3. See Orleck 2001; Friedman 2000.
4. For more on these issues, see Bagli 2009.

BIBLIOGRAPHY

Abramson, Stacy. 2010. "The Stories of One Brooklyn Block." *New York Times*, Metropolitan Section, July 23.

Alba, Richard D. 2009. *Blurring the Color Line: The New Chance for a More Integrated America*. Cambridge, MA: Harvard University Press.

Alexiou, Joseph. 2015. *Brooklyn's Curious Canal*. New York: New York University Press.

Anasi, Robert. 2012. *The Last Bohemia: Scenes from the Life of Williamsburg, Brooklyn*. New York: Farrar, Straus, and Giroux.

Anderson, Elijah. 1976. *A Place on the Corner*. Chicago: University of Chicago Press.

———. 1990. *Streetwise: Race, Class, and Change in an Urban Community*. Chicago: University of Chicago Press.

———. 1999. *Code of the Street*. New York: W. W. Norton.

———. 2011. *The Cosmopolitan Canopy: Race and Civility in Everyday Life*. New York: W. W. Norton.

Bagli, Charles V. 2009. "City and Developer Spar over Coney Island Visions." *New York Times*, February 17.

Basaran Sahin, Duygu. 2015. "Walking a Neighborhood: Safety, Inequality, Gentrification, and Lifestyle in Boerum Hill." Research Paper, Department of Sociology, City University of New York Graduate Center.

Bellafante, Ginia. 2012. "Where Optimism Feels Out of Reach." *New York Times*, January 14.

Berger, Joseph. 2001. *Displaced Persons: Growing Up American after the Holocaust*. New York: Washington Square Press.

———. 2007. *The World in a City: Traveling the Globe through the Neighborhoods of the New New York*. New York: Ballantine Books.

———. 2012. "As Brooklyn Gentrifies, Some Neighborhoods Are Being Left Behind." *New York Times*, July 9.

Bernstein, Fred A. 2011. "Pratt Institute Takes an Interest in Making a Neighborhood Nicer." *New York Times*, February 16.

Beyer, Gregory. 2008. "Living in Marine Park, Brooklyn: Isolation is Pretty Splendid." *New York Times*, November 16.

Brownstoner.com. 2012. January 2.

Buckley, Cara. 2006. "Brooklyn Community Is on Edge and in Spotlight after Hate-Crime Arrests." *New York Times*, August 12.

Calder, Rich. 2011. "It's Church Bada-Bingo!" *New York Post*, June 6.

Chiusano, Mark. 2014. *Marine Park: Stories*. New York: Penguin.

Cimino, Richard. 2011. "Neighborhoods, Niches, and Networks: The Religious Ecology of Gentrification." *City and Community* 10: 157–81.

Colley, David. 2013. *Prospect Park: Olmsted and Vaux's Brooklyn Masterpiece*. New York: Princeton Architectural Press.

Cordes, Kate. 2009. "Striking a Balance: Greenpoint, Brooklyn." Research Paper, Department of Sociology, City University of New York Graduate Center.

Dreyfus, Hannah. 2015. "Liberal Tikkun Olam Hits an Orthodox Stronghold." *Jewish Week*, May 29.

Duneier, Mitchell. 1992. *Slim's Table: Race, Respectability, and Masculinity*. Chicago: University of Chicago Press.

———. 1999. *Sidewalk*. New York: Farrar, Straus, and Giroux.

Dunn, Jancee. 2014. "A Brooklyn Bakery Named for No One." *New York Times*, New York Region, March 6.

Ehrenhalt, Alan. 2012. *The Great Inversion and the Future of the American City*. New York: Alfred A. Knopf.

Ellen, Ingrid Gould, Amy Ellen Schwartz, Ioan Voicu, and Michael H. Schill. 2007. "Does Federally Subsidized Rental Housing Depress Neighborhood Property Values?" *Journal of Policy Analysis and Management* 26: 257–80.

Foderaro, Lisa W. 2015. "Brooklyn Bridge Park Opening New Vistas." *New York Times*, July 27.

Foner, Nancy, ed. 2005. *Wounded City: The Social Impact of 9/11*. New York: Russell Sage Foundation.

Freedman, Samuel G. 1988. "From the Ground Up in East New York." *New York Times*, April 4.

———. 1994. *Once Upon This Rock: The Miracles of a Black Church*. New York: Harper Perennial.

Friedman, Robert I. 2000. *Red Mafiya: How the Russian Mob Has Invaded America*. New York: Warner Books.

Gamm, Gerald. 1999. *Urban Exodus: Why the Jews Left Boston and the Catholics Stayed*. Cambridge, MA: Harvard University Press.

Goldschmidt, Henry. 2006. *Race and Religion: Among the Chosen Peoples of Crown Heights*. New Brunswick, NJ: Rutgers University Press.

Gonzalez, David. 2010. "Still Taking to the Streets to Honor Their Saints." *New York Times*, June 6.

Gray, Christopher. 2003. "Recalling the Days of Knights and Elks." *New York Times*, August 24.

Gray, Geoffrey. 2012. "King Carl of Canarsie." *New York Magazine*, January 8.

Hamill, Dennis. 2010. Introduction to Brian Merlis and Lee A. Rosenzweig. *Brooklyn's Windsor Terrace, Kensington, and Parkville Communities*. Brooklyn, NY: BrooklynPix.com and Israelowitz Publishing.

Hamill, Pete. 1973. *The Gift*. New York: Random House.

———. 1994. *A Drinking Life*. New York: Little, Brown.

———. 1997. *Snow in August*. New York: Little, Brown.

Helmreich, Alan, and Paul Marcus, eds. 1998. *Blacks and Jews on the Couch: Psychoanalytic Reflections on Black-Jewish Conflict*. Westport, CT: Praeger.

Helmreich, William B. 1992. *Against All Odds: Holocaust Survivors and the Successful Lives They Made in America*. New York: Simon and Schuster.

———. 2013. *The New York Nobody Knows: Walking 6,000 Miles in the City*. Princeton, NJ: Princeton University Press.

Higgins, Michelle. 2014. "Dumbo Roars." *New York Times*, September 21.

Hum, Tarry. 2014. *Making a Global Immigrant Neighborhood: Brooklyn's Sunset Park*. Philadelphia: Temple University Press.

Ishayik, Edna. 2015. "The Aptly Named Irish Haven Survives in a Changing Brooklyn." *New York Times*, July 24.

Jackson, Kenneth T. 2010. *The Encyclopedia of New York City*. 2nd ed. New Haven, CT: Yale University Press.

Jacobs, Jane. 1961. *The Death and Life of Great American Cities*. New York: Vintage Books.

Jerolmack, Colin. 2013. *The Global Pigeon*. Chicago: University of Chicago Press.

Kasinitz, Philip. 1992. *Caribbean New York: Black Immigrants and the Politics of Race*. Ithaca, NY: Cornell University Press.

———. 1998. "The Gentrification of 'Boerum Hill': Neighborhood Change and Conflicts over Definitions." *Qualitative Sociology* 11: 163–82.

———. 2000. "Red Hook: The Paradoxes of Poverty and Place in Brooklyn." *Research in Urban Sociology* 5: 253–74.

Kornblum, William. 2002. *At Sea in the City: New York from the Water's Edge*. Chapel Hill, NC: Algonquin Books.

Kornblum, William, and Kristen Van Hooreweghe. 2010. *Jamaica Bay: Ethnographic Overview and Assessment*. Report, City University of New

York Graduate Center, Northeast Region Ethnography Program, National Park Service, Boston. December.

Kroessler, Jeffrey A. 2002. *New York Year by Year: A Chronology of the Great Metropolis*. New York: New York University Press.

Krogius, Henrik. 2011. *The Brooklyn Heights Promenade*. Charleston, SC: History Press.

Lees, Loretta. 2003. "Super-Gentrification: The Case of Brooklyn Heights, New York City." *Urban Studies* 40: 2487–509.

Lefkowitz, Melanie. 2011. "Bergen Beach: Connected, but Still Remote." *Wall Street Journal*, December 24.

Lethem, Jonathan. 2003. *The Fortress of Solitude*. New York: Doubleday.

Luken, Eleanor. 2015. "Williamsburg on the Boundary: A Neighborhood Study of Great Divides." Research Paper, Department of Sociology, City University of New York Graduate Center.

Manbeck, John, ed. 2004. *The Neighborhoods of Brooklyn*. 2nd ed. New Haven, CT: Yale University Press.

Mayer, Egon. 2010. *From Suburb to Shtetl: The Jews of Boro Park*. New Brunswick, NJ: Transaction Books.

Merlis, Brian, and Lee A. Rosenzweig. 2000. *Brooklyn's Bay Ridge and Fort Hamilton: A Photographic Journey, 1870–1970*. Brooklyn, NY: Israelowitz Publishing.

———. 2008. *Canarsie: Brooklyn's Last Village on Jamaica Bay*. Brooklyn, NY: BrooklynPix.com and Israelowitz Publishing.

———. 2010. *Brooklyn's Windsor Terrace, Kensington, and Parkville Communities*. Brooklyn, NY: BrooklynPix.com and Israelowitz Publishing.

Merlis, Brian, Lee A. Rosenzweig, and Oscar Israelowitz. 2011. *Brooklyn's Midwood: Farms, Film, and Falafel*. Brooklyn, NY: Israelowitz Publishing and Brooklyn Editions.

Merlis, Brian, Lee A. Rosenzweig, and I. Stephen Miller. 1997. *Brooklyn's Gold Coast: The Sheepshead Bay Communities*. Brooklyn, NY: Sheepshead Bay Historical Society and Israelowitz Publishing.

Morrone, Francis. 2008. *Park Slope: Neighborhood and Architectural History Guide*. Brooklyn, NY: Brooklyn Historical Society.

———. 2010. *Fort Greene and Clinton Hill: Neighborhood and Architectural History Guide*. Brooklyn, NY: Brooklyn Historical Society.

Mueller, Benjamin. 2014. "Eyes on Gaza, Tensions Flare in Brooklyn." *New York Times*, July 22.

Orleck, Annelise. 2001. "Soviet Jews: The City's Newest Immigrants Transform New York Jewish Life." In *New Immigrants in New York*, edited by Nancy Foner, 111–40. New York: Columbia University Press.

Poll, Solomon. 1962. *The Hasidic Community of Williamsburg: A Study in the Sociology of Religion*. New York: Free Press.

Powell, Michael. 2010. "Old-Fashioned Bulwark in a Tide of Foreclosures." *New York Times*, Metropolitan Section, March 7.

Pristin, Terry. 2010. "New Life and Uses for a Movie Palace in Brooklyn." *New York Times*, September 28.

Pritchett, Wendell. 2002. *Brownsville, Brooklyn: Blacks, Jews, and the Changing Face of the Ghetto*. Chicago: University of Chicago Press.

Rieder, Jonathan. 1985. *Canarsie: The Jews and Italians of Brooklyn against Liberalism*. Cambridge, MA: Harvard University Press.

Robbins, Liz. 2008. *A Race Like No Others: 26.2 Miles through the Streets of New York*. New York: HarperCollins.

Roberts, Sam. 2010. "New York's Haitian Diaspora." *New York Times*, Metropolitan Section, January 17.

———. 2011. "A Striking Evolution in Bedford-Stuyvesant as the White Population Soars." *New York Times*, August 5.

Rosenberg, Zoe. 2015. "Behind Booming East New York, Gentrification's Last Frontier." CURBED, January 28.

Rosenblum, Constance. 2011. "House of Strings and Feathers." *New York Times*, September 9.

Rothman, Aaron, and David Mandl. 2014. "The End of Brooklyn." *Places Journal*, October.

Satow, Julie. 2014. "Living in the Mix." *New York Times*, August 31.

Schiebe, Christoph. 2015. "Bedford Stuyvesant: Walking in Brooklyn's Little Harlem." Research Paper, Department of Sociology, City University of New York Graduate Center.

Singer, Isaac Bashevis. 1972. *Enemies, A Love Story*. New York: Farrar, Straus, and Giroux.

Sohn, Amy. 2009. *Prospect Park West: A Novel*. New York: Simon and Schuster.

Sorkin, Michael. 2009. *Twenty Minutes in Manhattan*. New York: Reaktion Books.

Spiegelman, Willard. 2013. "Cultural Connections in a Tour of Brooklyn." *Wall Street Journal*, August 5.

Stern, Robert A. M., David Fishman, and Jacob Tilove. 2006. *New York 2000: Architecture and Urbanism between the Bicentennial and the Millennium*. New York: Monacelli Press.

Thabit, Walter. 2003. *How East New York Became a Ghetto*. New York: New York University Press.

Williams, Alex. 2015. "Escape from New York." *New York Times*, May 3.

Yee, Vivian. 2015. "Dismay and Relief in Brooklyn over a Party That Won't Be Coming to Town." *New York Times*, February 13.

———. 2015. "Priced Out and Moving On." *New York Times*, Metro Section, November 29.

Zukin, Sharon. 1995. *The Cultures of Cities*. Cambridge, MA: Blackwell.

———. 2010. *Naked City: The Death and Life of Authentic Urban Places*. New York: Oxford University Press.

INDEX

Decent Medical Services, Medical & Dental, 285–86
Deity Event Space, 67
DeMarco, Domenico, 239
DeMeo, Roy, 246
Deutsch, Shaul Shimon, 294
Di Fara Pizza, 238
Diana, Princess, 185
Dillon Child Study Center, 126
DiMarzio, Bishop Nicholas Anthony, 126
Dime Savings Bank, 57, 58
Ditmas Park, 229
DKNY, 185
Dodger Playground, 154–55
Don Peppe restaurant, 325
Dorsey Gallery, 167
Douglas, Dan, 352–53
Douglas, John, 350, 353
Downtown Brooklyn, 56–59
Dracula, 322
Drinking Life, A, 109–10
DUMBO, 33–37, 87
DUMBO Moving and Storage, 121–23
Dutch Reformed Church, 334
D'Vine Taste, 101–2
Dyker Beach Golf Course, 311
Dyker Heights, 308–13
Dyker Park Playground, 311

Eagle Warehouse & Storage, 37
East Flatbush, 212–19
East New York, 188, 194–201
East Williamsburg, 16–21
Ebbets Field, 257–58, 322
Eckstine, Billy, 257
Eichler's Bookstore, 239
Eisenhower, Dwight, 257
El Puente, 26–27
Empire Mayo, 137–38
Erasmus, 213
Erte, 268
Essen New York Deli, 239–41
Eyup Sultan Cultural Center, 367

Farrell's Bar, 108–10
Federation of Jewish Philanthropies, 210

Feldman, Deborah, 292
Feldman, Hyman Isaac, 47
Fellner, Eugene, 263–65
filming, 7, 34, 52–53, 227, 228
Finding Jesus, 228
First Korean Church of Brooklyn, 335
Fishman, Jerry, 305–6
$5.00 Warehouse Shoes, 336
Flatbush, 210, 222–29
Flatbush Caton Market, 225
Flatbush Reformed Dutch Church, 228
Flatlands, 244–51
Flatlands Church of God, 246
Foam Center, 301–3
Fonzarelli, Arthur Herbert (the Fonz), 322
Footprints restaurant, 219
Forrester, Benjamin, 214
Fort Greene, 116–23
Fort Hamilton, 300
Fortress of Solitude, The, 63
Fountain Avenue dump, 246
Frankenstein, 322
Frank's Shoe Repair, 281–82
French, 67
French Connection, The, 315, 325
Fresh Creek Basin, 207

G & S Pork Store, 344
Gambino family, 246, 305
gardens, 5–6, 9–10, 43–45, 85, 143–44, 173–74
Gardner, Susan, 64–66
Garrison, Edward, 217
gays, 73–74, 229
Gehrig, Lou, 257
Gemini Lounge, 246
General Greene restaurant, 118–19
General Hospital, 315
gentrification, 18–20, 22–26, 68–69, 89–91, 97–101, 104–5, 127–28, 133, 136–37, 144–46, 148–49, 152–53, 155–56, 172–75, 188, 200, 228
Georgetown, 261, 262
Gerritsen, Wolfert, 349
Gerritsen Bagels, 354